# COMMON CREDO

ALSO BY JOHN E. SCHWARZ

FREEDOM RECLAIMED:
REDISCOVERING THE AMERICAN VISION

ILLUSIONS OF OPPORTUNITY:
THE AMERICAN DREAM IN QUESTION

THE FORGOTTEN AMERICANS
(with Thomas J. Volgy)

AMERICA'S HIDDEN SUCCESS

THE UNITED STATES CONGRESS IN
COMPARATIVE PERSPECTIVE
(with L. Earl Shaw)

# COMMON CREDO

★ ★ ★ ★ ★

*The Path Back
to American Success*

## JOHN E. SCHWARZ

LIVERIGHT PUBLISHING CORPORATION
A DIVISION OF W. W. NORTON & COMPANY
NEW YORK   LONDON

For information about permission to reproduce selections from this book,
write to Permissions, Liveright Publishing Corporation,
a division of W. W. Norton & Company, Inc.,
500 Fifth Avenue, New York, NY 10110

For information about special discounts for bulk purchases, please contact
W. W. Norton Special Sales at specialsales@wwnorton.com or 800-233-4830

Manufacturing by Courier Westford
Book design by Lovedog Studio
Production manager: Anna Oler

ISBN 978-0-87140-339-1

Liveright Publishing Corporation
500 Fifth Avenue, New York, N.Y. 10110
www.wwnorton.com

W. W. Norton & Company Ltd.
Castle House, 75/76 Wells Street, London W1T 3QT

1 2 3 4 5 6 7 8 9 0

*To my family—both here and gone—with
everlasting love and gratitude*

# CONTENTS

*Introduction*
*xi*

CHAPTER 1
HOW WE GOT HERE:
THE FAILURE OF CONTEMPORARY LIBERALISM
AND CONSERVATISM
*1*

CHAPTER 2
FREEDOM AND EQUALITY
25

CHAPTER 3
THE ECONOMY
53

CONTENTS

CHAPTER 4
COLLECTIVE ACTION VERSUS
INDIVIDUAL FREEDOM
87

CHAPTER 5
RULES FOR GOVERNMENT
117

CHAPTER 6
THE COMMON CREDO
147

CHAPTER 7
SOLUTIONS
163

CHAPTER 8
ATTITUDES ABOUT GOVERNMENT
209

CHAPTER 9
MOVING FORWARD CONFIDENTLY
225

Notes
235

Acknowledgments
261

Index
263

# INTRODUCTION

THE GOAL OF THIS BOOK is to transform the economic and political debate that has misdirected our country for most of the past four decades. Nearly everyone agrees we face immense challenges right now, but my reference to "four decades" may surprise some readers. It is tempting to trace our troubles in recent years to the onset of the Great Recession in 2008, or possibly to the 2000 presidential election and the political divisiveness that erupted in the wake of its controversial result. Yet as I'll show in the pages to follow, these developments represent symptoms, not causes, of a malaise that has actually been infecting our country since the early 1970s—a malaise that has produced a dysfunctional government that most Americans don't trust and an economy that has left a solid majority of working Americans out of prosperity for two generations.

In these and numerous other ways, America has lost its compass and gotten off track. Neither the left nor the right—not the Democratic or the Republican Party, not liberalism or conservatism—has successfully addressed the core issues or provided effective solutions, ones that can bring us back together as a nation of common ideals, enable Americans to feel government is truly in their hands, generate a vibrantly growing economy with widespread prosperity, and foster the actions necessary to attack the wide array of other damaging problems that have seemingly become intractable. In addition, the kind of government that would be required to attain these ends must also be carefully restrained, so as not to go beyond its proper bounds or become excessive. This requires a widely accepted, clear, and specific definition for what government's role is in society and the economy—a definition that citizens and politicians can use to hold government activity accountable. Providing this definition, of government that is neither too powerful nor too weak, is another area in which both modern-day liberalism and conservatism have failed, as evidenced by the bitter, ceaseless debate in Washington and the country at large over this very topic.

To get at the root of our troubles, I take us back to the political principles we all share that come directly from the Founding Fathers, principles that make up what I call the "Common Credo." Today, these principles lie dormant beneath the surface of our thinking. As a result, we have not merely lost sight of them, we have actually come to misunderstand them, as have both political parties and each of the dominant political ideologies. Our misunderstanding of these principles over the past forty years, in turn, has led to the most critical issues we face today, including the economy's near breakdown, languishing middle- and working-class income, health care that is both enormously expensive and leaves so many uncovered, the loss of our global lead in education, an aging infrastructure, an inability to agree upon climate control policies, long-term national deficits that are unsustainable, and a deadlocked, unequal political process itself. The list is a long one.

Backed by riveting new evidence and fresh analysis, this book identifies and explores the principles lying at the heart of our political identity as a nation and demonstrates exactly how departing from them has given rise to every one of the problems just mentioned. It then shows in detail how re-engaging these hallowed principles of our Common Credo and placing them back at the center of our political debate and political process will not only resolve the problems but prevent them from happening again.

The Founders' thinking is paramount here. Americans are inspired by the time-honored goals of individual freedom, equality among all, commitment to community, and a desire for prosperity. These basic goals, however, often come into conflict in ways that make it difficult to pursue them simultaneously.

The genius of the Founders' thinking, reflected in the Common Credo, lies in the way it combines these four great conflicting goals and harmonizes them so that they can all be pursued at the same time, enabling them to support and reinforce one another. Advancing one of the goals simultaneously advances the others; protecting one of them at the same time protects the others. Building from chapter to chapter, this book shows how to join these bedrock values together in order to achieve all of them. In the process, we discover both the root causes of the most serious problems we face today and powerful, efficient means to attack and surmount them.

I believe by book's end, readers will agree that the Common Credo alone can lead America back on the path to success.

## CHAPTER 1

# HOW WE GOT HERE: THE FAILURE OF CONTEMPORARY LIBERALISM AND CONSERVATISM

★ ★ ★ ★ ★

I HAVE BEEN A COLLEGE TEACHER for many years, but it is far from the only job I have held. Before becoming a political science professor I worked, most memorably, as a truck driver for a bakery, as well as a dishwasher, a receptionist, and a cab driver, not to mention a janitor in an electroplating plant and a customer service clerk in a department store. At one point I managed a small business. I took many of these jobs while finishing up college, and then to help pay for graduate school.

I vividly remember the long days that work as a truck driver took, when I would get up in the pitch dark at four-thirty in the morning for a workday that started at six. My fellow drivers and I would load the bread and baked goods into our trucks in Mount Vernon, New York, and spend the next ten hours delivering them all over southern Westchester County and the Bronx. If I was delivering to a building without a working elevator, which was all too frequently the case, it meant climbing up five or six flights of stairs carrying containers of food weighing thirty pounds or more on each arm, sweat pouring down my back. The work gave me the marvelous feeling of being physically fit, but it also left me thoroughly exhausted. I would get home at six or six-thirty in the evening, completely drained. And since this was a minimum-wage job in the 1960s, at the end of the day often all I had to show for my effort was $10 in my pocket. In some of the other jobs I held, it wasn't uncommon for me or my workmates to go for weeks on end without a day off and, in my case at least, to live off soda bottle returns at the end of most months.

Blue-collar work in this country has always been wearing and undervalued. And yet, as hard as the jobs were and as little as the return could be, the people I worked with in those years emanated a certain optimism. The men and women I worked alongside, most of them not heading toward a graduate degree and the job fields made available through such an education, took deep pride in their job and expected that if they continued to work hard their circumstances would continue to improve. And in the 1960s, they were right to expect so. At that time, minimum-wage pay was practically enough, coupled with a spouse employed half-time, to support a basic standard of decent living for a family of four. Of course, you couldn't go to Hawaii or buy a Cadillac on that salary, but you could provide sufficiently for yourself and your family, or come pretty close. And a worker who was industrious and reliable could anticipate an upward progression of solid raises enabling him or her to get ahead. In fact, real pay had risen sharply for nearly twenty years following World War II, and most diligent workers had good reason to believe that a bright light shone for them on the American horizon.

Sadly and ominously, this is no longer the case in America, and hasn't been for a long time. For those now employed in places similar to the bakery and the electroplating plant where I worked, the prospects are much bleaker. The arduous hours and low wages lead now to more arduous hours and equally low wages. The middle and working classes have been stunted in a profound and unprecedented way, and with calamitous consequences for the country as

a whole—indeed, for the entire world. This book, *Common Credo*—
the product of my forty-five years of teaching and research—aims
to shed light on how this painful contrast between our past and our
present came to be, how our politics have failed us in this and in
many other ways, and how we can get our economy and our politics
back on the path to success. There have been many other books,
and uncountable articles, with the same goal in recent years. Some
have been illuminating; many have been retreads of familiar partisan arguments from both ideological poles. The assessment and
solutions offered here, I believe, represent an original perspective
that uniquely closes the partisan divide, a perspective that has unity
and effective answers rather than political victory for either party as
its ultimate ambition. This book offers a fresh path forward while
addressing every fundamental concern of those on both sides of the
political standoff. It does so by uncovering the true sources of our
current malaise, which predate the Great Recession beginning in
2008 by decades and for which each party (and the philosophy it
espouses) shares responsibility.

Consider these two facts, both of which are crucial to understanding the state of our economy today, and yet neither of which
you have likely heard emphasized by any major political leader on
either side:

★ It is generally known that the percentage of unemployed
   Americans, including workers who had dropped out of the
   job market altogether, hit 12 percent of the whole labor
   force in 2010, one of the highest levels since the Great
   Depression. Much less well known, however, is that if we
   add in those Americans who were lucky enough to work
   but who occupied jobs that paid less than a living wage
   (the lowest hourly income required for a family with both
   spouses working to meet basic needs), the number with

inadequate pay or no pay at all soars far beyond 12 percent to 38 *percent* of all American workers. And that number hasn't significantly changed for the past four decades, since the early 1970s.[1]

★  Over the same four decades, since 1973, the real (inflation-adjusted) compensation of the average American worker has risen by barely 10 percent per hour, while how much workers produce on the job—or their productivity—has shot up by 80 percent.[2] That is, compensation for average workers has increased at only 13 percent of the improvement in workers' productivity. *Fully three-quarters of American workers, including even a majority of college graduates,* receive increases that are substantially beneath the gains in productivity. As their compensation has flatlined, most Americans today work for pay-per-hour that has changed hardly at all from what workers received forty years ago. Quite obviously, for most Americans a growing economy has not translated into a better standard of living built upon higher pay.

Given these facts, it is easy to see what an uphill battle so many American workers and families, including many of my former workmates, have gone through just to keep afloat, let alone get ahead. Tens of millions of Americans, significantly more than have been reported, are struggling to make ends meet. And this phenomenon has become dangerously worse in recent years. I am referring today not just to a minority of Americans, but instead to a large majority of Americans and American families who are now left out of prosperity. Their hardship and the inequities underlying it have bred division and combativeness in our society, reflected in the increased polarization of our politics.

Clearly, this situation betrays the long-held American notion that any man or woman who works hard and plays by the rules can expect to get ahead. This expectation is the very essence of the American Dream. The statistics above make a mockery of it. And the plight that all these Americans have suffered has had much wider effects. Their decades-long struggle, as this book will show, was the single greatest cause of the near breakdown of the economy in 2008, the consequences of which have been devastating both here at home and across the globe.

## HOW DID IT HAPPEN?

How have we gotten so far off track? This question has been at the heart of the vitriolic debate that has recently consumed the nation, though it has been asked without understanding or addressing the true nature of the problem. Those on the left blame the undermining of the American workforce by years of rising global labor competition and outsourcing, and the lack of sufficient economic regulation, especially of financial and banking practices. Those on the right blame "big" intrusive government—overregulation, overtaxation, and out-of-control public spending, and their suppressive effects on businesses, investment, and job creation. All these explanations largely miss the mark, and so have led to remedies that have actually compounded the real problems and made them even worse. The result, in effect, is that the true interests of a large majority of citizens have been abandoned by both parties. The voices of ordinary citizens have been drowned out by the clout of special interests and the clamor of misleading debate, and their basic concerns have not been addressed by either contemporary liberalism or conservatism. To the contrary, their concerns have been so marginalized that the very freedom of most Americans has been compromised. What I mean by this goes back to the way we actually define freedom in this country, how both parties have lost sight of that definition, and how we can reclaim it, which forms the backbone of this book. I return to the topic momentarily in this chapter and in greater depth in Chapter 2.

For now, think a moment about this: the decades-long inability of most American workers to get solid real pay increases, causing many of them to take on dangerous levels of debt as the only way to get ahead, should have provided a telltale sign of a deeply broken, untenable economy. After all, these distressing trends were hiding in plain sight, easily measurable and blindingly noticeable. Yet no major political leader from either party seriously addressed them. In the 1990s and 2000s I wrote three books pointing out that, even as we were experiencing strong increases in the gross domestic product (GDP), a shocking number of hardworking, responsible American families were getting left behind. I argued that the policies then in place were actually bringing economic hardship to a majority of Americans, and I worried about what would happen if we continued to operate such an economy, and how such an economy could possibly endure.[3] A meltdown of the economy finally did occur in 2008, but in terms of their pay most Americans had already been experiencing recession-like conditions for many years. I mention these books not to say "I told you so" (the actual meltdown itself, when it finally came, was as jarring to me as it was to all Americans) or to suggest I was the only one making these observations (I wasn't), but merely to reiterate that despite a rising GDP, red flags signaling forbidding economic difficulties were there all along. But they were largely ignored by both parties.

That these signs have been disregarded for so long speaks to the fact that our real problem is not solely economic in nature. In fact, at its root it is not an economic problem at all, but a political one. It is the inevitable outcome of a political system that, besides being severely fractured, is dominated by two internally flawed ideologies. In their current forms, as the coming chapters will demonstrate, neither liberalism nor conservatism is capable of delivering the kind of governance or policies required to build a sustainable, robust economy or to produce a healthy political process. As presently constituted, therefore, both are incompatible with America's true common interest. If we do not find an effective substitute for these failed ideologies, it will be impossible for the nation to move ahead successfully for any length of time, either economically or politically.

## The Failure of Liberalism and Conservatism

### The Role of Government

What does it mean to say that contemporary liberalism and conservatism are failed ideologies? The two essential rules for any governing ideology are, first, that it be based on concrete, logical principles (or values) that are widely shared and to which citizens can hold their government accountable; and, second, that it must be possible to apply these principles consistently. The latter is essentially the test of the former. If the principles cannot be consistently applied and referred to in justifying policy decisions, then they do not represent principles useful for governing, and better, truer principles must be found.

Consider contemporary liberalism, which violates the first rule: it has no well-defined foundation from which consistent policy decisions can be crafted. That is, contemporary liberalism provides no basis for determining the proper extent of government's role in people's lives or in the economy. In fact, it can't even identify clear goals for government or the nation, which would seem to be the most basic job of a governing philosophy. Ted Kennedy, the great liberal hero, believed that bringing greater equality to all facets of American society should be the nation's goal. And indeed, most liberals do believe that current income and wealth inequalities are too large and should be narrowed. Yet few if any liberals actually support full equality of property, wealth, or income, or anything close to it. But if complete equality is not the goal, then what income and wealth disparities would be acceptable, and why are those inequalities acceptable but not some greater level of inequality? Liberalism has no coherent answer to this basic question. And because it has no such answer, liberalism has no means for specifying how much action government should take to address these inequalities.

Liberalism's policy choices in general spring from vague rationales. For example, politicians on the left often defend public spending, regulations, and taxation on the grounds that because no individual makes it entirely on his or her own—because we are all mutually dependent and have a stake in the success of everyone else—obligatory collaboration and sharing are justified. Hillary Clinton delivered a speech to the 1996 Democratic National Convention with the title "It Takes a Village to Raise a Child." President Obama often reminds us that the wealthy have done well not solely because of their own ingenuity and hard work, but also because others invested in the education, research, and infrastructure required to make wealth creation possible. "We're not on our own," Obama has frequently pointed out. "And those of us who've been successful, we've always got to remember that."[4]

Most liberals applauded Elizabeth Warren, creator of the Consumer Financial Protection Bureau and now a U.S. senator from Massachusetts, when she offered the most widely acclaimed liberal argument of this kind during her 2011–12 Senate campaign. She was speaking about factory owners who had made large sums of money. Surely they should be congratulated, and they deserve to keep a large chunk of the money, she said, but they also have obligations to the community that paid for the roads the factory owners used to get their products to market, that educated the workers the factories employed, and that paid for the police and justice systems that protected the factories.[5]

The argument is valid. Yet it still does not provide a workable foundation from which to determine policy. It leaves central questions unanswered: To what degree are we dependent upon and so indebted to each other? That is, how much do we owe each other? Are all of us equally indebted, or are some more indebted than others? Why aren't the taxes we're paying right now enough, or perhaps even more than enough, to repay the debt we each owe? Do all the jobs that the wealthy create for others through businesses they own and their investments count as part—or maybe even most—of their proper contribution? Liberalism has no definition to apply to answering these important questions. It therefore gives the public no means of determining when government expansion into any given field—and into citizens' lives—has overstepped its bounds, with the consequence that liberals' arguments for government activism are susceptible to sounding arbitrary and fueling fears many Americans have of an ever-growing, unrestrained government with no bottom-line definitions or limits. It seemingly gives government a blank check to intervene as government deems fit, tailoring reasons to suit the action rather than tailoring action to principled reasons.

Meanwhile, contemporary conservatism *does* have a clear principled foundation, which has two prongs. The first is freedom as defined by mutual voluntary consent and limited government, which its proponents have erroneously made synonymous with *small* government. The second is deferment to free markets, which conservatives generally trust to provide the most efficient mechanism for individual and collective economic growth. The existence of this firm foundation has enabled conservatism to succeed where liberalism has not in creating a catchy, steady narrative about governance. And yet there is not a conservative politician in government who is able to adhere to the very principles he or she extols. No conservative representative with any hope of gaining office would claim that taxing for and public funding of Social Security, Medicare, Medicaid, unemployment assistance, or food stamps (now called the Supplemental Nutrition Assistance Program) should be abandoned and those programs left entirely or principally to the private market. Conservatives may propose taxing and spending less for these programs, but they still support taxing and spending substantial sums for them.

Indeed, while contemporary conservatives campaign on a philosophy of small government and deference to competitive free markets, they take a very different position on a wide variety of issues, either because in their own judgment it is the correct policy to pursue, or because they realize it is politically advantageous to do so. In neither case are they able to logically explain their conflicting stances. The inherently self-contradictory nature of contemporary conservatism, in fact, is how we wind up in a situation where a conservative presidential candidate like Mitt Romney has to vehemently oppose a health-care system based largely on the model he himself pioneered (which, in turn, borrowed from proposals formulated by conservative organizations like the Heritage Foundation and Republican legislators in the 1990s).

### The Economy

The flaws of the "small government" approach also lie at the heart of our economic struggles. In line with its mutual voluntary consent and small government model, free-market conservatism advocates allowing the free market to operate as unrestrictedly as possible, without regard to how uneven the distributional results are, so long as the results come from free exchanges. Consequently, it provides no way to discriminate between different paths to economic growth. In effect, free-market conservatism views economic efficiency and profits attained through increased layoffs and cheaper labor as equally valid as efficiency and profits reached through increased hiring and innovation. Such a flaw, if not corrected, leads to the deplorable statistics cited earlier: that for two generations in the United States, relatively few Americans have made substantial gains in pay-per-hour despite a soaring real GDP and the far greater productivity of the workforce. This condition, in turn, results in the loss of customers and demand in the market relative to what is produced—customers and demand that businesses need in order to function and grow—unless the reduction in demand is offset by individuals and families taking on increasingly burdensome debt.

As we've seen in recent years, though, this debt-based demand cannot last. Any economy operating upon such a condition is likely to collapse at some point, and this, more than greedy banking practices or the running up of national governmental deficits, explains the breakdown of the economy that ultimately occurred in 2008. Chapter 3 illustrates in depth how it happened.

That it happened is also a sad indictment of liberalism's inability to present a coherent economic alternative of its own. In its place, liberalism has a scattershot list of economic priorities—education, the infrastructure, and research, for example—but no core model explaining how to trigger the basic forces that make the economy run and what government's role should be in that process (the way conservatism focuses on incentivizing and empowering entrepreneurs to invest, produce, and generate economic growth, largely by government staying out of their way).

## A Way Forward

We are thus left with two competing ideologies: one (liberalism) that contains no clearly defined underlying principles by which the public can judge government action, and the other (conservatism) that either consistently violates its own principles as political expediency requires or operates on the basis of erroneous principles. Neither provides a successful measure for holding government accountable, either to its own goals or to the public. And such limited accountability opens the way for politicians on both sides to engage in obfuscation and even in dishonest debate while pursuing policies that end up serving primarily those who are most crucial to them: the most powerfully organized interests and largest campaign donors. The rest of us, the majority of Americans, have had our voices and our political and economic interests sidelined. Our government has become less responsive or representative, our politics cynical. The bulk of the furious rhetoric has come from the extreme right and to a lesser extent the extreme left, yet it is those many Americans in the middle who ought to be the most vehemently outraged, by their decades-long economic and political marginalization, by the political system's complete ineptitude in seeing and addressing problems that are vital to their lives, and by the disgraceful pettiness currently strangling our political institutions.

At bottom, then, the most fundamental political challenge we face as a nation today is that both ideologies dominating our politics are seriously flawed. They are not able to govern effectively. We need an alternative, one based on solid principles that are widely enough shared that our leaders can act consistently on them and expect to win office with real mandates that reflect meaningful majority interests. This alternative must have the ability to define our goals as a nation clearly enough both to guide the development of government policy (or nonpolicy) in the most important areas of our lives and to be held accountable to those goals. And it must provide effective solutions, laying the groundwork for sustainable economic growth and widespread prosperity for all Americans, the resolution of other major pressing problems, and a politics enabling everyone to both be and feel included.

Such an alternative exists. It resides in the middle of American politics, and is based on an understanding of freedom that goes all the way back to the Founders, an understanding that has been lost in the past forty years, forgotten by one party and subverted by the other. For reasons I will explain shortly, I call this alternative philosophy the Common Credo.

It is important first, though, to consider why the Founders should play a crucial role in the foundation of any model for governing we would want to use. When I speak of the Founders, I am referring, of course, to men such as Thomas Jefferson, James Madison, George Washington, John Adams, Benjamin Franklin, and George Mason. The Founders are of such significance that both the right and the left frequently try to "claim" them for their ideology. Conservatives and liberals make these claims because the thinking of the Founders takes us back to essentials, to true fundamental values. The Founders' thinking describes the vision that gave birth to the nation. It expresses the nation's soul, the source of identity toward which the nation has historically strived. At the heart of this vision is a specific definition of freedom that is neither ambiguous nor dated, and that recognizes when government is required to intervene to secure freedom and when its very presence represents an intrusion upon freedom. It is neither freedom as small government nor freedom as some indeterminate striving toward equality.

By building from this fundamental definition, the Common Credo has a systemic, consistent means of determining both the obligations of and limitations on freedom, something that neither contemporary liberalism nor conservatism can claim. In the example of my former workmates at the bakery where I drove a truck or at the electroplating plant where I was a janitor, the Common Credo as a governing model would ensure conditions in which compensation from their employment would be sufficient not only to allow them to make ends meet decently through full-time work, but also to optimize their ability to get ahead with the general improvement in worker productivity. It would do so while simultaneously providing a hard cap on the government's role in this process, preventing government from intervening any further than the minimum necessary to attain these conditions—conditions, not coincidentally, that are also indispensable to nourishing and sustaining a vibrantly growing free-market economy. This is to say that while the Common Credo would fully achieve the basic level of economic equality just described, it would not seek in any way to prevent substantial and, indeed, unrestricted economic inequalities in pay, income, or personal wealth from occurring thereafter, all of which are appropriate once the threshold of economic equality has been fully met.

Chapter 2 uncovers the definition of freedom that permits this seemingly contradictory combination—of a genuinely meaningful level of basic economic equality for all and unrestricted economic disparities thereafter—by taking us back to the nation's birth. The definition reflects what has popularly become known and venerated as the promise of the American Dream, whose fulfillment is actually mandated in the Declaration of Independence. Analyzing the words and policies of the Founders themselves, the chapter sheds new historical light on the Declaration of Independence and the intentions and meanings contained within it.

Using this principle of freedom, a principle we all share intuitively today, the book then shows how we can better understand and finally come to grips with the numerous challenges presently facing the nation. These include issues of low-paying jobs and flatlined wages;

sustainable economic growth; government's role in health care, the environment, education, and research innovation; budgetary deficits; and basic processes of government, such as rules regarding campaign finance and elections. The book will reveal how we veered off course nearly forty years ago, leading ultimately to the breakdown of the entire economy, and how the Common Credo and the specific policy solutions tied to it provide a path for the nation to get back on track. Indeed, the solutions presented here would have avoided the problems from developing in the first place.

Focusing on several root principles of the Founders and the Common Credo, Chapters 2–5 start the story by detailing how the problems arose and became intractable, due primarily to the nation's departure from those principles. Taking off from there, Chapter 6 lays out all ten principles of the Common Credo. Chapter 7, in turn, demonstrates how the ten principles lead the way to specific and effective solutions to every one of the problems.

The Common Credo does not summarily discard either liberalism or conservatism. To the contrary, it captures much of the essence of both ideologies. In the manner of a true philosophy of the center, it bridges the core meanings and strengths of the two ideologies, joins them together, and eliminates the auxiliary failings of each. In this way it enacts the sort of deep compromise that has become so difficult in our era of venomous, debilitating partisanship. Its ability to do this stems from the legitimacy of the principles at its core, which, rooted deeply in our history, are indeed clear, logical, and widely shared.

## THE COMMON CREDO AND AMERICAN THINKING

That last description brings me back to why this philosophy deserves the name "Common Credo." I believe that, while the Credo is submerged beneath the surface of political discourse and is thus generally dormant today, nevertheless nearly all Americans intuitively subscribe to the ethos it represents. It is grounded in the instinctive beliefs that practically all Americans hold in common. Built upon a set of potent values, they come down to us directly from the thinking of the Founders stretching back to the Declaration of Independence and its transcendent premise that "All men are created equal."

It is obviously a risky proposition to claim that any philosophy's principles are shared by most Americans, especially when the current intensity of political debate suggests otherwise. How can we tell? Following the tradition of Jefferson, I believe you, the reader, will find the principles and beliefs making up the Common Credo, set forth in the chapters to come, to be virtually self-evident; that is, they will be what you yourself consider fundamentally right and true either immediately or upon just a little reflection. Where that cannot be expected to be the case in particular instances, I aim to show convincingly through historical evidence and analysis of polls and public attitudes that each such principle is indeed valid: backed by the Founders, endorsed by nearly all Americans, and consistent with the Credo's other principles. Ultimately, though, its viability lies with your assessment: Does it speak to political principles and values you hold dear? Do its policy proposals serve interests you feel are valid and important? I believe you will find, regardless of your political identification, level of income, or any other background characteristics, that it does, and they do, or nearly always do.

Americans subscribe to the Common Credo as instinctively and widely as they do because it is a complete and compelling philosophy. It has the ability to appeal not just to the center, but to liberals and conservatives as well, for it contains within it the best features of both ideologies. It respects and indeed prioritizes the need both for a government that is strictly limited and for one with all the authority necessary to deal effectively with national problems. The Common

Credo calls for a government that can address these problems successfully while operating with the lowest cost and intrusiveness, and the greatest decentralization, practicable. At the same time, it shows how the economic models of Adam Smith (hailed by conservatives) and John Maynard Keynes (hailed by liberals) are predicated on the same principles, not conflicting ones. With these principles in mind, the Common Credo identifies, and the book empirically shows, when strong government action is needed, and when it isn't, for the competitive free-market economy itself to work successfully. I take pains throughout to detail what those on both sides of the political spectrum stand to gain from implementing the Common Credo in a range of areas, and what both sides would be expected to cede.

The principles of the Credo, though, differ fundamentally from the surface views that many political leaders and citizens express today about how America's politics and economy should work. To bring this point home, Chapters 2 through 5 begin with a contemporary belief that Americans take as almost axiomatic today—about the proper role of government, the idea of freedom, or the aim of the economy—and then go on to show that it is mistaken and inconsistent with the principles held by the Founders as well as the deeper underlying beliefs to which Americans truly subscribe. In the process, the chapters reveal how the thinking of the Founders also stands fundamentally at odds with each of the ideologies that presently dominate our politics.

Because the principles of the Common Credo are instinctively held by nearly all Americans, they represent a common ground upon which to build consensus and reengender civil discourse. Attaining consensus through the Common Credo will not end the need for public and legislative debate about exact processes and policies, of course, which is a fundamental purpose of democracy. But it will end the notion that we are a nation deeply divided by basic values and goals. The Republican vice-presidential candidate in 2012, representative Paul Ryan, said that "the fight we are in here, make no mistake about it, is a fight of individualism versus collectivism." On the Democratic side, while stumping for reelection in 2012 President Obama stated that "this election is not just a choice between candidates or parties but two very different visions of this country we love."[6] Many campaign ads carried the same message. The Common Credo rejects such a stark dichotomy, and defuses the antagonistic mentality behind it, from both sides, that has led to our current political stalemate.

Can the Common Credo succeed politically? Is it a practical solution? My argument has been that many Americans intuitively subscribe to its principles, far more than subscribe to either of today's two contesting ideologies, neither of which can garner real majority support. What is more, as Chapter 3 on the economy shows, the Common Credo speaks to the basic economic interests of most Americans in a visceral way and to a degree unmatched by either liberalism or conservatism. In appealing simultaneously to the core values and key economic interests of most Americans, as well as the larger interests of the nation, it has the ability to move people's minds and hearts at the same time in a way neither of the current ideologies can. Of the political alternatives available to us today, only the Common Credo has the potential to inspire and deliver solid, continuing majorities that are essential to govern. Any political party or movement committing to it will be in a position to reap substantial political advantages over any opposing alternative that does not.

## A PERSONAL REFLECTION

A final personal reflection before we dive in. There have been many, many instances in recent years demonstrating the failure of our contemporary politics to produce responsible government that citizens can have faith in. In March 2012, partisan warfare in Congress prevented the new transportation bill, once among the most routine of congressional matters, from being approved, despite the fact that there were then over 70,000 structurally deficient bridges in the country and nearly three million jobs at stake. It was only after *ten temporary extensions* of the prior inadequate funding during the previous three years, and with time nearly up, that another short-term and imperfect solution was worked out, one that will certainly mean further horn-locking in the near future.

With respect to the equally routine matter of addressing the debt ceiling, we weren't even that fortunate: the standoff between the parties in Congress and the White House took our government to the brink of a total shutdown, and resulted in the first ever downgrade of our country's credit rating, an outcome that not so long ago would have seemed unthinkable. It is no wonder that, in late 2011, 89 percent of Americans said they distrusted government to do the right thing.[7]

It's gotten so bad that all too often now Congress is unable to reach consensus on important matters in the absence of a full-on crisis setting. Recognizing its own dysfunction, and in order to force itself to reach the minimal consensus needed to make crucial tax and spending policies, Congress in 2011 set two fiscal time bombs to go off at the start of 2013. If no plan to reduce deficits had been agreed on by then, policies that everyone detested and recognized would possibly cause a recession—a $400 billion tax hike on all Americans from the expiration of the Bush tax cuts and an across-the-board reduction of nearly $100 billion of spending each year for a decade, called a sequester (half the cuts from domestic and half from defense spending)—would automatically take effect. In other words, Congress had to resort to actually holding itself hostage by manufacturing a crisis in order to ensure that it would be able to make basic policy decisions, an unprecedented action in modern politics.

Remarkably, even that failed. Congress did decide to make most of the Bush tax cuts permanent except for the highest earners, yet was unable to agree upon an overall deficit-reduction plan. As a result, the sequester, which everyone said was a terrible idea that we should do anything to avoid, took effect. According to many projections, it was likely to cut economic growth, cost hundreds of thousands of jobs over the period of the sequester, curtail assistance to the most economically vulnerable children and senior citizens, and reduce military readiness, all at the same time. Of course, there is always the possibility that the two sides will rethink and eventually come together on a different course of action.

For me, however, the full horror of our current situation was brought home two years ago, when my own Democratic congresswoman, Gabrielle Giffords, a thoughtful, admirable legislator who identified herself as a moderate and earlier had been a Republican, was the target of an attempted assassination in January 2011 that badly wounded her and eleven others, killing six. It took place during a routine "Congress on Your Corner" session held with constituents in the parking lot in front of a local supermarket in Tucson, Arizona. This came seven months after Giffords's office, along with those of several representatives from other districts, was vandalized immediately following the 2010 vote on health-care reform. A bullet was shot through the glass front door to her main office in the district. In a cruel irony, an American flag, the symbol of our nation's unity, stood serenely in the background behind the bullet hole in the shattered glass. The pain I felt seeing a photo of that scene, and then hearing of the tragedy that followed seven months later, was visceral and profound.

Giffords returned to the House floor in the summer of 2011 for the first time since the attempted assassination in order to vote on ending the standoff over the debt ceiling. Her right arm was bandaged, and she steadied herself on a cane. Words coming to her only with great difficulty, she said of the weeks and months of stalemate during her hospitalization and recuperation that she despaired at the complete collapse of bipartisanship in Washington. Her appearance brought a moment of dignity to the proceedings, a feeling of genuine fellowship across partisan and ideological lines. The grave concern she expressed represented far more than the views of her constituents in southern Arizona. They expressed the feelings of nearly all Americans.

We have reached a critical point. Unless we work to identify and reclaim our shared elemental values, we risk more of the same political discord and paralysis and more of the same economic stagnation that has engulfed Americans for so long. For the many reasons mentioned above, both contemporary conservatism and liberalism have failed as governing philosophies. Over the past four decades, they have not enabled the nation to progress in all too many areas. To the contrary, the ideas contained in them have been associated with massive failures, dearly paid for by the average American. We deserve something better. Indeed, the nation cannot ultimately succeed without something better.

## CHAPTER 2

# FREEDOM AND EQUALITY

★ ★ ★ ★ ★

*Mistaken Belief 1: Freedom is the right of every*
*person to choose as he or she decides.*

*Mistaken Belief 2: "All men are created equal" argues*
*for equal rights and equal opportunity, nothing more.*

NO WORDS IN THE DECLARATION of Independence are more majestic or beloved among Americans than "We hold these Truths to be self-evident, that all Men are created equal, that they are endowed by their Creator with certain unalienable Rights, that among these are Life, Liberty, and the Pursuit of Happiness." Yet when the Liberty Bell rang out on that warm summer day in Philadelphia and the Declaration of Independence was read aloud in public for the first time, this sentence was not the same as the one that the Declaration's author, Thomas Jefferson, had originally penned. At the time, few were aware of this difference, or of the profound relevance it would one day come to have for American politics and for the individual lives of a substantial majority of Americans.

The Declaration that Jefferson originally drafted was more specific in places, and accordingly more cumbersome. Because quite a few of these specifics were struck from the final version, some of the soaring phrases at the heart of the Declaration, such as "all men are created equal," may seem a bit vague to us. For the Founders, however, the spirit and the intentions behind the words were quite clear.

To the grave disadvantage of most Americans today, the more specific meaning that the Founders had in mind in adopting the Declaration of Independence has now been all but forgotten. It is practically lost in our contemporary political life, save for the promise of the American Dream that lives on, and the Common Credo, both of which now lie passively beneath the surface of our thinking. Rediscovering and reasserting that more specific meaning of the Declaration, as this chapter sets out to do, will provide the framework for determining what the most fundamental goals of the country and government are, where the nation has gone astray in meeting them, and how to find our way back on course. It is thus the vital first step.

## FREEDOM

The very first principle that the Founders derived from the transcendent truth that "All men are created equal" was the right of each person to individual freedom, a term used synonymously here with the word "liberty." If all men are created equal, each of us having inviolate dignity and worth equal to everyone else's, then it directly follows that every person must be free to choose for him- or herself and not be under the arbitrary will or control of any other, including the government. To the Founders, the equality of all men and right to freedom were self-evident, unalienable, and eternal. They had their origins in natural law.

The right of every individual to freedom spanned two crucial spheres. Both have become the subject of considerable confusion and misunderstanding today, over what they mean and what they involve. This confusion is partly attributable to the outright manipulation of the definition by politicians and groups serving their own causes.

The first sphere of freedom was the right to individual auton-

{ 28 }

omy—for example, one's right to believe and decide for oneself; to determine one's convictions and religion; to think and speak one's thoughts; to purchase, own, and control property; to choose one's occupation; to travel where one wants; and to marry and have children if one decides.

Obviously, though, individual autonomy had limits. Nobody was free to wrongfully harm others. An individual's personal will and ability to choose extended only so far as they did not encroach on someone else's autonomy. As John Locke, a major philosophical influence on the Founders, succinctly put it, "Freedom is not license." James Madison, in *The Federalist Papers*, termed such encroachment "abuses of liberty."[1] Freedom, this is to say, is reciprocal: it gives priority to individual autonomy yet at the same time sets restrictions and obligations upon each of us that are required to ensure the same autonomy for others.[2]

Everyone knows this underneath, but the language commonly used in political discourse these days often neglects or entirely disregards the reciprocal nature of freedom. The more widespread conception today is summed up by this pithy excerpt from the influential columnist George Will: "Modernity teaches freedom is the sovereignty of the individual's will—personal volition that is spontaneous, unconditioned, inviolable and self-legitimizing."[3] By this description, freedom is highly individualistic: the sovereignty of the individual and the unconditional, inviolable right of each individual to choose and do as he or she wants. It is freedom as pure voluntary choice. There is no mention of the limits freedom places on our behavior to ensure that no one else's freedom is compromised.

A similar view is reflected in many of the organizations in the United States with the word "freedom" or "liberty" as part of their name: FreedomWorks, Institute of Liberty, Frontiers of Freedom, Liberty Central, and Freedom's Lighthouse, to mention a few. Every one of them promotes an individualistic view of freedom. For example, the website for FreedomWorks, the largest and most influential of the organizations, says that it "believes individual liberty . . . provides individuals with the greatest control over what they own and earn" and that FreedomWorks is "leading the fight for lower taxes, less government, and more freedom."[4]

Yes, freedom does involve individuals' having the greatest control over what they own and earn. At the same time, less government and lower taxes do not necessarily mean more freedom. The limits, restrictions, and obligations that freedom entails might well require more government and higher taxes.

For example, the way in which some people use their property could necessitate government regulation in order to protect other individuals' autonomy from wrongful harm. Such harms might involve the next-door neighbor letting trash pile up endlessly in the front yard and scatter all over; an industry neglecting to attend to workplace safety; or a company putting contaminated food onto the market. Examples like these abound in society, and we take for granted that government is able to set regulations and intervene if necessary to protect us from such abuses of autonomy by others. Strictly equating freedom with less government, however, as is so frequently done today, undermines this protection. It downplays and even challenges the limits, restrictions, and obligations that freedom legitimately places on each of us in order to assure the same autonomy for all people. It opens the door for the "abuses of liberty" that Madison warned against.

This takes us to the second sphere of freedom, in which the neglect of freedom's reciprocal side has had disastrous consequences. It is here that Thomas Jefferson's edited wording of the Declaration of Independence becomes relevant, illuminating how far we have strayed from the thinking of the Founders and how substantial the costs of doing so have been to most Americans and to the country at large.

This second sphere asserts that freedom is not simply a sink-

or-swim, you're-on-your-own proposition in the way that the individualistic view generally regards it today. Yes, freedom does involve self-reliance and the obligation of individuals to take care of and be responsible for themselves. But the Founders believed there was a necessary reciprocal context for such self-reliance and individual responsibility to occur. That context was the availability of sufficient economic opportunity. Rather than being a sink-or-swim proposition, freedom requires the presence of enough economic opportunity to enable every willing individual to "swim"—to make a decent living and get ahead through his or her efforts. There must be enough opportunity for all willing individuals to be self-reliant.

This key goal of freedom and the call to achieve it, though never expressed in those exact words, underlie the Declaration's powerful mandate for the nation. To our considerable loss, many of our leaders and most influential political media figures now give little more than lip service to this fundamental goal of the Founders. They have done so for many decades notwithstanding how crucial the goal was to the Founders' thinking, and with scant understanding of how harshly the neglect of that goal would end up injuring most Americans' lives or damaging the economy right down to its foundations.

## HISTORICAL BACKGROUND OF
## THE DECLARATION OF INDEPENDENCE

The stirring idea at the heart of the Declaration, that "All men are created equal" and therefore that all individuals have certain unalienable rights, took various forms at the time the nation announced its birth. What listeners in Philadelphia heard that day—what the Founders had written and signed in the final draft of the Declaration of Independence—was that timeless idea presented only in its most distilled form. The refined beauty of the final Declaration, which has inspired so many Americans since then and so many other human beings around the globe, came from the editing of Jefferson's draft by a working committee of the Continental Congress, known as the Committee of Five.

In writing his draft, Jefferson was building upon the thinking of his generation. Indeed, there had been other renditions of the idea prior to his.

First among them was George Mason's. For some years before 1775, Mason had endeavored to avoid public service both because of problems with his health—he suffered severely from gout—and because of his frustration with the outsized egos that he felt infected political life. In 1775, however, he became deeply involved again in trying to express the ideal of individual freedom. He formulated his own belief about individual rights in the spring of 1776 for Virginia's Declaration of Rights, which began: "All men are by nature equally free and independent, and have certain inherent and natural rights . . . namely, the enjoyment of life and liberty, with the means of acquiring and possessing property, and pursuing and obtaining happiness and safety." The new state of Virginia went on to enact Mason's words in early June of 1776. Jefferson had already described Mason as "the wisest man of his generation," and he was intimately familiar with the wording when he began writing his draft of the Declaration later that month.[5]

In Mason's formulation, all individuals had not only the right to pursue happiness but also a right to *the means* to obtain happiness. Similarly, with regard to property, Mason's formulation included not just the right of all individuals to acquire and possess property but also a right to the *means* to acquire property. And alongside being equally *free* by nature, the formulation asserted that all men were equally *independent* by nature.

In fact, having the means to obtain rather than merely pursue happiness, as well as having both the right and the means to acquire property, followed from what it meant to be independent. The term "independence" had an economic as well as a political dimension: it entailed having the ability to provide a customary, dignified living and to get ahead through means under one's own control—thus being free to make choices on one's own and not being under the arbitrary will or control of any other. If individuals were independent, it followed that they would have the basic means necessary to acquire property and, in terms of means, to obtain happiness.

Natural law and natural-rights thinking, as championed by philosophers such as John Locke, greatly influenced the Founders and continues to exert a strong presence in American philosophical, political, and legal thinking today. Independence had been the condition of all individuals in the beginning, in the state of nature, when every individual had the right of access to the commons—to the Earth—to attain the resources necessary to provide for him- or herself in a manner customary to the times. To be independent was the natural condition of every individual, and every individual was equal in this regard.

Support for the words of the Virginia Declaration of Rights was widespread in the newly emergent nation. John Adams used nearly the same words in crafting the Massachusetts Declaration of Rights, asserting that "All men are born equally free and independent." Elsewhere Adams had observed that "equal liberty" required enabling "every member of society" to acquire land "so that the multitude may be possessed of small estates." Whether or not he believed independence to be an absolute right, a society based upon citizens who were economically independent was undoubtedly, in Adams's eyes, the best-organized and freest of all societies. James Madison believed so, as well. In Madison's words:

The class of citizens who provide at once their own food and their own raiment may be viewed as the most truly independent and happy. They are more: they are the best basis of public liberty . . . It follows, that the greater the proportion of this class to the whole society, the more free, the more independent, and the more happy must be the society itself.

And Benjamin Franklin voiced the same view that Mason had, affirming that "All men are born equally free and independent." In August 1776 those words became part of Pennsylvania's Declaration of Rights and constitution.[6]

## THE MEANING OF THE DECLARATION

What exactly did Jefferson mean when he wrote the Declaration of Independence? This question brings us to the differences between his original draft and the final document that the Committee of Five and then the entire Continental Congress enacted and read aloud in Philadelphia.

Jefferson's original draft did not assert: "All men are created equal." Instead, his draft stated: "All men are created equal and independent."[7] This wording is nearly identical to the principle expressed by Mason, Adams, and Franklin, in their declarations of rights, that "All men are born equally free and independent." In the natural-law thinking that heavily influenced Jefferson, "equality" presumed the condition of independence. The one incorporated the other. It is likely that this was the way Jefferson understood the revised phrase "All men are created equal": "equal" encompassed the condition of independence, making the latter word superfluous.[8] There is no doubt, in any case, that a majority of the Committee of Five that finalized the document believed that the condition of economic independence was fundamental to freedom. Jefferson, Adams, and Franklin all subscribed to this belief, and they constituted a majority of the committee that edited the final phrase.

The practice of slavery of course, which many Founders willingly condoned and even engaged in, brutally insulted the vaulted vision that the Declaration expressed. The ideal that "All men are created equal" was proclaimed by a society that did not practice the principle, in the worst way possible, with regard to most blacks and Native Americans. At the same time, the Declaration of Independence was a statement asserting an ideal that Jefferson, its primary author— who himself owned slaves—believed the nation should pursue, and fervently hoped the nation would ultimately achieve, despite not then being true to it.[9]

The ideal that the Declaration conveyed had been familiar in America right from the start. At the settling of Jamestown, John Smith wrote that in America, "Every man may become master and owner of his owne labour and land." The same sentiment prevailed in America in the wake of the Revolutionary War nearly two centuries later, when Noah Webster wrote, echoing the thinking of Jefferson, Adams, Franklin, and numerous others, "A general and tolerably equal distribution of property is the whole basis of national freedom." George Washington, too, frequently spoke of every man's having the ability to live and provide under his own proverbial fig tree.[10]

The words of the Declaration of Independence, then, inferred an epic vision, a vision of a nation where individuals could be and were free and independent, and where every person was equal in this fundamental way. This is to say, *freedom entailed not simply a particular political or economic process but also the societal attainment of a certain economic condition.* Freedom would thrive with the availability of sufficient opportunity to permit all willing individuals to be economically independent.

The economic condition the Founders envisaged had a moral power they believed was compelling enough to be regarded as a self-evident truth. Its moral force resided, first, in the basic natural right of every free individual to the fruits of his or her own labor and improvement. Second, it lay in the ready access that nature gave all individuals to the economic means needed for independence, through the common access that every individual had to the Earth at the beginning, a right affirmed in natural law. The condition of independence meant that no individual would be economically under the arbitrary will or control of any other. Third, its moral force emanated from the fact that, for freedom to have any real meaning, such economic opportunity had to be available. Absent the availability of that opportunity, individuals were not free to attain independence.

Adding further moral power was the basic stricture of reciprocity enunciated by Adam Smith in 1776, in his magnum opus *Wealth of Nations*. Regarding the proper return from an individual's work, Smith wrote: "It is but equity that they who feed, cloath, and lodge the whole body of the people, should have such a share of the produce of their own labour as to be themselves tolerably well fed, cloathed and lodged."[11] In terms of today's economy, Smith is saying that individuals who work full-time at jobs producing commodities and services that others want but don't wish or have time to produce on their own deserve at least a tolerably decent living themselves. Even the server at McDonald's is doing a strenuous job that requires a good bit of fortitude, a job that eases others' lives but that most others do not want to do themselves.[12]

The Founders cared deeply about independence and the pivotal role it played in securing the autonomy of the individual and the success of a free society. Indeed, Jefferson believed it to be imperative:

Whenever there is in any country, uncultivated lands and unemployed poor, it is clear that the laws of property have been so far extended as to violate a natural right. The earth is given as a common stock for man to labour and live on. If, for encouragement of industry we allow it to be appropriated, we must take care that other employment be furnished to those excluded from the appropriation. If we do not the fundamental right to labour the earth returns to the unemployed.[13]

Regarding any who had been excluded, Jefferson argued that the right to the means of providing a tolerable living *came prior to and took precedence over* the right of property ownership of any others who own in excess. It was up to society to ensure the required availability of opportunity—if need be, through accessibility to public lands or to additional employment—so that a condition of independence would in turn be broadly available.

The access of all individuals to economic independence and the means of self-reliance was, therefore, of more than simply theoretical or even material importance to the Founders. It was a moral imperative and as such needed to be an objective of public policy. Accordingly, Jefferson proposed that every individual who had never owned property be granted fifty acres of public land, enough in most locales to support a dignified living for a family in terms customary to the day, well above mere subsistence;[14] he supported public works of various kinds to spur commerce and prosperity; and he initiated the Louisiana Purchase, ensuring the ideal of a nation, as he had described in his First Inaugural Address, "with room enough for our descendants to the thousandth and thousandth generation." Thus granted the availability of opportunity, workers in manufacturing in America, if they lost work or suffered from depressed wages, would be "as much at ease, as independent and moral as our agricultural inhabitants, and they will continue to be, so long as there are vacant lands for them to resort to."[15]

Jefferson's purchase of the Louisiana Territory in 1803 may thus have been the largest and most enduring public assistance program ever in the nation's history. Sixty years later, the Louisiana Purchase made possible the Homestead Act of 1862 under Abraham Lincoln, which was later updated by Congress through the Enlarged Homestead Act of 1909. Following Jefferson's prescription, the Homestead

Act granted freehold title of public lands in the Louisiana territories and beyond, in parcels ample enough to support a dignified living, to all families willing to settle, work, and improve them.

The idea of economic independence, as the Founders understood it, had two related dimensions. One dimension was the ability to provide a dignified customary living through means under an individual's own control, so that the individual would not be under the arbitrary will of another. Understood here, too, was the necessity of retaining adequate time for other aspects of life, including family, civic, and spiritual life. A second dimension was the ability to get ahead by dint of improving one's efforts—that is, the ability to receive the return from one's labor rather than having someone else receive it. The latter possibility—of the return from one's efforts going somewhere else without one's consent—was a clear violation of freedom. Freedom, as the Reverend Garrison Frazier, a former slave, put it, meant precisely "placing us where we could reap the fruit of our own labor."[16] The ready availability of economic opportunity was indispensable to attaining these two dimensions of independence and thus, in the Founders' eyes, crucially important to attaining the vaulted aim of freedom.

## ONE AREA THAT JOINS THE RIGHT AND THE LEFT

Where do the left and the right presently stand on these issues? Here there is some positive news to report, at least at one level. Both liberals and conservatives today share something vital: they both subscribe to the same goal for the nation and the economy, the goal that the economy should operate to benefit *all* who contribute or are willing to contribute, not just some.

Asked in August 2008, just as the presidential election campaign was heating up, whether he could identify a Democratic narrative, and, if so, what it was, candidate Barack Obama answered this way:

I think I can tell a pretty simple story. Ronald Reagan ushered in an era that reasserted the marketplace and freedom. He made people aware of the cost of government regulation or at least a command-and-control-style regulation regime . . . George Bush took Ronald Reagan's insight and ran it over a cliff. And so I think the simple way of telling the story is that when Bill Clinton said the era of big government is over, he wasn't arguing for an era of no government. So what we need to bring about is the end of the era of unresponsive and inefficient government and short-term thinking in government, so that the government is laying the groundwork, the framework, the foundation for the market to operate effectively and for every single individual to be able to be connected with that market and to succeed in that market . . . Now, that's the story. Now, telling it elegantly—"low taxes, smaller government"—the way the Republicans have, I think is more of a challenge.[17]

Here's the Republican version, told by N. Gregory Mankiw, senior economic advisor to President George W. Bush. He begins from the individualistic view of freedom characteristic of convervatism today, in the tradition of philosophers led by the most prominent contemporary proponent of individualist freedom, the late Robert Nozick of Harvard:

From [the conservatives'] perspective, it is not the proper role of government to fix income distribution . . . They believe, instead, that in a free society, people make money when they produce goods and services that others value and that, as a result, what they earn is rightfully theirs . . . Despite their rejection of spreading the wealth, Republicans recognize that times are hard for the less fortunate. Their solution is not to adjust the slices of the economic pie, as if they had been doled out by careless cutting, but to expand the pie by providing greater opportunity for all.[18]

There are plenty of differences between the Democratic and Republican viewpoints in these two stories, but one thing is evident: no matter how different the viewpoints are, each aims to attain the same end result—a market economy that provides opportunity for all and not just for some. At least in theory and in the abstract, Democrats and Republicans share this same goal.

## FREEDOM AND EQUALITY BECOME ONE

The Founders were pretty clear about what this goal involves: in a free society, opportunity for all necessitates that all willing individuals have access to the means of achieving self-reliance, enabling them both to provide at least a minimally dignified living in terms customary to the day, above sheer subsistence, and to improve their standard of living on the basis of their own efforts.[19] This vision of the Founders has come down to us in the form of the promise of the American Dream, to which so many Americans subscribe.

An essential component of this vision involved the relationship between the values of freedom and equality. Today, these two values are treated as being quite different, different enough that they come into conflict at critical junctures. Indeed, they are often seen as being directly opposed: either we can choose to prioritize personal freedom, or we can choose to prioritize equality. As the Founders saw it, however, prioritizing the availability of economic opportunity for self-reliance and improvement is the very point where the two great fundamental values—the freedom of all individuals and the economic equality of all individuals—fuse and become one. We needn't choose between them.

Being equal under freedom, then, is not simply the fulfillment of equal opportunity, or having an "equal chance," as it is often considered to be today. Yes, equal opportunity and an equal chance are essential, but there must also be *enough* opportunity—a level of availability of opportunity that is sufficient to meet the bottom line of equality that freedom calls for. Suppose there are too few jobs for those out of work. Where such opportunity is insufficient or lacking, it follows that treating every individual consistently with equal opportunity must leave some individuals out, and thus unfree, because there is not enough opportunity for all. Equal opportunity, then, does not suffice. The American Dream does not promise equal opportunity alone. It does not promise just an equal chance. It also promises *"sufficient opportunity."* It promises enough opportunity for every person who is willing to be diligent and work hard to attain a decent living and to get ahead by dint of his or her efforts.

It is important to note that once this foundation of sufficient opportunity is met—once a condition of sufficient opportunity does in fact exist for all—there should and will still be considerable inequalities of income and wealth upward from the base condition, without restriction. Great differences of income and wealth are entirely appropriate and consistent with freedom—any person or any number of people can become as affluent as possible—so long as sufficient opportunity to be self-reliant and get ahead by dint of one's efforts is and continues to be readily available to everyone.

## THREE KEY IMPLICATIONS OF EQUAL FREEDOM

### The Free Market Is Not the Equivalent of Freedom

So what kind of economic arrangement does this model of freedom call for? It is tempting to think of a free-market economy as the pure expression of freedom, partly because it contains the word "free," but mostly because the free market is based upon the voluntary choices of people. That is a highly important attribute, to be sure. Nonetheless, a different conclusion follows from the thinking of the Founders, as a brief historical account enables us to see.

In 1776 America, the economic condition of freedom was usually attained through farming and access to landed property or, secondly, through small enterprises and skilled trades. In a good part of early America, large numbers of white males enjoyed a condition of economic independence.

An industrial market setting, which began to emerge in the 1800s, is something vastly different from an economy based on land. As an industrial market economy advances, farming and access to land are no longer the means to independence and self-reliance for most; rather, these conditions increasingly stem from access to sufficiently remunerative employment and a ready choice among jobs. An individual earning at least a living wage or higher, with compensation improving commensurate with productivity, and who can also easily choose among other similar openings so as not to be dependent upon any one job, is self-reliant within the Founders' understanding of independence. In addition, individuals must be left with enough time to engage in other important aspects of their life.

From the Founders' era through the industrial expansion of the nineteenth and early twentieth centuries, the availability of open lands in the West made independence at least theoretically attainable by every American. But with the vicious unemployment of the late 1920s and 1930s, the Great Depression renewed the basic issue of independence and self-reliance in the starkest terms. The New Deal was in part an attempt to restore and adapt the Founders' vision of freedom and independence to an economy no longer grounded in land and farming but rather in wage-earning employment in an industrial market setting. Franklin Roosevelt said as much when defining his aim in creating public jobs, establishing a minimum wage, setting up programs like unemployment insurance, Social Security, and housing assistance, and instituting collective bargaining. "True individual freedom cannot exist without economic security and independence," Roosevelt declared in his penultimate State of the Union Address, echoing the way he had described the New Deal in the Second Inaugural Address eight years earlier: that our forefathers "established the Federal Government in order to promote the general welfare and secure the blessings of liberty to the American people. Today we invoke those same governmental powers to achieve the same objectives."[20]

Following the New Deal and the extraordinary effort involved in World War II, the nation entered a period of widespread prosperity. The minimum wage of the 1950s and 1960s was, in fact, quite close to a living wage (a wage capable of supporting a modest, customary standard of living), and coverage of the wage was expanded to encompass workers in an ever-greater range of economic sectors. Unemployment was moderate, and the total growth of the economy and productivity corresponded with the substantial growth in real wages and incomes of nearly all Americans.[21] In those decades, the social contract of the New Deal remained broadly intact.

At the same time, some Americans were egregiously left out, with the result that the struggle for civil rights took center stage in the late 1950s and the 1960s. It became the dominating force in politics for much of a generation. In the spirit of the founding principles, it was enunciated, foremost, as a movement for freedom, with "freedom marches" as its most visible organizing tool. Liberal thinkers, though, increasingly came to view the movement as emphasizing the aim and end goal of equality, such as equal economic opportunity and equal access to public accommodations, and liberals focused more and more on achieving equality without mentioning the broader notion of freedom. In time, the goal of freedom practically vanished from the liberal lexicon as regards economic relationships and issues. This left a vacuum for the individualistic view of freedom to fill.

It was in this context, in 1980, that Nobel Prize–winning economist Milton Friedman authored a book with his wife, Rose, called *Free to Choose*.[22] It defended the thesis that because free choice and voluntary exchange form the foundation of the free market, the free market is in effect the equivalent of freedom in the economic realm. The book became an instant bestseller, a basic text for conservatives, and did much to boost the gathering ascendancy of the individualistic view of freedom. Other eminent conservative thinkers, like the philosopher Robert Nozick and the economists Friedrich Hayek and N. Gregory Mankiw, shared its view. With the book, Friedman came to be seen as the most notable contemporary economist of the free market.

This chapter, however, has demonstrated why freedom is never about individual choice alone. Among other things, freedom involves restrictions and obligations placed upon all of us—necessary for ensuring the same freedom for all—that are not matters of voluntary choice. Similarly, individual choice within a free market, by itself, takes no account of the availability of economic opportunity, particularly the kind of sufficient opportunity the Founders deemed essential to secure individual autonomy and the natural condition needed for freedom and self-reliance. This kind of opportunity has never pretended to be the objective of the free market. A free-market economy might well produce growth, indeed substantial overall growth, but its distribution is another matter. Narrowly distributed, even substantial growth will fail to achieve the goal.

Likewise, nothing in the objectives of a free market speaks to paying a living wage or ensuring a proper return for an individual's labor as efforts improve. To the contrary, the whole idea of market efficiency, which is the market's express goal, is not only for the purchasers of labor to pay as little as they can, but also for employers to get along with the least amount of labor possible.[23]

On what grounds, then, without external intervention, is it reasonable to expect that the market economy on its own will lead to the widespread opportunity for self-reliance and improvement that is central to the Founders' understanding of freedom? In the following chapter, we will see how very distant from that goal the contemporary economy actually is and has been for many years. More than that, we will see how the failure to bring about the sharing of prosperity to the degree the Founders' definition of freedom requires became the originating cause of the economy's collapse in 2008, the economy's relatively poor performance for quite a few years before that, and the difficult recovery the economy has experienced ever since. Identifying the root cause will, in turn, lead to the steps that must take place in order for the economy to attain strong sustainable growth again in the future.

This is not to condemn the free market, which can accomplish many worthwhile ends through its demonstrated dynamism and creativity. The very fact that the free market is based on the free, voluntary choices of individuals is a powerful asset. It is only to say that the free market is not the same as freedom—it is aimed neither at necessarily creating nor at broadly distributing the kind of economic opportunity that freedom as envisioned by the Founders requires. For that to happen, a free-market economy cannot generally just be left alone to its own devices. It must be coupled with a certain amount of public guidance targeted to attain the core goals lying at the heart of the Founders' beliefs.

### Freedom Is Morally Absolute, Not Morally Relativist

Just as equating freedom with the free market represents a mistaken understanding, so too does equating freedom with moral relativism. Relativism of values troubles and even scares many Americans, for if morals are relative to each person, there then can be no bedrock societal standard, no unswerving expectations to which everyone would feel compelled to adhere. Where would limits come from? In a morally relativistic world, nothing would be out of bounds.

The notion of freedom appears to present that real possibility. If individuals are free, it seems to follow that values, too, must be relative and up to each individual to accept or reject. How otherwise can individuals be autonomous and free to choose for themselves? On this view, freedom suggests that there is no external moral order—no absolute and timeless morality that everyone is obliged to accept and follow.

Moral absolutes generally require a higher perspective. They depend upon a preexisting, fixed, and eternal truth, which is sometimes considered the special province of religion and theology. Yet if this is so, and if a free society protects religious choice as it should, then a diversity of religious beliefs—or no belief at all, for some—would seem to rule out societal-wide agreement on such an eternal truth.

Freedom as understood by the Founders, however, is not a relativist belief. It is instead based upon an absolute, fixed truth, which the Founders termed "self-evident" and also considered transcendent and unending: that all of us are created equal.

Many religions hold that this same timeless truth came first from God and represents the word of God, grounded in the creation of each human being in the image of God. In this way the underlying premise of the Common Credo has both a secular and a sectarian foundation, understood equally well as being self-evident or as deriving from divine teaching. Indeed, the Founders themselves acknowledged each root of this truth in the Declaration of Independence; in the same sentence, they described this truth as both self-evident and "endowed by [the] Creator."[24] From either perspective, the underlying premise of the equal creation of every individual leads to each individual's unalienable right to freedom as well as each individual's unalienable duty to others—a moral code delineating the restrictions, obligations, and responsibilities we each have in relation to every other person that are needed in the name of equal freedom.

Inevitably there are disagreements about precisely what the strictures mean and how far they extend. When does self-defense override the prohibition against murder, for example? When and how should producers be held liable for defective products? Under what circumstances is it acceptable for an individual to breach a contract? How clean should the air we breathe be to be considered healthy, and how should the costs of cleanup and enforcement be paid? Disagreements over many questions like these occur just as disagreements occur over the interpretation of religious strictures. Yet beyond such disagreements, the principles as well as the premise from which they flow remain both absolute and eternal.

## Both Conservative and Liberal Ideologies Today Face Fundamental Dilemmas That Neither Can Resolve

The fact that the theory behind the free market cannot promise the delivery of sufficient opportunity even when the economy is growing poses major dilemmas for today's ideologies. With respect to contemporary conservatism, as Mankiw pointed out, conservatives believe that outcomes produced by the private market are necessarily legitimate if they follow from voluntary exchanges and free choice. As a result, many conservatives are opposed to obligatory sharing to alter outcomes of the private market. Indeed, conservatives often view such obligatory sharing as a form of public theft.

Instead, Mankiw says, conservatives call for increasing the size of the pie. They call for growth in the economy. However, if the pie is being very unevenly shared, increasing its size may well do nothing for most, or even leave quite a few worse off. That certainly has been the case for the past four decades, as GDP has more than doubled per capita while middle-class and working-class wages have stagnated. What then?

Contemporary conservatism has no immediate answer, at least not one consistent with its individualistic idea of freedom. While most conservative politicians advocate at least some social insurance and public assistance programs, they do so *against* the philosophy they otherwise so vocally promote. Individualistic freedom, as we've established, places its focus on the voluntary consent of individuals in market exchanges, to the stark exclusion of other considerations. In other words, individualistic freedom as a model provides no downward limit on how little we can spend or tax for social insurance or public assistance programs. In fact, it provides no basis for taxing or implementing such programs *at all*, except, perhaps, to preserve the sheer capacity to stay alive; nor does it identify any situation in which a person might be unfree despite participating in a market exchange. For example, the most notable contemporary conservative philosopher of individualistic freedom, Robert Nozick, has reasoned that an individual voluntarily selling him- or herself into slavery comports with freedom if the individual believes that doing so will improve his or her situation. Similarly, the celebrated conservative economist of individualistic freedom, Friedrich Hayek, concluded that voluntary exchange leaving an individual "at the mercy of the only man willing to employ me" was entirely compatible with freedom.[25]

"Compassionate conservatism," the hallmark of George W. Bush's 2000 campaign for president, was an attempt to respond to this difficulty of pure individualistic freedom. It was intended to address those myriad instances when market outcomes grounded in free voluntary choice still leave individuals in need. Yet invoking "being compassionate toward others" (or, alternatively, appealing to what "a civilized, decent, and caring society must do") as the justification for obligatory social assistance offers no defined *upward* limits on that assistance. It establishes no boundaries on the areas covered by that obligatory assistance or the amount that can be spent on its behalf. This is the same kind of problem, as we will see in a moment, that afflicts liberalism.

Milton Friedman advanced a different way of trying to justify obligatory sharing within the frame of individualistic freedom. He defended programs to counter poverty, such as a guaranteed minimum income, on grounds that he was mentally distressed by poverty and therefore benefited from its reduction. As a result, if the reduction of poverty were left to individual compassion and philanthropy instead of to obligations set by public policy, those who contributed to philanthropy would essentially become free-givers, letting Friedman off the hook to benefit as a free-rider—a form of market failure.[26]

Once again, though, this way of thinking could justify literally any kind of governmental intervention and any amount of governmental spending, without limitation at all, in order to eliminate whatever happens to distress an individual. (Not to mention that there are some who are not so disturbed by poverty, when they believe it is the fault of the poor themselves, yet would still be forced to pay to alleviate it.) The absence of any upward limitation on government, and the logic leading to such a result, places Friedman's rationale wholly outside the frame of individualistic freedom—thus making it a rationale that the adherents of individualistic freedom themselves would roundly reject. In rejecting it, however, the adherents would find themselves once again stuck with the sink-or-swim philosophy that contains no downward limit on spending for the very same kinds of programs.

Conservatives might then reply that government is not the proper actor to serve in these situations of need in any case. Rather, voluntary philanthropy is. Individuals who are in need can turn to many different charitable services. But even if charity were widely enough available and sufficient to the need—hardly the case in reality—the dignity of equal freedom requires that individuals have access to sufficient economic opportunity as a matter that is due to them, not as a matter left to the voluntary choice of charity (which by definition cannot be assured to be forthcoming). Philanthropy can never suitably substitute for something that is due to individuals.

Liberals, meanwhile, don't regard outcomes from the private market as necessarily sacrosanct in the first place, so they have no problem with obligatory sharing to rectify limitations of the private market. On the other hand, as the previous chapter made clear, to the degree that liberals seek either equality or the reduction of inequality as the ultimate goal of government, or some other undefined idea of either interdependency or the common good, there is no philosophical limit within liberalism as to the amounts of government intervention and obligatory sharing that are permitted. The questions that contemporary liberalism leaves unanswered are "What are the proper upper limits of the welfare state?" and "From what specific principles do those upper limits follow?"

Today, both choices provided by the nation's two governing ideologies are fundamentally unsatisfactory: either follow private-market outcomes faithfully, regardless of what they are, because the exercise of free exchange has produced them; or intervene to change the outcomes of the private market on grounds of equality, interdependency, or the common good, but without any clear goal or upper limit tied to a defined underlying principle for that intervention. The first has led to the crippling of the middle class and a majority of American families. The latter has led to a widespread concern about government as being unaccountable and as growing in size without boundaries or limits. The nation, effectively, has been asked to choose between two non-answers, both of them woefully inadequate.

These non-answers, along with a continuing neglect of freedom's reciprocal side, have resulted in an ever-greater distortion of the American economy over the past forty years, through a dramatic narrowing of the prosperity of most American workers and their families. That, we will see, was the proximate cause of the near-breakdown of the economy and its weakening for years before that. It is to this process leading to the economy's breakdown—and the path it reveals to a healthy, sustainable recovery—that we now turn our attention.

# CHAPTER 3

# THE ECONOMY

★ ★ ★ ★ ★

*Mistaken Belief: To boost wages and salaries, we want
to focus on generating growth in GDP.*

MOST AMERICANS PROBABLY VIEW growth in GDP and
the general success of the economy as pretty much the same thing.
Asked to recall the strongest periods for our economy in recent
decades, many would undoubtedly hearken back to the 1980s under
President Reagan or the 1990s under President Clinton. And indeed,
those periods reflected the most dramatic rises in GDP in recent history; during the 1980s, for example, the real gross domestic product
rose by a whopping 40 percent, leading President Reagan to bless
the decade as "Morning Again in America." Many still think of it
nostalgically that way.

When solid growth in the economy is considered the equivalent
of rising prosperity, it is only natural to believe that growth ought
to be our primary goal for the economy. Yet ask average American
workers during the 1980s if the decade felt like a sunny "morning"
to them. The stories many of them would tell of struggling in vain
to get ahead and improve their families' lot would sound more like a
shadowy dusk, indeed sometimes even an outright nightmare. And
their stories are the far more common ones of that, and this, period.

The truth is that there is a gigantic difference between a growing GDP and a society that is prospering according to the Founders' standards, the promise of the American Dream, and the tenets of the Common Credo. The difference is so vast that it has worked to considerable economic disadvantage for more than two of every three Americans over the past forty years. In turn, the economy's poor performance for so many Americans, as measured by the Founders' benchmarks, created the conditions resulting in the erosion of the economy's very foundations and then the economy's eventual collapse in 2008. The experience of the entire period, both before and during the collapse, reveals that the models we presently use to understand the economy and set economic policy are flawed at their core.

## THE ECONOMY'S PERFORMANCE RELATIVE TO THE FUNDAMENTALS OF FREEDOM

We discover these flaws only by being specific. Recall that the Founders' understanding of a prosperous and free society required that opportunity be broadly available for individuals to provide themselves a dignified living and advance through means under their own control—an economy, that is, in which everybody who is diligent and works hard can live decently and get ahead. Applying this foundational idea of prosperity and freedom to today's conditions suggests that a willing worker must have access to, first, a job—indeed, a ready choice of jobs—and the educational opportunities that enable individuals to occupy jobs successfully; second, to wages capable of supporting minimally decent living standards or better through full-time work, including, based on reasonable inference from the Founders' principles, access to standard health care and a basic retirement;[1] and third, to jobs whose pay increases in some reasonable fashion with overall increases in workers' productivity. There are other requisite features as well, such as safe working conditions and time for satisfying lives off the job, but for now let's focus on these first three.

How well has the American economy been doing in meeting these three fundamentals? Needless to say, almost no one would argue it has been doing remotely well in recent years. But few realize just how stunningly poor the economy's performance has actually been or for how long it has done so poorly. We tend to think first of the unemployed, those workers the economy has left out. When the nation was coming out of recession in 2009–10, 12 percent of American workers, including those who had stopped looking for employment altogether, were unemployed. That's the section of the labor force that has topped the national debate about jobs and the economy.

Yet remember the alarming statistic from Chapter 1: if we add in those Americans who are employed but who hold jobs that pay less than the living wage of $11.70 per hour (which is the lowest wage for full-time work required just to support basic needs at a modest level), we are then speaking about 38 percent of all American workers, including the unemployed—practically four in every ten.[2] It is a substantially higher proportion than occurs in other industrialized countries. Virtually every year before the Great Recession hit in 2008, going back for decades, no fewer than 30 percent of American workers found themselves in this predicament, either unemployed or working in jobs paying beneath a living wage—many of them for long periods, year after year on end.[3] It is not a short-term or cyclical situation. It has not mattered whether GDP was experiencing a period of solid growth or not.

No nation whose economic processes leave such a large number unemployed or earning less than a living wage can rightly be considered a land of freedom and opportunity, at least not as the Founders understood those terms. Such a failure also violates Adam Smith's stricture that a person who does a job from which others want the product or service but don't wish to do the job themselves deserves a tolerably decent living, which is what a living wage measures. As Smith points out, that's the very essence of what reciprocity and treating another's labor with dignity mean.

Amazingly, the fact that so many Americans earn less than a living wage is not even the full extent of the problem. Because individuals rightly own their own labor, they are supposed to receive the fruits of their labor. This is to say, improved performance on the job should bear some relation to pay received on the job. And those assumptions bring us back to the other statistic introduced in Chapter 1, this one possibly even more disturbing than the first: since 1973, the real (inflation-adjusted) compensation of the average American worker has risen by 10 percent while the output of workers per hour—or their productivity—has climbed by 80 percent. Compensation for the average worker, that is, has risen at only 13 percent of the improvement in workers' productivity. The disparity has been so great that fully three-quarters of American workers, including most college graduates, have been receiving pay increases that are not simply beneath the gains in productivity, but substantially beneath them.

When we speak of pay or compensation, of course, we are referring to what employees from the highest-paid managers to the lowest-paid workers receive for their work. Compensation paid to employees, therefore, does not encompass what investors receive as their proper return on capital investment and the contribution it makes to innovation and new productivity. Returns to capital instead come in the form of profits, dividends, and interest. Employee compensation also does not include any grants of capital stock or stock options that are sometimes directed to management. Compensation for employees in 2010 amounted to around three-fifths of GDP.[4]

Until 1973, no such gulf between the compensation received by the average American worker and the overall productivity of the workforce had ever been recorded. From 1945 to 1973, for example, real compensation for the average worker went up pretty much in tandem with gains in worker productivity, coming to about 80 percent of productivity gains—quite a contrast with the paltry 13 percent for the average worker after 1973.[5] As a result, despite the large improvement in workers' output per hour, a majority of American workers in 2010 were paid little better in real wages per hour of work than American workers had been paid forty years earlier during their *grandparents'* generation. The once-standard condition of workers' pay moving ahead with improved productivity had all but vanished.

For two generations, the nation's economy has performed in ways quite different from the principles that the Founders believed crucial for ensuring widespread freedom and prosperity. Yet during the years since 1973, the level of GDP has more than doubled per person in real terms. At least up to 2008, most observers would probably describe the prior thirty to forty years as generally prosperous ones in America. One of the periods of hottest growth came in the last six years of the Reagan presidency, from 1982 to 1988, when the real GDP climbed by 27 percent, averaging a strong 4.5 percent growth annually. Nevertheless, at the end of the period, 36 percent of American workers were either unemployed or working at jobs paying less than a living wage, and the median real pay of workers rose by a meager 3 percent in those six years, barely one-quarter the growth in worker productivity.[6] Indeed, a sizable majority of workers who began the period in year-round full-time jobs paying less than a living wage ended the period still in such jobs, no better off. This was true even among workers who had gained some higher education.[7]

## EXPLANATIONS

Before exploring how the conditions just described led directly to our economy's meltdown in 2008–09, it's important first to figure out how this situation developed to begin with. What happened? Why over the past four decades has the economy performed in a way that has left so many workers out, for so long, and at such variance with the basic principles the Founders held dear?

Four explanations deserve discussion—the first of them because it is the correct one, despite the fact that until recently it has received hardly any national attention, and the other three because they are the explanations that have received the greatest attention, despite being ultimately incorrect. Incorrect diagnoses lead to incorrect policy solutions, ones that don't fix (and in many cases have exacerbated) our economic tailspin. Uncovering the true nature of the problem, then, is a crucial step to prescribing the policies necessary to get back on the path to real prosperity for all.

Briefly, the four explanations focus on how workers are paid, mounting global competition, inadequate education and skills, and the heavy cost of government.

### How Workers Are Paid

The first explanation for why so many American workers have been left out is that almost all the raises in employee compensation during the past four decades have gone to those at the very top. This in and of itself is probably not surprising to anyone. But just how critically unaligned these compensation trends have become, and especially how severe the consequences have been, have largely escaped the nation's attention and debate.

Consider, again, that the productivity of American workers in the nonfarm economy has risen by 80 percent since 1973, but the inflation-adjusted compensation received by the average American worker, or real median compensation, has risen by only about 10 percent, roughly 13 percent of workers' productivity gains.

What happened to the remaining money that the substantial productivity improvement helped generate? We have been speaking about median compensation, which focuses on the average worker—the worker right in the middle. It says nothing about those at the top. In contrast to median compensation, total compensation per worker averages the compensation that goes to everyone, including those at the top. Since 1973, total compensation per worker has advanced by 50 percent, or five times more than median compensation has increased.[8] As a result, total compensation per worker has come to a little over 60 percent of the gains in productivity, much closer to the approximately 80 percent of recorded productivity gains before 1973. That is, the money to compensate employees has been there, or at least much of it has, but it has been distributed among workers very differently since the early 1970s than it was before.

Here's what has happened to pay for chief executive officers at the very top: Forty years ago, the pay of CEOs of major companies was 20 to 30 times more than pay for the average worker. Today the pay of CEOs hovers at 150 to 250 times that of the average worker.[9] By 2011, the median pay of the top 100 CEOs was $14.3 million, compared to the earnings of the average American of $45,230.

Those at the top of the pay scale are a relatively small share of all workers, just 1 to 5 percent of the total, with employers, executives, and high-level managers accounting for the largest share of them. How much of the total compensation could 1 to 5 percent of all workers possibly account for?

A huge amount. The real compensation going to the top 1 percent in salaries, benefits, and bonuses (not including grants of stock or stock options) shot up by an amazing 200 percent from 1973 to 2007, from an average of about $200,000 annually in 1973 to approximately $600,000 annually in 2007, even as the pay for most Americans remained practically flat.[10]

The annual cost to business operations in 2007 to fund just the average real $400,000 in raises to the top 1 percent amounted to

$560 billion. Add in the raises that went to the next 4 percent, and we're talking about nearly $1 trillion spent by businesses in that single year alone just to finance these raises—and that figure does not include the money spent on the base salaries of the top 5 percent.

If businesses used this money differently, yet still directed it toward employee compensation each year, the raises that the top 5 percent earned beyond average raises for others would be sufficient on their own to fund 16 million additional full-time jobs in perpetuity at $40,000 per year. That's enough jobs to eliminate unemployment completely by itself, and there would still be ample money left over to give the people at the top pay raises at more than double the rate of growth that other workers receive. (I hasten to add that this is not the solution I propose in this book, which is detailed in Chapter 7; I merely aim to illustrate here just how remarkably skewed compensation trends have become.) The nearly $1 trillion in outsized raises amounts to about $7,300 per American worker at year-round full-time hours and to $11,000 annually for each American family with one year-round full-time and one half-time worker.

So the raises to the top tier of employees may involve only a relatively small number of people, but aggregated they total an immense amount of money.

It's often difficult to say, of course, whether an individual's high salary matches his or her productivity, if only because so much of economic production involves collaboration among many individuals from the top to bottom of an organization, where the separate contributions are impossible to disentangle. Salaries that are at a ratio of more than 50 times the median worker's, however, essentially represent an assumption that it takes a middle-level worker an entire year to be as productive for the business as the high-level manager is in a single week. For salaries at 250 times the median worker's wage, merely replace a single week with a single day.

There are dozens of CEOs paid salaries in the millions whose businesses do markedly less well than their competitors', so that it would be very hard to argue that their pay matched their merit or productivity—their marginal product. An example at the extreme is Leo Apotheker, fired by Hewlett-Packard as the CEO after less than a year for doing a "disastrous" job, in the words of the *New York Times*. He was paid $13 million in termination benefits.[11] That is, Hewlett-Packard paid $13 million for the conspicuous failure of one single individual, an amount it would take a median American worker, whose wages have remained stalled for decades, more than 300 *years* to earn. Free-market proponents say that the market pays people according to the marginal product they contribute, but the loose relationship between CEO pay and the performance of their companies reveals so many exceptions that the connection appears nearly lost.

A proxy for productivity that is sometimes used is level of education. Yet, as we will see momentarily, compensation even for workers with a college degree fell far below the overall productivity of the workforce over the past four decades.

To summarize, the bottom line for this first explanation is that total compensation received by workers has actually largely kept up with what the productivity gains of the workforce could support. In this regard, compensation relative to productivity has stayed largely consistent since World War II. What changed most following the early 1970s is that its distribution became dramatically skewed. As a result, even before the economy's collapse in 2008, median American workers remained in pretty much the same economic condition per hour of work as workers nearly forty years earlier.

Why did pay become increasingly skewed after the early 1970s? Most of the wage gap has appeared in the private sector. Consider that in the public sector, the president of the United States receives $400,000 annually. On average, it now takes the CEOs of many major companies barely two or three weeks to make what the president receives for an entire year.

In the private sector, partly because of a steady decline in union membership and the eroding power of collective bargaining, individual workers were left far more on their own than in the period from 1945 to 1973. With the decline of unions, those in stronger bargaining positions within companies—executives and upper management—were able to push their interests to considerably greater effect than were individual workers.

At the same time, as the influence of the free-market model grew, the era witnessed a steady retreat of government as a countervailing force in the private sector. This trend is demonstrated by the significant reductions in the real minimum wage, the elimination of direct job-creation programs, a retreat from full-employment policies, and the greatly disproportionate cuts in tax rates on high salaries and gains from investments relative to the tax rates on the pay of average workers. Few holds were barred in shifting the balance away from the average American worker in favor of those at the top. There is no arguing with the fact that disparity in the growth rates of the top- and average-earner wages has widened to an unprecedented level. The evidence is starkly clear. But how do we know that this imbalance— along with the corresponding decline of labor power and the rise of the free-market model—was the primary cause of the economic struggles that so many Americans have experienced, rather than some other cause? Let us turn now to the three most common alternative arguments, to see why none of them provides a satisfying answer.

## The Global Marketplace

A far more commonplace explanation for the stalled wages of American workers emphasizes the stiff competition coming from an increasingly globalized marketplace—both from advanced economies like Japan and Germany and from low-wage developing countries like Mexico and Singapore. This competition, it is said, has caused businesses in the United States to clamp down on labor costs in order to be able to compete. The result has been both a loss of American jobs to lower-wage countries and a general suppression of pay increases for jobholding Americans. Hence, wages have hardly increased over the past forty years. Thomas Friedman, the *New York Times* columnist, calls globalization along with information technology the most important trend taking place in the world.

Maybe so, but we've seen that total pay for employees hasn't actually been suppressed by very much. The increased compensation has simply gone in huge sums narrowly to the top. Globalization hasn't forced executives, directors, and managers to pay themselves such a highly disproportionate share of the total compensation increases as they have, and it hasn't happened to nearly the same degree in most other developed economies, like Germany or France. Indeed, median wages have advanced considerably more robustly in most other developed economies that have faced the same low-wage global competition that we have.

As for lost jobs, it is true that jobs have migrated. Foxconn, for example, employs one million Chinese workers, paying them $150–300 per month, to make Apple iPads, Hewlett-Packard computers, and other electronic devices. Smaller companies do the same. Taphandles, of Seattle, employs 450 workers in China producing equipment it sells to breweries in the United States and elsewhere around the world.

At the same time, however, many foreign producers have set up shop here, such as Toyota and Volkswagen in Tennessee, Rolls-Royce in Indiana and Virginia, and BMW in South Carolina. The real question is whether there has been any suppression of job creation in the United States and, if there has been, how much.

Here's a stunning fact: despite global competition, there were 63 *million* more jobs in 2007, the year before the economy's collapse, than in 1973. There were about 30 million more jobs in 2007 than in 1990, normally supplying enough or nearly enough jobs for those seeking work. The annual unemployment rate never rose above 6 percent from 1995 to 2007. In 2007, unemployment stood at a modest 4.6 percent, near to what many economists consider to be full employment, and half its level at year's end in 2011.

Globalization does not account for why so many Americans have been left behind economically for so long, with wages flatlined for typical workers and disproportionate numbers of jobs paying beneath a living wage. It possibly does help tell us why total compensation per worker has fallen to a little over 60 percent of productivity gains since 1973, rather than the approximately 80 percent that occurred before 1973. That would go part of the way toward explaining flat wages, but it still doesn't account for why very little of the total compensation increases that productivity did generate went to the average American worker—again, only 13 percent, far below either the total compensation per worker of 60 percent of productivity gains since 1973 or the 80 percent that the average worker received before 1973.[12]

### Education and Skills

A third explanation, most effectively popularized by Harvard economist Lawrence Katz, is that American workers have been left behind because their education and skills have not improved as much as they did in the past.[13]

Periods of great economic growth in the United States have generally been marked by substantial increases in education. The United States was the first nation where graduation from high school became nearly universal. After that, we became the first nation where large rather than tiny minorities earned higher degrees. Over the past several decades, by contrast, we have ceased to surge ahead in educational attainment, and other nations have caught up with and even passed us.

It is true that college-educated workers do considerably better in terms of pay. They also experience relatively low rates of unemployment. When the unemployment rate in the United States was at 9.1 percent in 2011, college graduates had an enviable 4.5 percent rate of unemployment.

It is equally true that there are some areas experiencing shortages of workers with the appropriate skills, such as occupational therapy and nursing. At a little more than one million, however, the total number of job openings that have remained permanently vacant would accommodate barely one in fourteen unemployed Americans, including those who have stopped looking for work.

If educational attainment were a major factor leading to pay inequality, we ought to find that college graduates have fared reasonably well relative to the median worker in attaining pay raises; and they indeed have done somewhat better. However, at an inflation-adjusted pay increase per hour of 19 percent since 1973, equaling 24 percent of overall productivity gains, college-educated workers as a group remained far closer to the median worker's 13 percent than to the total compensation growth per worker of 60 percent of productivity gains.[14] In other words, even a majority of college-educated workers received pay increases that were far below both total compensation growth per worker and overall productivity gains. Even if every American citizen had obtained a college degree, most workers still would have been left far behind.

### The Heavy Burden of Government

A final explanation holds that American businesses, business owners, and the private sector have been held back from creating jobs and granting pay increases to workers because government taxation and regulations place too heavy a burden on them. This has been a longtime concern. Two decades ago, the Cato Institute's *Handbook for Congress* told legislators: "[The federal government's] taxes and regulations are sapping the strength and vitality out of the economy and harming our standard of living."[15] Given that diagnosis, then and today, the obvious prescription is "the more free market the better" as Scott Walker succinctly put it just a few days after his election in 2010 as governor of Wisconsin.[16] The argument is that lowering taxes and easing up on regulations would save owners and businesses large amounts of money and jump-start the private sector, giving business more to put into new investment, greater job creation, and wage increases.

This explanation does not answer—it doesn't even attempt to answer—why the compensation increases that businesses have been able to afford have gone so narrowly to the top. Although this disparity is crucial to the pay most Americans end up receiving, the "heavy burden of government" explanation has nothing to say about it. Nor does the explanation tell us why any money that businesses would save from future reductions in taxes and regulations wouldn't simply continue to go narrowly up to the top, rather than to median wage increases or the creation of new well-paying jobs.

Far from being unusually onerous, in fact, tax rates have actually been dropping throughout most of the period in question, especially for the well-off. Since 1970, marginal tax rates have been cut *in half* for top-income groups.[17] Taxes are presently at or near their postwar lows not just on incomes but also on capital gains and dividends. Beyond that, corporate tax payments as a proportion of GDP have declined virtually continuously since 1973. Taxes paid by corporations relative to GDP in the United States rank near the bottom of all developed nations, notwithstanding a 35 percent nominal rate.

Studies show that, as with taxes, regulations also aren't decisively restricting business growth. A Bureau of Labor Statistics (BLS) analysis of the first half of 2011 concluded that only 0.18 percent of job layoffs (roughly 2 of every 1,000) were due to regulations. More than 100 times as many were attributable to poor business demand.[18] Most businesses seem to agree with these studies. In surveys conducted by the BLS and the National Federation of Independent Business at the time, only 13–15 percent of businesses said that regulations played a major part in layoffs or were the major problem they faced.[19] A 2011 McClatchy survey found that even a smaller percentage of businesses were concerned about regulations as a major problem, some actually saying that without regulations there would be even less growth.[20]

Over the past four decades, those at the top have received both highly disproportionate gains in their compensation and steep reductions in their tax rates. One can reasonably ask: If getting significantly more income with steeply lower tax rates is not enough to spur growth from the top down, what then would be? As Nick Hanauer, a venture capitalist and former member of the board of Amazon.com put it, "If it was true that lower taxes for the rich and more wealth for the wealthy led to job creation, today we would be drowning in jobs."[21]

Government operations can be improved, certainly, and indeed must be, as this book will go on to argue. But the notion that the heavy hand of government is crushing businesses and holding them back does not begin to explain the crucial phenomenon of our era: the tiny increases in compensation for most American workers and families over the past forty years, during a time when the productivity of the workforce has grown sharply and compensation for the highest-paid has risen by leaps and bounds. The presence of government is not a main reason why the economy, particularly within the private sector, has performed at such variance with the basic principles espoused by the Founders.

## Why the Economy Collapsed

Only our first explanation, focusing on the widening gulf between the economic fortunes of the average worker and the overall productivity gains of the labor force, takes us a major step forward in understanding why most Americans have done poorly in the economy. Workers have been left behind not because global competition has greatly suppressed job creation and growth in total compensation, or because in a technological age pay increases have gone mostly to those with educational attainment, or because government taxation and regulation have strangled businesses. Rather, average workers have fared poorly because the large increases in compensation that productivity gains did generate have gone narrowly to the top. In an age when collective bargaining has been in steep decline and the government has been in retreat as a countervailing force, increases in compensation within businesses have gone almost exclusively to those at the top, who are in the strongest bargaining positions.

What choices, then, were left to regular American workers over the many years leading up to the 2008 collapse if they wanted to get ahead? With rising productivity eliminated for many families as a means of significantly lifting their standard of living, there were only two possibilities: average families could try to work more hours, or they could go into ever-increasing debt relative to their income.

As it was, they did both. Families started working longer hours. As second earners streamed into the market, work hours for married couples with children climbed by about 20 percent from 1979 to 2000—about 12 more hours of work per week. Pay for those families, though, rose only by about 25 percent, barely 5 percent more over those years than the increased hours.[22] Even then, much of the income gain was eaten up by the extra costs that the additional work involved, such as for transportation, clothing, and child care, not to mention the greater strain the increased working hours put on families. By the late 1990s, both husbands and wives were working in about 70 percent of all families with children. At that point, working still longer hours was simply not a feasible option for them, and thereafter their working hours no longer increased.

Most families also began taking on more debt. Americans' loans on credit cards and cars proliferated. They bought houses with little or no money down, and homeowners used the growth that took place in housing prices to refinance their homes and get more credit.

By 2007, the debt ratio for the median-income American family had soared to over 140 percent of income, almost double the 75 percent level of the early 1970s. All household debt, taken together, mushroomed in inflation-adjusted dollars from about $3.7 trillion in 1990 to $7.4 trillion in 2000 to nearly $14 trillion by 2008, pouring on average nearly $500 billion in new consumer demand per year into the economy, and even more in those final years before the economy crashed.[23] The amount was so large that it was able to offset the demand of at least $500 billion per year that was drained out of the economy as a result of the disproportionate compensation received by those at the top. (The spending habits of low- or median- and high-income families differ dramatically: higher-income households spend significantly less on consumption goods and services and far more on savings and assets expected to appreciate in value.)[24]

Here, then, we get to the crux of the problem, and also to the originating cause of the economy's collapse and the Great Recession that followed. Because two-thirds of our economic activity comes from people purchasing goods and services, the growth of the economy depends upon robust consumer demand. In a healthy economy, expanded consumer spending is based on real pay gains generated through increased productivity. Under the conditions of the past four decades, however, compensation for most American workers experienced so little real growth relative to improved productivity that, simply on the basis of the gain in their hourly pay, they weren't even able to buy the output their increased productivity had produced. Pay for most Americans hadn't advanced much beyond what it had been two generations earlier. Instead, to move appreciably ahead, families had to borrow. The economy's expansion, in turn, came to rely increasingly upon artificial consumer demand, fueled by mounting debt.

Economies resting upon such artificial foundations cannot easily survive, and, in 2008, our economy fell off the cliff and crashed. The collapse was preceded by a six-year stretch during which the economy grew more slowly than it had during any nonrecessionary period since before World War II.

While it lasted, though, the constant rise in household debt undoubtedly had the effect of helping dull the reality that real hourly pay was not growing by very much. It enabled families to feel they were still getting ahead, at least to some very hard-won degree, and that the economy might actually be doing all right. And it calmed what otherwise could have become mounting anger and resentment at the actual experience of continuously stalled pay, only now beginning to be articulated as the days of rising debt have passed and the reckoning has come. One must wonder what would have happened politically in America had families not been able to borrow to the hilt but instead had actually had to face the unvarnished reality of living for years on end with their pay and buying power flatlined, despite the rise that was taking place in productivity.

## TODAY'S PARADIGM
## REQUIRES AN ALTERNATIVE

### Today's Economic Paradigm

The free-market paradigm as a model for the economy has been ascendant in America for forty years. The idea behind the model, as articulated today, is that free exchange in the market sets up positive incentives for individuals to produce, invest, and create jobs that generate powerful growth and improve economic well-being. Intervention by the government tends only to get in the way of those incentives, distort them, and diminish growth.

During the past four decades, in line with the free-market model, government regulations have been reduced in a wide array of sectors; trucking, airlines, energy, telecommunications, and banking and finance are just a few examples. Tax rates on incomes and on capital gains have been slashed. Welfare was reformed and cut, public jobs programs ended, and collective bargaining weakened. All sorts of public economic props, such as the minimum wage and unemployment benefits, were allowed to fall way behind inflation.

This approach hasn't succeeded for a solid majority of working Americans. The free-market proponents' answer to this, however, has been to argue that if the economic fortunes of average Americans have stalled, they have done so because a full-throated free-market approach has not yet been tried. Were it attempted, were taxes further lowered and regulations further cut back, it would fuel greater economic growth that would spread to all.

It is worth emphasizing again, though, that overall tax levels as a proportion of GDP in the United States are near the lowest of all developed nations and that individual tax rates in the United States have declined significantly over the past four decades. Since an optimal tax rate that is appropriate to a free-market model hasn't yet been defined, and comparative rates either historically here at home or relative to other nations don't seem to qualify, one is left wondering whether there is a level of tax other than zero that would provide an absolutely clear test.

Just take a look at recent history. The Bush tax cuts of 2001 on both income and capital gains were substantial. And they have largely remained in place. Free-market proponents claimed that such tax reductions were required to spur investment, job creation, and wage growth.

However, after the tax cuts were enacted in 2001, compensation for the average American worker remained stalled, increasing at barely one-tenth of the rise in workers' productivity while pay at the top continued to soar. Family income for most Americans hardly budged. The suppressed pay and income trends of the previous thirty years, as free-market influence gained force, simply continued throughout the remainder of the Bush presidency until the economy eventually collapsed.[25]

As for regulations, listen to what the National Federation of Independent Business had to say in 2011 about what was hampering business and entrepreneurs during recent years, following from surveys of its 350,000 members:

Remember, there was much hiring and expansion [before 2008] based on spending by consumers who [borrowed and] did not save. Now there is "excess capacity" and it has not yet been rationalized. It is simple: when sales pick up, owners will have a reason to hire more workers to take care of customers, to produce more output and will have reason to invest in new equipment and expansion.[26]

Businesses need customers and there is no question that lack of demand has been a central concern of businesses. As Ron Nelsen, who operates the Las Vegas business Pioneer Overhead Door, put it this way: "You know what makes jobs? Consumer demand . . . I hire people when demand necessitates it."[27]

## An Alternative Economic Paradigm

Four decades of poor economic results in the private sector for most Americans, measured by the Founders' standards, ought to be enough. The nation needs a different model. The free-market approach, as it is currently interpreted, cannot be displaced without one. Consider how widely the unfettered free-market model was discredited after the economy's collapse in 2008, only to be passionately revived just one election cycle later as the central rallying point of the 2010 congressional elections.

This isn't to say we should abandon free markets, of course. Virtually all Americans would agree that the free market must be at the center of any economic model that we follow. The reasoning behind the free-market model regarding self-interest, competition, and incentives and the way they generate growth is broadly valid and widely accepted.

At the same time, the free market needs external guidance. While free-market reasoning cares deeply about growth, ultimately economic efficiency is its actual goal. From an efficiency standpoint, the economic interest of employers is to produce with as few workers as possible getting paid the lowest wage possible.[28] Workers have the reverse interest. In the end, the goal of efficiency says nothing about the ready availability of opportunity for self-reliance and self-improvement. Nor does the goal say anything directly about the sustainability of growth.

To get on the right path, the first step is to identify and then aim at the goals we most want to reach. What exactly do we want the economy to achieve? The next step is to think afresh, in the context of those goals, about what exactly enables the competitive free market and private sector to attain the impressive successes in the areas that they do.

***Focusing on the Right Goals***   An alternative perspective would start by focusing on the goals the Founders envisaged, goals that have come to define the American Dream as nearly all Americans perceive it. Those goals describe an economy that produces not just growth but freedom for all individuals. And freedom as understood by the Founders entails opportunity existing for all individuals both to be self-reliant—and thus able to live in dignity through their efforts—and to get ahead by receiving a proper return from improving their efforts.

This, then, needs to be our bedrock definition of a successful economy—no more and no less. That last phrase is not simple rhetoric: just as it is essential that the economy we build fully attains the minimum requirement of equal and sufficient opportunity for all, based on appropriate returns on one's labor, it is also essential that we don't force the economy to create more equality than that. Once equal and sufficient opportunity for all citizens exists, fully so—meaning all citizens can be considered free—there still will and ought to be considerable disparities in pay, income, and wealth. Any government impositions that seek to extend beyond the minimum level—for example, policies that would raise the minimum wage beyond the base living wage, at the expense of those with higher incomes—would be in themselves a violation of freedom. But the basic level of opportunity just identified must be fully met for our society to be deemed widely free and prosperous. In addition, assistance would be needed to help those who are not fully able to survive in the economy, such as the elderly or seriously infirm, as is generally agreed upon by both liberals and conservatives.

Furthermore, sharing prosperity in this manner is essential for another reason quite apart from the critical importance it has for freedom. Simply put, doing so is indispensable for the free market, itself, to operate effectively. This is because private investment rooted in self-interest generally requires the prospect of adequate demand to encourage it. To survive and prosper, both small and large businesses depend upon demand being adequate. Moreover, for growth to be sustainable, the demand must be based upon a solid foundation, not reliant upon ever-escalating debt. That's why the International Monetary Fund (IMF), in a global study, found that economic inequality within a nation—at the extreme, the failure to share prosperity at all—puts limits on the sustainability of economic growth. "A ten percentile decrease in inequality," the IMF analysis concluded, "increases the expected length of a growth spell by 50 percent."[29]

**What Makes the Free Market Work**   To see the importance of sharing prosperity within society in order for the free market to work effectively, you don't need to look any further than the free-market icon himself, Adam Smith. When he wrote the *Wealth of Nations*, describing the basic theory behind the free market, the most famous metaphor he used was that of "the invisible hand." He later described the example of a local baker who provided bread to neighbors not out of altruism or benevolence but out of his self-interest in making a living, intending only his own gain. As if led by an invisible hand, Smith explained, free exchange transforms an individual's self-interest and personal economic gain into the common good of others.

But what is this invisible hand? For today's free-market proponents, the key force is the entrepreneur and his or her energy, initiative, and creativity—Smith's baker being the archetypical example.

Yet Smith's baker would not buy an oven along with the ingredients to make bread for others in the first place unless he believed there would ultimately be enough purchasers for the bread he made. The self-interest of entrepreneurs, then, requires a decent prospect of enough customers. That—whether a producer believes there will be sufficient customers, and thereby sufficient consumer demand—is integral to the "invisible hand" that lies at the root of the free-market model. In this way, demand provides the context required for self-interest to be transformed into investing and producing goods and services. Expecting investment or job creation to come from a prudent entrepreneur who sees no decent prospect of demand is like expecting applause to come from a single hand. Without customers—who are their economic lifeblood—entrepreneurs cannot succeed. And the reverse is equally true: customers need entrepreneurs. From this vantage point, both customers and entrepreneurs are indispensable to job creation.

Families with average or below-average incomes spend significantly greater proportions of their income on consumption than do high-income families. For this reason, the demand that is necessary for a successful free market will weaken if families with average or below-average incomes receive ever-smaller shares of pay, and if that trend is allowed to persist.[30] The result will continuously drain demand from the economy. In these circumstances, supply cannot create its own demand, and supply-side economics cannot work.[31] Demand, in addition, must remain real. It must be based upon work and the improvement of work and not become reliant upon ever-rising debt. Otherwise the prosperity that has been generated cannot continue.

For these reasons, economic prosperity cannot be sustained in a free market without the sharing of prosperity within society that freedom, as understood by the Founders and defined by the Common Credo, calls for. This basic truth is key to the success of any economy built upon free exchange. It is the link that joins economic freedom to economic prosperity. Just as freedom is reciprocal, so is the functioning of a successful economy.

Over the past forty years, the kind of sharing needed has not occurred. To the contrary, the trend within the private market has moved continuously in the opposite direction. By the 2000s, the effects of the growing disparity between median compensation and workforce productivity had become so substantial, reducing consumer demand to such a degree in the process (by $500 billion or more yearly),[32] that they more than offset the effects that the Bush tax cuts were intended to have in increasing consumption. Recovery during the Bush administration showed the lowest rate of growth for any comparable period of recovery since before World War II—with far worse to follow.

The economy slowed, that is, because the amounts of deficient demand had grown so large—building up continuously into hundreds of billions of dollars, year after year—that they overwhelmed the effects of even the large Bush tax cuts, effectively removing tax cuts as an answer. To create new demand of the kind needed, the only alternative was for individuals and families to engage in ever-rising debt relative to their incomes that could not be sustained, thus eventually resulting in the economy's breakdown.

Here in a nutshell is the story that the Common Credo conveys about the economy: Americans can be free, as the Founders understood freedom, only when prosperity is shared in a particular way among all those who have worked for it, those whose work created the goods and services we enjoy and on which we rely. That sharing of prosperity comes in the form of the ready availability of opportunity for independence to all, enabling all willing individuals to obtain a dignified living through work and to get ahead through becoming more productive. Unless economic growth is shared to that extent among those who have contributed to it, prosperity cannot be maintained in a market economy, and average American workers cannot claim freedom as the Founders envisioned it. Consumer demand will wither and with it both large and small businesses will slow, their self-interested incentive to invest, produce, and grow becoming increasingly choked off. Even tax cuts will not be enough. If expanding consumer debt falsely substitutes for demand so that what we produce doesn't overtake our purchasing, the reckoning may take longer, but the economy will still inevitably collapse. As the escalating debt becomes unsustainable, the economy will at some point slow and then fall into deep recession that requires many years to overcome.

The economic approaches of Adam Smith and John Maynard Keynes are sometimes regarded as rival models in politics, the former supported by conservatives, the latter advanced by liberals. Smith, however, presumes Keynesian conditions with regard to demand, just as Keynesian economics presumes Smithian conditions of voluntary exchange, free enterprise, entrepreneurship, and predominantly private markets. The two models are closely connected rather than fundamentally opposed, and in this respect there is no need to choose between them. Rather than focusing on either one of them, the paradigm we need must attend to both the importance of individual responsibility and entrepreneurial activity and the relevance of sufficient and sustainable consumer demand.

Similarly, there is sometimes considered a tradeoff in economics between equality, on the one hand, and efficiency, generally meaning growth, on the other.[33] Economic growth requires that there be disparities in income and wealth to serve as effective incentives for individuals to invest and innovate, yet these very disparities work against equality. Recall from the previous chapter, though, the way freedom and equality join together at a certain point and become one. That is also the case for equality and economic growth, as this chapter has shown. Economic growth requires consumer demand, which

requires that individuals have sufficient opportunity to obtain a minimally decent living through work and get ahead as their productivity improves, rather than having gains in compensation flow almost
exclusively to the top. Economic growth, that is, depends upon a
threshold of equality at least up to this point in the distribution of
compensation in order for growth to be sustainable. Just as there is
no tradeoff necessary between freedom and equality when the two
intersect, the same is true for equality and sustainable economic
growth at the point where those two intersect and become one.

The key to restoring sustainable growth in the American economy
today and averting another collapse of the economy down the road
involves dealing with the originating sources of the debt explosion
and the economy's dependence upon an ever-rising tide of debt as
a means for sustaining demand. Chapter 7 proposes specific policies to ignite this restoration, policies that involve active government
intervention but also mechanisms for minimizing and strictly moni-
toring that involvement.

The originating sources of our economic woes, to recap, are the
severed links between workers' compensation and the substantial
productivity gains of the labor force over the past four decades, during which time compensation has gone narrowly to the top (where
the propensity to consume is lowest); the resulting stagnant pay
increases for most Americans, including a profusion of low-paying
jobs; and the greatly inflated borrowing relative to income that followed, aided by an increasingly deregulated financial market, which
became necessary to provide the consumer demand that businesses
and the economy rely on in order to grow.

Until and unless those problems are addressed, little can or will
change for most Americans. And, if little changes for most Americans, the economy cannot and will not become genuinely prosperous, healthy, or congruent with the aims that the Founders believed
were essential.

## Benefits for the Right and the Left

This new perspective delivers important benefits for both the right and the left in America today. The right speaks of two different priorities. First, the right wants to ground government and public policies solidly in the vision and thinking of the Founders—the very source of the new perspective. Second, the right seeks to optimize conditions for the private sector, businesses, and entrepreneurship so that they can prosper and thrive. That cannot happen without turning from the old perspective to this new one.

True, the right would need to welcome government involvement to the degree it is required to create the societal economic context necessary for the private sector and business to prosper. Welcoming government would mean prioritizing this necessary context over "small government" as an end goal in itself. It would no doubt help the right to take this step if government itself were to give bottom-line priority to operating in the way a limited government should—that is, as minimally as necessary (a topic we come to in Chapter 5). As long as government does not make operating as minimally as necessary a crucial priority, the right will react both ideologically and politically to that failure. Those on the right might also appreciate that the call for government action and for a reworking of our economic model are both directed toward an express purpose that conservatives regard as an overriding goal of the nation: enabling all Americans to be self-reliant and independent through means they have earned.

With respect to the left, this new perspective identifies and persuasively justifies certain activist roles for government engagement in the economy, roles that the left ordinarily supports. They are all firmly grounded in the Founders' vision of freedom and indeed the deeper view of freedom that most Americans accept today. To gain that advantage, however, the left would need to accept definitional limits and boundaries to the welfare state that are now absent in its way of thinking about economic equality and fairness. Liberals would need to agree, in effect, that the availability of sufficient opportunity for all able-bodied individuals is what equality and fairness in the economy mean—nothing more. They would also need to accept—indeed emphasize and act to ensure—that government assistance in fully achieving this condition of sufficient opportunity involves the lowest cost and level of restrictiveness needed to attain the goal. I believe many liberals could readily accept these strictures. If they do, liberalism would then contain a clear definition of the limits and upper boundaries of the welfare state, one emanating not from largely undefined values of equality and fairness or the indeterminate fact of interdependence, but instead from the Founders' ideal of freedom.

## SOCIAL IMPLICATIONS FOR FAMILIES AND THE NATION

Even more is at stake here than America's formative idea of freedom, widespread economic prosperity, and economic growth that can be sustained, though surely they are enough. Low-paying jobs and the stalled wages for most workers, along with rising inequality, have still farther-reaching effects.

For one, it becomes far more difficult for government to function effectively. When the middle and working classes feel they are falling behind, or are going deeply into debt, they become more self-protective. Cutting spending on programs that benefit them or raising taxes to finance such programs faces even stiffer political resistance than usual. Within such a context, unmanageable budget deficits become more likely.

For another, people whose flatlined pay makes it hard to get ahead are likely to grow demoralized after a time, feel rising resentment, and develop a sense that the system does not represent or pay attention to them—feelings that have indeed grown and become hugely influential in American politics.

In addition, low-paying jobs and growing pay inequality exacerbate a wide range of family and societal dysfunctions. The British epidemiologists Richard Wilkinson and Kate Pickett examined a series of social indicators: level of trust for others, mental illness (including both drug abuse and alcohol addiction), life expectancy, educational performance, obesity, homicides, teenage pregnancies, and violent crime and rates of imprisonment. They placed these indictors into a single measure of social problems and examined them in twenty-one advanced nations, including the United States. They also examined them in all fifty states within this country.[34]

The authors found that there was no connection whatsoever between the level of average income per person in the advanced nations or American states and the level of social problems the nation or state experienced. A nation's or a state's absolute income per person had no effect.

The authors saw a very different result, however, when they examined income inequality within each nation or state, rather than the absolute level of income. Those nations and American states with higher levels of income inequality experienced more serious levels of social problems on the combined measure. The same pattern also occurred on virtually every individual social problem in the measure taken in isolation. In many cases the level of a social problem doubled or tripled in seriousness in nations and states with higher income inequality. For example, in the United States, which has the highest level of income inequality of the nations analyzed, the rate of teenage pregnancy is four times higher than in nations like Canada, Germany, and France, where levels of income equality are closer to the median. And within the United States, states with the highest income inequality have significantly higher teenage birthrates than states with lower levels of inequality. The same trend occurs in areas such as educational performance, mental illness, drug abuse, and violent crime and rates of imprisonment. High-school dropout rates within the United States are three times greater in the most unequal states than in the least unequal states.

An extremely disturbing development that has accompanied wage stagnation in the United States concerns the nearly two-thirds of American adults who have a high school but not a college degree. They are what the sociologist W. Bradford Wilcox calls "middle Americans."[35] With respect to most aspects of family instability and dysfunction—ranging across divorce, out-of-wedlock births, single parenting, partner conflict, and troubled children—the families of "middle Americans" in the 1970s were similar to families headed by college graduates. Thirty years later, by the 2000s, the families of these middle Americans experienced a far higher incidence of many of the dysfunctions, including divorce, out-of-wedlock births, and troubled children, than did the families of college graduates. The prevalence of the dysfunctions in these families now nearly matched those of high-school dropouts. Wilcox attributes a good part of this dramatic change directly to the reduction in wage growth and decline in job security.

Lacking a healthy economic foundation, including sufficient well-paying jobs and avenues to get ahead, both individuals and families understandably become more prone to experiencing debilitating social difficulties of all kinds.

## WE MUST REVERSE COURSE

Moving away from the Founders' idea of freedom over the past forty years has done individual Americans and their families, as well as the nation as a whole, enormous damage. That has been the case with respect to the poor level, breadth, and sustainability of economic growth, the profusion of low-paying jobs, the flatlining of wages for most Americans, and the many kinds of dysfunctional effects on families and the larger society connected to these developments. All these developments took place rather silently, even as the real GDP was more than doubling, making the economy itself look quite healthy until crisis hit.

But things were not healthy. They have not been healthy for many years. A solid majority of Americans have been reduced to the Sisyphean task of working harder and harder, producing ever more, while receiving hardly any greater return than generations before them had many decades ago. And their circumstances have only worsened following the economy's collapse. Now, after all these years, it has become clear to Americans that the nation has gotten off track. We will remain unable to find our compass and correct course as long as we hold to policies that lead the nation further and further away from the Founders' idea of freedom, and further away from the Common Credo.

# CHAPTER 4

---

# COLLECTIVE ACTION VERSUS INDIVIDUAL FREEDOM

\* \* \* \*

*Mistaken Belief: Being required to do things collectively,*
*by force, is against what America stands for.*

AMERICA HAS INDEED GONE BADLY off course. At least
in part, that's because our present frame of thinking lacks a way to
appreciate the essential role that collective public action plays in
the success of individual freedom—freedom viewed reciprocally
the way the Founders did rather than as an "anything goes" or "sink
or swim" proposition. Abraham Lincoln made the point this way:
"The legitimate object of government is to do for a community of
people whatever they need to have done, but cannot do at all, or
cannot do as well for themselves in their separate and individual
capacities. In all that individuals can individually do as well for
themselves, government ought not to intervene."[1] The great apos-
tle of the free market, Milton Friedman, believed the same. The
purpose of government, he wrote, "is to accomplish jointly what we
would find it more difficult or expensive to accomplish severally."[2]

As free individuals, joining together collectively is necessary in
order to set rules to protect against wrongful harm and to establish the free market—rules that define and enforce property rights,

secure contracts, establish a national currency, protect the owner-ship of inventions, and prohibit various forms of theft, fraud, and libel. The free market, in other words, *is itself* a collective societal act—backed, if need be, by governmental coercion (coercion here referring to the government's ability, through laws and the judicial system, to enforce the rules by imposing penalties on actions such as committing fraud or libel, counterfeiting, breaking contracts, pro-ducing dangerous goods, and many others involving private market exchanges).

Likewise, there must also be collaboration to assure sufficient economic opportunity to support self-reliance for all, as well as to ensure the education needed for that opportunity to be real-ized.[3] Such opportunity, in turn, is required to create the aggre-gate demand necessary for a vibrant economy and sustainable prosperity.

Those are the basics, but the need for working together in order for freedom to succeed extends to many other areas, all of them fit-ting Lincoln's statement about the appropriate role of government in a free society. Economists often call these areas "market failures" or "market deficiencies." At the root of the difficulties America has experienced in coming to grips with many of its most serious challenges—for example, the skyrocketing costs of health care and the stalemate over carbon emissions—is the absence of a proper understanding about the need for strong public involvement, in the very cause of freedom, in these areas involving market failures.

## FOUR KINDS OF MARKET FAILURES

Four general kinds of situations make it extremely difficult or impos-sible for individuals, if acting independently of each other, to attain the goals they seek effectively or efficiently.

## Natural Monopolies

There are certain situations in which the level of competition that is essential to the free market's success cannot occur, situations in which monopoly or oligopoly is actually called for. The general defense and security of the nation cannot result from free-market competition, for example, or from separate and independent action by individuals to provide a national defense.

The same holds true for much of the infrastructure. Competition among a superfluity of roads, bridges, electric power lines, and gas and water pipelines makes little sense. Since fire stations need to be readily accessible to a nearby area, they can't compete effectively across town. While individuals can purchase supplements to protect their homes and persons, many competing police forces would, by dividing up the market, be far more expensive and, by dividing up resources, be much less effective. In general, services with high fixed expenses that are very costly to duplicate, such that competition cannot drive down prices, are ill suited to a competitive free market.

In these and other similar areas, the full-blown competition necessary for the successful operation of a free market cannot take place efficiently. Since producers within a free market who don't face intense competition can potentially coerce consumers through extortionate pricing or other abuses, some form of societal collaboration is necessary to prevent such coercion—either public regulation of private producers, public contracting for private services, or outright public ownership and provision.

## Free-Givers and Free-Riders

Two other situations exist in which collective action may be more effective than individual action. In one, called free-giving, individuals are expected to produce for others without any assurance that all or even any of the recipients who benefit would pay the costs. In the reverse situation, called free-riding, individuals are able to shirk the costs of their activities and push those costs onto others.

Free-giving can occur in the area of education; for example, a worker receiving education paid for by one company subsequently goes to work for another company that then benefits from the worker's education without having to pay the costs. Or it can occur in the area of basic research, where inventions resulting from new knowledge need not compensate the discoverer of that knowledge. In areas like these, a free market will not produce either education or basic research at optimal levels because producers of the goods cannot be sure that they will be compensated. Here again, public subsidy, regulation, or actual ownership is needed to provide these goods at optimal levels. (In the case of education, of course, public subsidization is also needed to make an effective education affordable, given the pivotal role it plays in both the availability of economic opportunity and the fostering of civic involvement.)

The situation of free-riding is no better. This happens when, for example, individuals with the flu go out to work or to enjoy a ball game, risking the health of others who happen to be near them; or when they receive health-care services in emergencies even if they have no insurance and cannot pay the costs; or when companies save money by selling tainted food through distant outlets, making purchasers suffer the consequences; or when an industry pollutes the surroundings and passes the costs of the damage its pollution creates onto others.

### Perverse Economic Incentives

A fourth problematic situation occurs when the rational self-interested motives essential to the proper operation of a free market have perverse, negative effects that hurt others and oftentimes even the initiating actors themselves. An example is the rational incentive of an individual business to cut back production and employment when demand falls. That action, however, adds to the loss of demand, which then causes the business and other businesses to cut back further, resulting in a spiral that can continue downward into recession or depression, harming everyone unless there is external intervention to support demand. The same applies to financial markets if they get out of balance and experience panic.

Or consider health care. The health-care system's primary goal is to treat the ill, but private insurance companies have a rational economic incentive to save money by covering only those least likely to get ill and avoid covering individuals at high risk of getting ill, such as the elderly, the poor, and individuals with prior conditions. People covered by fully paid health insurance, for their part, have an economic incentive to consume health-care services without regard to cost. Similarly, doctors paid on a fee-for-service basis have an economic incentive to recommend marginally needed or even unneeded services.

The numerous areas affected by the four kinds of market failures, which thereby warrant some form of collective intervention in line with Lincoln's injunction regarding freedom, takes the breath away. The stakes within many of the areas are enormous. And it is the middle Americans who have been most severely harmed, both economically and politically, by the perpetuation of these failures. These are the citizens who, when disease or illness strikes, lack sufficient financial resources, even with insurance, to purchase the proper care in our inflated private market, and who also lack the political clout to compete with special interests like insurance company lobbyists. For such citizens, these market failures often act as chains binding them indefinitely to conditions of financial hardship, or even bankruptcy, and political marginalization.

## HEALTH CARE

A prime example of an area in which market failures have drastic consequences is health care, which accounts for about one-seventh of our entire economy. Because freedom is now commonly associated with individual decisions resulting from voluntary exchange, the American health-care system is primarily privately funded. We are the only nation in the developed world whose health-care system operates mainly through competitive private markets.

How well has it worked? It's hard to find even a silver lining. America now has the most costly medical care per person, by far, of all advanced nations. How much more expensive? No one else comes close. We spend nearly twice as much per person ($7,900 in 2009) as do citizens in Germany ($4,200), France ($4,000), or Great Britain ($3,500).[4] The cost of a normal childbirth in the United States averages $8,435 as compared to $2,147 in Germany; $13,123 versus $3,284 for an appendectomy; $1,009 versus $632 for an MRI; and $14,427 versus $4,718 for an average hospital stay.[5] With respect to cost, we are in a class by ourselves, up there in the stratosphere. Amazingly, even then, many Americans (15.7 percent, or nearly 50 million in 2011) have no health-care coverage at all, while millions more are woefully undercovered.

On top of this, despite spending nearly double the money per person, Americans, on average, do not typically receive higher-quality health care. Most Americans get neither superior overall medical results nor superior overall satisfaction from the health care they receive than do people in other countries. In fact, we are often pretty far down the list of developed nations on many measures of health outcomes. For example, cross-national studies find that the United States falls well below the average of advanced nations in infant mortality and ranks no better than the middle of the pack in the percentage of heart attack patients who die in the hospital within thirty days of admission; we are well beneath the average again regarding the survival rate for cervical cancer; and, although near the top for breast cancer survival and for timely access to specialists, we rank below the average both in the proportion of patients who experience medical errors and who encounter problems because of uncoordinated care.[6]

The high cost of our health-care system inflicts a terrible price. As it presently operates, it has become a substantial financial burden on our families, our businesses, and the nation as a whole. Soaring health-care costs are a leading cause of bankruptcies among American families, even for families who have health insurance. They are a major concern of businesses as well; in 2004, for instance, the costs for employee health care added $1,525 to each vehicle built by General Motors.[7] If health-care costs are not better contained, they risk eventually bankrupting the government itself because of their effects on Medicare and Medicaid. In fact, without the projected rising costs in the single area of health care, the budget deficits forecast for the federal government would be low enough to border on being manageable.

We have confused private funding and the private market with individual freedom and economic efficiency in the delivery of health care. That mistake has ended up imposing exorbitant and unnecessary costs that have placed a heavy burden on virtually all Americans, American businesses, and the government. The costs result in good part from a morass of market failures that infuses the health-care sector, from top to bottom.

At the top, insurance companies have an obvious economic incentive to insure only those who are the least likely to get ill, even though addressing the needs of those who become ill is what a health-care system is for. Nonetheless, the very opposite economic incentive lies at the center of a health-care system that is based upon private insurance. To overcome this incentive, governmental intervention is needed either through direct financial aid from the government itself or in the form of regulations requiring the insurance industry to cover citizens most vulnerable to illness at affordable prices—those with preconditions or most likely to become ill, such as the elderly.

Similarly, a great asymmetry exists between physicians and their patients. Patients depend upon information from doctors about their need for medical services. However, a fee-for-service system gives doctors an economic incentive to render more services, an incentive that continues to operate even for second opinions. Absent countervailing pressures to restrain health-care providers, an oversupply of medical services by doctors and hospitals will occur. An overconsumption of those services will also take place at the bottom of the system among patients who have prepaid health insurance that will cover their medical costs yet, to the same degree, also give the insured a disincentive to cut their individual costs. One projection estimates that overtreatment wastes more than $200 billion annually in unnecessary health-care spending, or almost 15 percent of all spending on health care.[8]

Together, market failures such as these lead to increasingly high but also disproportionately ineffective spending on health care, yet with great undercoverage at the same time. With respect to such spending, it is only through collective governmental actions that the rising costs, which now so burden American families, businesses, and the government and threaten ultimately to price most Americans out of the market altogether, can be restrained. One example of such an action might be a government mandate that both Medicare and most private insurance plans implement data-driven medicine (that is, medicine transparently linked to empirical evidence of success, not to highest profits). The mandate would also require providers to implement better coordination systems in their practices, to avoid duplication of services and the extra costs (and often worse outcomes) that result. Alongside the mandated plans could be some private insurance options under no such mandate.

As things stand today, however, collective answers such as this are rejected as limiting freedom of choice and individual decisions in health care, when in fact they or others like them are needed for the very purpose of securing freedom with respect to keeping the choice of health care itself available and affordable. Without the collective solutions that could overcome the serious market failures affecting transactions in health care, it is no surprise that Americans end up spending substantially more money than citizens in other developed countries without getting either superior overall results or greater patient satisfaction. And to boot, our system leaves many more people uninsured than that of any other developed country.

### The Health Insurance Mandate

Recently the most-discussed market failure in health care involved the problem of free-riders who receive health-care services but are unable to pay because they lack adequate insurance coverage. The argument focused mainly on whether or not to take action against those individuals in the form of a mandate to purchase insurance. The primary argument against the insurance mandate held that requiring individuals to purchase insurance violates their freedom to decide for themselves whether or not to obtain such insurance coverage. If the government can require the purchase of private health insurance for the purpose of controlling health-care costs or making a more rational health-care system, then why, as Justice Scalia observed, couldn't it require eating broccoli or other foods that the government deems healthy so as to reduce health-care costs? When the mandate was in the appeals stage in 2011, Judge Stanley Marcus of the 11th Circuit Federal Court of Appeals asked: "If they [the federal government] could compel this, what purchase could they not compel?"[9] If the government, to moderate costs, can control the behavior even of individuals who are not engaged in commerce at all, who are inactive—in this case, who are not in the market for health insurance—would anything, then, be beyond the government's power?

That was the core question asked by opponents of the insurance mandate and by federal judges who ruled the mandate unconstitutional.

The insurance mandate, though, did not have improving health or lowering health costs per se as its immediate aim. The immediate aim was to prevent free-riders within a market sector. To protect against free-riders is a perfectly legitimate interest of freedom. Often the only other recourse for providers is to withhold their services in what are usually emergency and excruciating circumstances, the very instances in which we would agree that services should not be denied. Indeed, it is frequently impossible when individuals are in serious pain for service providers to determine whether or not patients will be able to pay. Partly for that reason, the denial of medical services in these circumstances is currently not permitted under the law; providers are legally required to give service while being unable to anticipate the instances in which they may not be compensated. Some or all of these unpredictable losses are ultimately shouldered not by the providers but by those who *do* pay for their services and by taxpayers at large. The mandate's objective, then, was to reduce or eliminate free-riders so as to prevent their costs from being shoved onto providers and others who would have to pay higher prices than they otherwise would pay. The problem is drastic enough that even Newt Gingrich castigated individuals who didn't purchase health insurance yet could afford it as free-riders, writing in a 2007 op-ed: "Personal responsibility extends to the purchase of health insurance. Citizens should not be able to cheat their neighbors by not buying insurance, particularly when they can afford it, and expect others to pay for their care when they need it."[10]

Likewise, in a 2006 *Wall Street Journal* op-ed regarding his enactment of a similar mandate as governor of Massachusetts, Mitt Romney distinguished between the freedom enabled by an insurance mandate and the "anything goes" freedom championed by those who opposed such government intervention. "Some of my libertarian friends balk at what looks like an individual mandate," he wrote. "But remember, someone has to pay for the health care that must, by law, be provided: Either the individual pays or the taxpayers pay. A free ride on government is not libertarian.[11]

Under the Affordable Care Act, implementation of the mandate on all citizens can be expected to reduce the problem significantly. Individuals unable to afford insurance, the majority of whom are employed but without benefits, will be provided with assistance for insurance consistent with the principles of opportunity and freedom discussed in Chapters 2 and 3.

The objectives just described are all reasonable to seek in the name of freedom. It is indeed essential to regulate free-riders, where there are large numbers of them, for a free market to be able to operate properly. For this reason, it was the Heritage Foundation—a fierce advocate of the private free market—that was among the first organizations to propose mandating the purchase of health insurance.

At the same time, the objectives provide clear grounds for distinguishing the mandated purchase of health insurance from myriad other purchase options in markets that do not share the same free-ridership issues—including the commercial market for broccoli, or the ones for healthy foods, and indeed the great majority of markets for other commercial products—in which it is generally a simple matter to exclude and prevent free-riders at the point of sale. There is by no means a "potentially unbounded assertion of congressional authority" going on here, as the 11th Circuit Federal Court said it feared. Commercial markets where inactivity results in free-ridership that a competitive market cannot restrain or prevent is the limited range of this power.

There remains the oft-mentioned concern that persons with unhealthy habits, such as those who become seriously overweight and so push up the costs for health insurance for everyone else, could, by the reasoning regarding free-ridership, become the legitimate objects of federal regulation. That concern misconstrues what free-ridership is. Free-ridership becomes a problem only when free markets cannot restrain or prevent it on their own, which was the case regarding the provision of medical care in the circumstances that were under the court's review. In the case of personal habits affecting individuals' health, by contrast, free markets can deal with such problems effectively on their own. For example, commercial insurance companies and businesses have every opportunity to charge individuals a higher price for health insurance (and they do at times) according to such specific personal characteristics as smoking, weight, and participation in particular exercise programs.

In June 2012 the U.S. Supreme Court ruled in *National Federation of Independent Business v. Sebelius* that penalizing individuals for failing to purchase insurance was a proper power of Congress under the Constitution. Although its decision was castigated by opponents of the insurance mandate as a grave defeat for individual freedom, in fact the opposite is so.

The Court, in effect, ruled against the one-sided individualist autonomy of free-riders, who were exercising license and not freedom, and safeguarded the freedom of health providers, enabling them to avoid being subjected to what is essentially a form of theft. The providers otherwise would be legally required to deliver services to free-riders without knowing whether they would be compensated. To be caused to work without compensation is a characteristic of forced labor. The providers would then need to see whether they could finagle other third-party consumers and their insurers—innocent bystanders—to pay for some or all of the free-riders' costs by charging them higher prices than they would otherwise pay.

Had the Court ruled otherwise, the Founders would have been aghast to learn that they had created a central government unable to root out such activities occurring in commerce among the states. The decision was not a defeat for freedom. It was, however, a defeat for an anything-goes notion of freedom that is amoral, and thus mistaken, and a vindication of the reciprocal, moral ideal of freedom that the Founders set forth.

It is important to add about this case, though, that the Court ruled that Congress had the power to deal with free-ridership in interstate commerce under the *taxing powers* of Congress but not under the *interstate commerce powers* of Congress. The Court came to this conclusion on the basis of the argument that regulating "inactivity" in commerce (the nonpurchase of a product) would mean that little would stand beyond the reach of the interstate commerce power— that it would in effect become a limitless power and thus unconstitutional.[12] As the syllabus to the decision of the Court put it:

> The Framers knew the difference between doing something and doing nothing. They gave Congress the power to *regulate* commerce, not to *compel* it. Ignoring that distinction would undermine the principle that the Federal Government is a government of limited and enumerated powers. The individual mandate thus cannot be sustained under Congress's power to "regulate Commerce."[13]

The Court was, and is always, correct to fear limitless powers. Such powers have no place in a limited government.

The argument just made in this chapter, however, is that the power to regulate the kind of inactivity *that specifically results in free-ridership* is indeed necessary in order to effectively regulate inter-state commerce generally. Moreover, this power is very clearly and definably limited. It is by no means the unrestrained power that the Court would otherwise be correct to fear. This is to say, there is no need to separate the taxing power from the interstate regulatory power of Congress as the Court did in this case. This is an important point in the context of the Court's concern about unlimited power because placing the mandate instead under Congress's power to tax potentially leaves that power substantively unbounded. That is, the Court appears to introduce the very type of open-ended power that it wrongly feared the interstate commerce power would become. If so, then the Court's decision may actually create the possibility of taxing people who fail to buy broccoli for reasons of promoting good health, as long as the tax does not become so steep as to meet the definition of a penalty. In contrast, had controlling abusive free-ridership in commerce been the basis of the Court's decision, the Court would have reached the same verdict regarding the individual mandate but without opening the door to a potentially dangerous expansion of government power.

## Controlling Health-Care Costs

The health-care system in the United States operates through private markets far more than is the case in any other advanced nation. Given the American health-care system's dramatically higher costs without achieving either better overall medical results or higher patient satisfaction, it is clear that relying upon voluntary exchange in private markets has some serious drawbacks as a basis for producing and delivering health care, and that collaborative societal approaches deserve consideration. Greater societal collaboration would not necessarily violate or impinge upon individual freedom but, to the contrary, could easily bolster it, assuming that private options also remain, for precisely the reasons Lincoln cited regarding the legitimate role of government.

Consider the examples of France or Germany. Though they have largely collective systems, no serious argument can be made that they either ration health care or restrict personal choice in any way beyond what is already customary here in private commercial health insurance. If our costs were the same as the health-care systems in France or Germany, even if we kept the higher American compensation for doctors and nurses and the steep prices paid here for pharmaceutical drugs, the savings would still come to about $1,200 annually for each American—nearly $5,000 per year for a family of four, and between tens of thousands and many millions of dollars for most American businesses, a national savings of nearly $400 billion annually—with no overall reduction of choice, beneficial medical results, or patient satisfaction.

Some say that stronger private competition in a free market would hold down health-care costs as or more effectively. It is true that private competition in the area of pharmaceuticals did dampen costs when pharmaceuticals were brought within the scope of Medicare, yet even here entirely government-run programs (Medicaid and the Veterans Health Administration) pay and cost considerably less for pharmaceuticals.[14] It is typically within private competitive markets that overall health-care costs have soared most. While costs have also risen within Medicare and collective systems elsewhere in the world, they have generally grown markedly more slowly than within private markets in the United States.[15] Given the market failures stemming from the numerous perverse economic incentives that characterize private, for-profit health care, it is doubtful that increased competition *alone*, unaccompanied by societal collaboration, can effectively hold down costs, let alone make health care affordable for all.

## The Environment

In the mid-1960s, breathing the air in Los Angeles was equivalent to smoking more than a pack of cigarettes a day. Other American cities were heading in the same direction. The waters of Lake Erie were so polluted that the lake stood on the verge of death.[16]

The effect that any one individual or any one business has in polluting the environment is normally trivial. Aggregated, however, the effects are enormous enough to make Lake Erie unlivable and Los Angeles well on its way to becoming so, were the trends of the 1960s to have continued.

The problem is that pollution in the aggregate carries large negative costs for health and property, but, in exchanges taking place within a free market, pollution is not part of the cost of production and price, so there is nothing to restrain its growth. Those who create the pollution do not bear most of its costs and so do not price their products or services to reflect those costs. It's what economists call an "externality" because it happens outside of prices in the voluntary exchange of goods and services within a free market. In effect, each of us who pollutes shoves the costs on to someone else, in the form of poorer health or property damage.

This externality would be of little consequence if pollution had only small effects. But we can see from the examples of Los Angeles and Lake Erie that such is not the case. The costs are substantial. According to the American Lung Association, "the estimated annual health costs of human exposure to all outdoor air pollutants range from $40 billion to $50 billion, with an associated 50,000 premature deaths."[17]

The effects of pollution are not necessarily limited to the present. If the consensus that exists among knowledgeable scientists is correct, carbon emissions are in the process of causing future changes in global temperatures and weather that may well be lasting, profound, and very costly to adapt to—if we can adapt to them at all—unless carbon emissions are reduced well below present levels.

Because pollutants are externalities, the price mechanism of the free market cannot control them unless there is external intervention to tackle the costs through some form of public mandates, regulations, taxes, or charges. That intervention began in the United States with actions at the state and local levels in the 1950s and 1960s. When they proved insufficient, federal regulation followed, first in the form of public command-and-control regulations of air and water pollution and then in the form of governmental taxes on pollution.

The results have been generally positive and in some cases quite striking. During the first twenty-five years of air pollution regulation, since the 1960s, measured pollution declined on average by more than 30 percent even as the population grew by more than 25 percent. The number of days of excessive peak air pollution dropped by 35 percent in the nation's urban centers. During the twenty years since pollution charges were established in the early 1990s to control acid rain, acid rain has declined by 50 percent and saved an estimated $120 billion per year in reduced deaths and illnesses and healthier rivers, lakes, and forests.[18]

Water pollution has been more problematic. While quite a few rivers and lakes have been brought back to life, nearly 40 percent of them still don't meet at least one of the four standards regarding drinking, swimming, fishing, and ability to support aquatic life.

Just as all individuals have a legitimate interest in being protected from assault and theft, so they have a legitimate interest in being protected from pollution that may harm their life, health, or property. Virtually no one disputes this proposition. It is a fundamental reading of personal freedom. Because no free market can deal with externalities like pollution without intervention from the outside, disagreements about the need for governmental intervention in controlling pollution normally center upon the questions of whether there is pollution, the degree to which the pollution is having a harmful effect, and the lowest cost and restrictiveness necessary for mitigation of the harm (command-and-control regulations, taxes or charges, a cap-and-trade system, subsidizing forms of energy using less carbon, or some combination of these).

The most serious environmental issue presently facing the nation involves the relationship between growing carbon emissions, primarily from the burning of oil and coal, and global climate change. The United States is far and away the largest per-capita contributor of carbon emissions of any nation. Opponents of governmental action to address this problem argue that the human impact on the climate has not been demonstrated and so does not yet require governmental attention. The evidence for climate change, and also for the impact of human emissions on the climate, is not convincing, they say, despite a consensus approaching unanimity both among knowledgeable scientists (including even serious former skeptics) and in peer-reviewed scientific research that the issue is real and severe.[19] Nevertheless many opponents of action by the government continue to regard much of the scientific evidence and its interpretation as fraudulent or manufactured in some way; thus one politician in 2012 characterized global warming science as "one contrived phony mess."[20]

Whyever, though, would scientists engage in such a conspiracy? More to the point, given the scientific process itself and the way it operates, how would a widespread conspiracy like this among scientists even be possible?

More likely is that opponents find such a conspiracy view attractive because they realize the necessity of governmental intervention if in fact problems of pollution leading to climate change do exist—or even if there is a reasonable chance that such problems exist. (After all, people are normally considered prudent to insure themselves against eventualities that might prove devastatingly costly.) With this in mind, consider the words of Newt Gingrich when he switched his earlier stance to argue against a cap-and-trade approach to address global warming: "Cap and trade," Gingrich said, "was an effort by the left to use the environment as an excuse to get total control."[21]

The American instinct is to be suspicious of imposed collective action and expanded governmental power as invasions of one's freedom. Given that basic instinct, there is no question that the claims raised against the scientific consensus on climate change have made it considerably more difficult for the nation to come to agreement on this leading environmental issue. It can reasonably be debated what level (the federal government, state and local governments, incentivized private markets, or some combination of these) is the most effective and efficient for attaining the necessary results. Indeed that question must be asked, debated, and answered, and will be in a discussion of solutions in Chapter 7. But such willful outright dismissal of overwhelming evidence is effectively a betrayal of the freedom of others whose lives and property could be seriously harmed as a result of collective inaction. It is another example of a system in which the ideological battle over the size of government dominates and distracts from addressing the substantive issue of how individual lives are affected. Protecting against the possible infliction of harm upon others is a legitimate issue of freedom; as we will see in the next chapter, attaining small government as a goal in and of itself is not.

## INNOVATION IN THE ECONOMY

If there was ever an area in which Americans are prone to think that free competitive markets require no external assistance, it is the area of technological advances and product innovations. But, here again, things are more complicated.

Since we purchase products in the market, we are naturally inclined to conclude that they originated there. Yet often that is not the case. Consider the technologies and products that have come in whole or in part from outside the market, that relied heavily upon spending or research activities within the public sector. They include jet air transport, penicillin, the computer, the semiconductor and microelectronics, the Internet, global positioning systems and cell phones, nuclear power, aspirin, oral contraceptives, the suspension bridge, anesthesia, polio vaccine, MRIs, stethoscopes, the Web browser, the CT scan, and superconductors. And these are just a few on a very long list.

In all these cases, the innovations would not have happened or would have been significantly delayed if they had relied solely on the operations of private enterprise and the private competitive market. They all depended mightily upon contributions available only through the public sector.

Much innovation does occur within private commercial markets, of course. It is encouraged by substantial financial incentives made possible through legally protected patents and trademarks. Those same protections, however, can also create boundaries that limit innovation. Patents and trademarks essentially give their owners a monopoly over what is legally protected. No one else can use the patent or trademark without permission from and payment to the owner at the owner's discretion. Trade secrets, indeed, do not have even that level of openness.

Rules outside the private market are very different. In public settings, there is far less financial incentive because nothing is commercially protected in the way that patents and trademarks are. The absence of financial incentive is often seen as a disadvantage for innovation. At the same time, the result is that pretty much everything is open for anyone to use (with attribution) and thus to build upon. Cross-fertilization and creativity can take place between otherwise separate networks of people, even large numbers of them, in ways that are impossible in private commercial market settings.

Some kinds of knowledge and information are sufficiently general that they are not easily subject to patents and trademarks and so cannot be effectively protected, which removes or significantly reduces the financial incentive commercial markets require in order to produce them. Such knowledge and information are often called basic research. Because its results are open to all and are not patented, basic research tends to be created more in the public sector than in commercial settings, but can be used by anyone for commercial purposes. For example, the ability to map and sequence DNA resulting from the development of genomic science, which came about largely through basic research done in academic and other public settings, will lie behind hundreds of future pharmaceutical products in the commercial market and many billions of dollars in profits.[22]

Markets also require sufficient demand to operate effectively. That fact can pose problems for innovations that have huge upfront research and development costs but few immediate customers and no sure sizable market even in the distant future.

At times, when pursuing its other aims, the government ends up providing the missing but needed demand. In the early years of air flight, for example, the postal service was the fledgling airline industry's largest source of demand and the foundation for its future growth.

Consider the computer, too. Early computers were enormously

large and enormously expensive. A fair amount of the exploratory research on computers was governmentally sponsored. More important, according to economist Richard R. Nelson, government "was practically the sole market for the early operational computers . . . Few of the companies involved in the early work for government believed that there would be a large civilian as well as governmental market. Of course, later a very large nongovernmental market developed. The massive governmental support to computer technology provided U.S. companies with a head start that still has not been surpassed by foreign companies."[23] Similarly, work on integrated circuits and the semiconductor, necessary for the development of personal computers, took place only with the assurance that, if successful, a large governmental market would be there to support future sales.

The DuPont company today manufactures windmills, fenders for NASCAR racing cars, superstrong rope, and many other products from a material called Kevlar, which DuPont developed in conjunction with the needs of the Defense Department to provide soldiers with better protection on the battlefield. Teflon came about in the same way. Governmental involvement can truthfully be described as an "invisible hand" behind a large number of popular products in the private market. Similarly, many little-known but highly successful companies grew out of publicly funded programs in the academies, like Ventana Medical Systems, the multimillion-dollar company that is the world's leading supplier of automated diagnostic systems in the anatomical pathology market.

Fortunately, regarding technological and product innovation, there is no need to choose between commercial markets and public settings. We can and do have both. The synergistic connections between them have achieved amazing things. Progress in technological and product innovation has been the result not of either the private market or the public sector alone, but of the silent and normally seamless collaboration that routinely takes place between private markets and the public sector.

A lack of understanding of this key dynamic, resulting in a failure to attend to the public sector, will hinder future economic innovation within the United States and our success in commercial markets around the world. Public-sector research and development spending relative to GDP has declined steadily over the past four decades in the United States.

Given present trends, according to journalist Adam Davidson, founder of the podcast and blog "Planet Money," China will pass the United States in total research and development spending in about ten years, the first time on record that any nation will have forged ahead of us in total spending. He advises:

> China already has plans to focus on exciting but vague ideas now—like green energy and bio- and nanotechnology—that will most likely become products in the 2020s. And if U.S. government labs, university departments, and corporate researchers aren't already on top of the *next* generation of breakthroughs, the country will likely fall behind in 10 or 20 years when those innovations become marketable products. Our global competitiveness is based on being the origin of the newest, best ideas. How will we fare if those ideas originate somewhere else?[24]

## IMPLICATIONS

Collectivism and individual freedom are commonly considered to be opposites. They are not opposites, however, and Americans, down deep, do not really believe they are. After all, collective action is required to pass and enforce laws against common crimes, and such laws are universally accepted as fully compatible with freedom, in fact required in the name of freedom.

Following the same logic, collective societal action is legitimate in the name of individual freedom not just in addressing wrongful harm and sufficiency of opportunity but in any area in which freedom is undermined by collective inaction. Market failures—situations in which rational actions on the part of individuals acting separately from one another will end up creating ineffective or inefficient results, often leaving individuals vulnerable to greater harm—are precisely such areas. They closely fit Lincoln's assessment of 150 years ago. Public action is legitimate, in the name of freedom, "to do for a community of people whatever they need to have done, but cannot do at all, or cannot do as well for themselves in their separate and individual capacities. In all that individuals can individually do as well for themselves, government ought not to intervene."

Although we have emphasized areas that are appropriate for government to take action, the same principles spell out clear limits to legitimate action by government. Anything that is not either (1) addressing a genuine market failure, (2) needed to bring about sufficient economic opportunity, (3) required to protect against wrongful harm (including protecting the nation from foreign harm and individuals from civil liberties and civil rights abuses), or (4) necessary for educating citizens to take advantage of opportunities and fulfill the duties we have toward others as citizens (discussed in the next chapter) cannot be assumed to be a rightful action of government, and indeed should be treated as highly suspect.

For example, we have seen why a government regulation mandating individuals to purchase broccoli falls outside the boundaries of legitimate government action.[25] So, too, does government assistance to able-bodied individuals as an unending entitlement, such that it discourages recipients from taking adequate employment even when it is readily available. This is essentially how the nation's welfare system was permitted to operate before the 1996 reforms. Although those reforms had their own problems, the older welfare system was indeed subject to routine abuses that were incompatible with freedom.

Likewise, requiring religious institutions to provide benefits that violate their religious convictions lies outside the bounds of government, so long as other reasonable and similarly affordable options are available to recipients to obtain the same benefits. In addition, redistribution of wages or income for the sole sake of generating greater economic equality after the base levels of equal and sufficient opportunity already exist for all—such as lifting the minimum wage above a living wage—is expressly disallowed under the Common Credo. Finally, condemning one person's private property in order to transfer it into the private ownership or use of another, or into public use, even with proper payment, is outside the boundaries of government unless it can be shown to be clearly necessary to achieve one of the four purposes above. In sum, it runs counter to freedom to impose collective action where the protection of freedom is not at stake.

Those who oppose collective action often ridicule it as socialistic. Yet, in the worst sense of the term, nothing is as socialist as "free market socialism"—where individuals and industries make others pay for the costs of the economic activities from which they benefit. Such socialism can be countered *only* through collective action. Nor is anything more socialist than the collective manner of paying and providing for national defense, the infrastructure, and the protection of private property, which proponents of individualist freedom not only approve but deem essential to freedom.

If collective action is required and acclaimed in these areas in the name of freedom, what could the principled objection to collective action possibly be for similar purposes elsewhere: to achieve ends that people want to achieve as free individuals but cannot achieve, or achieve so well, acting separately and independently of one another?

What hinders individual freedom is not collective action so much as the pretense that acting together collectively is somehow the opposite of individual freedom. Notwithstanding their longstanding suspicion of collective action and the power of government, Americans intuitively understand this. As a result, by large margins, the American public does positively support collective action—that is, governmental programs—in every market-failure area in which the government has acted, from controlling environmental pollution and food safety to defense and police protection to the provision of education and health care (including large majorities of support among Americans for both Medicare and Medicaid, whether those responding are receiving benefits or not).

At the same time, opponents who have played to Americans' natural suspicion of collective action have made it nearly impossible for the nation to advance in dealing with two of the gravest situations it faces today—controlling the costs of health care and limiting pollutants that affect or might be affecting climate change. The latter inaction, if reversed, would also confront a third major problem by reducing or eliminating the nation's dependency upon oil and our subjection to the wildly fluctuating prices of the global oil market. On top of that, an unhealthy level of suspicion about collective action threatens to cost the United States the lead it has always held in basic research and development, which has long been one of the keys to the American economy's continuing power and success. This is all apart from the relevance that collective public action has more generally in establishing the societal conditions conducive to the creation of economic prosperity and its sustainability.

Getting the relationship between individual freedom and collective action straight is essential for the nation to attack and surmount many of its most serious problems, not the least of which is the inability otherwise to protect and enhance freedom itself.

## BENEFITS FOR THE RIGHT AND THE LEFT

Once again, as with the economy, core concerns of both the left and the right have something substantial to gain from the principles of the Common Credo as described throughout this chapter. For the left, the principles establish a compelling foundation for activist government and engagement as a collective society across a broad array of collaborative efforts. For the right, the same principles establish limits and boundaries to the areas and purposes of governmental activity. Both the chapter to come and Chapter 6 add further limiting conditions: that government, even within its appropriate areas, operate with the lowest level of cost and coerciveness necessary to accomplish the mandated goals of freedom, and that the government action be as localized and decentralized as possible, consistent with attaining the end goals and achieving them nationwide.

Will the left be willing to put explicit limits on government's activism? If the areas and purposes for societal collaboration listed above match the broad priorities of those on the left, which I believe they largely do, then keeping government confined within those areas and using the least costly, coercive, and centralized means possible should well be acceptable, too.

In the case of the right, market failures, by definition, identify areas where private competitive markets contain serious flaws and cannot function effectively. For this reason, conservatives in the past have supported policies calling for intervention by government in many of these areas, including pollution control, health care, and basic research, as well as the infrastructure, police, and national defense. Therefore, if conservatives oppose government involvement to address these problems, they do not do so on the basis of any principle about free markets. To the contrary, principled support for free markets means that conservatives ought to support external intervention in the specific areas where market failures exist. They should be even more likely to do so with a government obliged to operate at the lowest level of cost and restrictiveness necessary to get the job done, an obligation to which the Common Credo gives unstinting priority. The next chapter explores what steps we can take to hold government accountable to this key priority and, further, to achieve desperately needed reforms required both to elevate our politics and enable our government to work effectively again.

## CHAPTER 5

# RULES
# FOR
# GOVERNMENT

★ ★ ★ ★ ★

*Mistaken Belief 1: "That government*
*is best which governs least" calls specifically*
*for "small" government.*

*Mistaken Belief 2: Everyone should vote*
*according to his or her own self-interests.*

THE SAME MAN WHO PENNED the words "That government is best which governs least," Thomas Jefferson, also accused the British king, George III, of refusing to "assent to laws [that are] the most wholesome and necessary for the public good" and forbidding "his governors to pass laws of immediate and pressing importance." The Declaration of Independence cited these as the very first reasons for proclaiming the birth of a new nation—not the presence of the king's overbearing or tyrannical government, but the lack of sufficient governance. Not until much later does the Declaration mention anything smacking of tyranny.

It is nevertheless true, of course, that the Founders were also very much objecting to tyranny—to "absolute despotism" and "arbitrary authority." The power of government to coerce and its potential to intrude on freedom, which the Founders believed they had experienced firsthand, were ever-present concerns in their minds.

## LIMITED GOVERNMENT

The Founders obviously recognized the necessity of having a government with authority sufficient to protect liberty and promote the public good. They had said as much in the individual grievances they listed and the reasons for government they gave in the Declaration of Independence. They said the same again in 1787–1789, when they rejected the minimalist government established under the Articles of Confederation and replaced it with the considerably more powerful and far-reaching federal government of the Constitution precisely, as they wrote, "in Order to . . . secure the Blessings of Liberty to ourselves and our Posterity."

The Founders did not favor small or minimalist government per se. What they favored was limited government, controlled government, the least government necessary to do the job, and representative government. None of these is the same as small government; nor are they the same as unlimited, bloated, or wasteful government.

Rather, the Founders saw government as a means toward another goal: the securing of liberty in its various components. A government that effectively and efficiently served that goal was what they were seeking; ineffective or inefficient government, or government expanding beyond such proper goals, was to be avoided. Thus, limited government could well be large—even very large—as long as it was directed toward securing freedom in the least costly and restrictive way necessary to achieve the aim, and did not go beyond that aim. Obviously there were differences of opinion among the Founders about the exact role of government, but the very fact that they protested in the Declaration of Independence against insufficient government and then set up a federal government that was both bigger and far more powerful than what preceded it demonstrates that small government in itself was not their goal.[1]

However large government needed to be, efficiency (the lowest cost and restrictiveness it took to succeed, with no more taxing and regulating than was required for that success) was essential. Clearly, any government that either taxed more or was more restrictive than required constituted a diminution of the freedom of citizens. In this light, Jefferson's observation that the least government is the best government, and his condemnations of the king for providing insufficient government, are compatible and not contradictory.

The Founders attempted to control government through separation of powers, checks and balances, and federalism. By splitting power among different institutions and levels of government, James Madison wrote in *The Federalist Papers*, the Founders hoped that each institution and level, pitting ambition against ambition and the drive for power against the drive for power, would challenge, limit, and contain the others.[2]

## LIMITED GOVERNMENT IN CONTEMPORARY LIBERALISM AND CONSERVATISM

Despite bulwarks such as separation of powers and checks and balances, the Founders understood that institutional arrangements could go only so far in enabling government to do its job while simultaneously keeping it limited. Ultimately, decisions taken by human beings—leaders from all branches of government as well as members of the public—would determine what government would do and how powerful and extensive it would become. In dealing with this area, both liberalism and conservatism as practiced today have pivotal weaknesses.

For its part, except where civil rights and liberties are concerned—such as free speech and religion or freedom from unreasonable searches—liberalism rarely speaks of controlling government and avoiding governmental excesses in the domestic economy as a basic principle of its governing philosophy. Instead, concerns about rooting out governmental overreach, waste, and inefficiencies in domestic economic and social programs, when expressed at all, tend to be framed in pragmatic terms rather than as matters of firm principle.

For example, while outlining a series of reductions in unnecessary governmental activities in the autumn of 2011, President Obama explained: "At a time when families have had to cut back . . . we thought it was entirely appropriate for our government and our agencies to try to root out waste, large and small."[3] This statement implies that if families had not needed to spend less and tighten their belts, wasteful activities within government would have been acceptable.

Elsewhere, Obama has frequently spoken of needing to reduce wasteful spending so that the public will have more trust and confidence in government and become more willing to support initiatives that Democrats care about in other areas. Democratic initiatives may indeed benefit, but, again, it's not a principled reason for trying to reduce unnecessary spending in government.

Announcing a waste-cutting initiative, Vice President Joe Biden said: "We can make our government more efficient and responsible to the American people. If we're going to spur jobs and economic growth and restore long-term fiscal solvency, we need to make sure hard-earned tax dollars don't go to waste."[4] The suggestion here once more is that, except for the need to spur jobs or reduce deficits, waste in government would be tolerable. It overlooks the view that waste is wrong virtually whatever the circumstances because when government costs, taxes, or regulates more than is necessary it diminishes the freedom of its citizens. One possible exception might be when government attempts to reverse a dearth of private spending through public spending; spending, even if some is wasteful, might arguably be more tolerable in that single circumstance.

According to findings of the General Accounting Office (GAO), in 2011 the federal government had eighty-two separate programs to improve teacher quality and another fifty-six separate programs intended to help people with financial literacy. According to a panel of experts, federal "agencies paid private contractors at least $539 billion in fiscal year 2009, much of it with little or no competition or performance evaluation. An additional $660 billion-plus in grants to states, local governments and non-profits has undergone no systemic Congressional review."[5]

The accountability of government is no small matter. These areas of potential extravagance should be addressed *as a matter of principle*. Such an undertaking ought to involve, at a minimum, designing a process to comprehensively review and reduce waste in all areas of government in a coherent and comprehensive way, followed by producing an annual written report on the basis of those reviews, summarized orally to the public each year by the president.

It should also involve establishing an entity somewhat like the Congressional Budget Office (CBO) to analyze all new programs and reauthorizations of existing programs and giving its conclusions the same legislative weight now accorded to CBO analyses of revenues and costs. The office would examine whether programs are achieving their purposes at the lowest practicable cost and restrictiveness. The General Accounting Office, congressional auditors, and inspectors general of the departments and agencies now do elements of such studies, but not in the coherent or comprehensive manner just suggested, or given the same legislative weight and level of publicity through the president that I am proposing here.[6]

Conservatives have something of the reverse problem. They aim to reduce taxes and also overall spending and regulation for domestic economic and social programs. Calling for cuts in taxes, spending, and regulation as a bedrock principle and end goal in itself, however, risks constricting government to such a degree that it cannot carry out its proper aims.

For example, during his career, Senator Orrin Hatch of Utah, a conservative, attempted to keep dietary health supplements exempted from federal safety reviews before the products went to market, while still allowing the producers of supplements to make health claims about their products. In 2011 an official of the GAO, arguing in support of tighter regulations, pointed out that companies marketing the pills claimed falsely that the ingredients could cure cancer, diabetes, and the common cold. Senator Hatch responded that those claims were outlawed already. "No one is more interested that this industry works properly in the best interests of our people than I am," the senator said. He then went on to acknowledge that "the F.D.A. doesn't have the money to really do what it should do."[7]

Just as wasteful spending and overregulation in government infringe upon freedom, so, too, does failing to provide government the powers or resources it needs to properly do its job. There are numerous areas where we see this problem. They include underfunding of the infrastructure; uncompetitive pay that then fails to recruit the most able into teaching; the improper administration of labor regulations; inadequate funding of legal aid; and the failure to supply government with sufficient resources, including the necessary regulations and dedicated personnel, to investigate, prosecute, and convict individuals of the sort of financial wrongdoing that was the proximate cause of our economy's collapse. Examples such as these merely scratch the surface.

Few conservatives, however, support giving regulatory and other domestic programs more funding or power. It runs against their general goal of cutting government. Nearly all conservatives in Congress have signed Grover Norquist's pledge never to vote to raise tax rates no matter what the fiscal circumstances. The idea, Norquist boasted, is to make the federal government small enough so that "we can drown it in the bathtub."[8] Conservatives have signed the pledge without making the least effort to demonstrate how it comports with the proper functioning and needs of government. True, some signers of the pledge voted to allow the Bush tax cuts to expire on top incomes, thereby permitting those tax rates to go back to the former higher level. They did so, however, as the sole remaining option to prevent still broader tax hikes for everyone had the Bush tax cuts expired.

Many balanced-budget amendments supported by conservatives, including every Senate Republican and a majority of House Republicans, call for a limit on federal spending of 18 percent of GDP from the former year, or about 17 percent of the current GDP.[9] During the year before the economy's breakdown, in 2007, federal spending was 19.6 percent of GDP and was virtually the same as a decade earlier. Throughout the Reagan presidency, federal spending relative to GDP ranged from 20 percent to 23 percent. No one explains why 17 percent of GDP is an optimal figure for today. Making such proposals in the absence of careful analysis, including spelling out the concrete implications of such a limit, is no way to run a country— not a healthy country at any rate.

In signing the Declaration of Independence and establishing the Constitution, the Founders indicated that they wanted to encourage government to be sufficiently powerful with enough resources to achieve its properly constituted aims, but at the same time limited and controlled enough to attain its aims with as little cost and restrictiveness as possible—what the Founders would have considered "economy in government." Both are first principles for government. A philosophy that fails to embrace both principles as bedrock rules—defining upper and lower boundaries for government— becomes especially vulnerable to interest-driven decisions. As they are practiced today, neither liberalism nor conservatism considers both of them to be bottom-line principles—a serious weakness for any worldview that claims to be a governing philosophy.

## Civic Virtue and Representative Democracy

The problem is that government itself is in some ways contradictory to freedom because the decisions government makes, by their very nature, are coercive. Laws and regulations require citizens to do certain things and typically back up the requirements by force, through fines or imprisonment. The esteemed Judge Learned Hand understandably looked upon taxation as "enforced extraction, not voluntary contributions."[10]

Yet at the same time, government is needed to make collective societal decisions in the many situations in which freedom cannot be achieved through individuals' acting alone. Even setting up a free market requires a series of collective decisions delineating rights of property, contracts, and patents, as well as the responsibilities of liability and honesty, and the enforcement of such rights and responsibilities. All these actions depend upon the coercive power of government to enforce compliance. Many are high-stakes decisions that will be applied even to those who disagree with them, by compulsion if need be.[11]

How, then, do we keep this coercive agent under control so that its actions stay within the aims of freedom? The Founders recognized that while dividing power and judicial review could put checks on government, nothing could assure limited government in the final instance except a specific mindset in both leaders and citizens: what the Founders called "virtue." In Benjamin Franklin's famous words: "Only a virtuous people are capable of freedom."[12] The word we use today might be "character." James Madison viewed it thus:

> But I go on this great republican principle, that the people will have virtue and intelligence to select men of virtue and wisdom. Is there no virtue among us? If there be not, we are in a wretched

situation. No theoretical checks—no form of government can render us secure. To suppose that any form of government will secure liberty or happiness without any virtue in the people, is a chimerical idea.[13]

Despite his faith in pitting self-interest against self-interest, and power against power, Madison recognized that ultimately, if they failed, only virtue could come to the rescue.

John Adams held the same belief: "Public virtue cannot exist in a Nation without Private, and public Virtue is the only Foundation of Republics."[14]

And what was virtue? To quote the historian Eric Foner, it was "the willingness to subordinate private passions and desires for the public good."[15]

In other words, freedom can ultimately be protected only if leaders and individual members of the public are virtuous—that is, only if they are able to rise above advancing their own self-interests in order to care about others and the public good. That surely means respecting and protecting the legitimate interests of others in their freedom wherever those interests are at risk. In the end, the commonplace notion that individual citizens should vote their own narrow self-interests, or that leaders should advance the particular interests of their constituents, has stringent limits. Both individual citizens and leaders also need to practice virtue. We have an obligation to vote, act, and speak in a way that cares about and gives proper weight to the rightful interests of others in their freedom. If these matters are at stake, it is neither appropriate nor acceptable for citizens simply to follow their own private interests, or for leaders to serve solely their own constituents' interests.

Recall the example of Orrin Hatch defending the position taken by the supplemental dietary pill industry to keep the industry exempted from FDA authority. Steven Novella, a clinical neurologist at the Yale School of Medicine, observed that "Orrin Hatch certainly has a right to fight for his constituents," notwithstanding the fact that slick, dishonest methods of an unregulated market cause people harm and abuse.[16]

To the contrary, Senator Hatch has no such ultimate right. According to the Founding Fathers, above and beyond any right Hatch has to advance his constituents' (or his own) interests, he has an obligation to distinguish freedom from license against freedom, even if doing so might moderate his constituents' (or his own) interests. Hatch himself recognized this obligation and the principle behind it when he responded to Novella, according to the *New York Times*, that he had repeatedly demanded that federal regulators step up their enforcement of existing laws and even worked to expand their powers. No relationships directed his policy positions, he said.[17]

Americans generally understand and accept the same principle. Most Americans believe, for example, that their representatives should support national needs and not solely the interests of their own constituents, let alone simply the representative's own individual political or economic interests. In our own everyday lives, most of us show each other mutual respect in myriad ways rather than pressing for self-advantage. To give just a few illustrations, we routinely defer to others who are standing in lines, or to other drivers, or to requests that we refrain from smoking; we participate in campaigns to recycle waste; we turn off cell phones in a movie; and we refrain from interrupting others in conversations.

Ultimately, advancing one's own interest and perspective *above all*, with little concern for others' interests, encourages intellectual dishonesty—that is, the willingness to defend one's interest or perspective without regard to integrity or consistency or evidence—if acting otherwise would harm one's own interest. Where intellectual dishonesty is widespread, and political power is divided, leaving no available majority, paralysis must result; worse, in the context of widespread intellectual dishonesty, a determined and enduring majority occupying all institutions would likely produce a form of tyranny.

Polls show that a substantial majority of Republicans today do not want their representatives to work with President Obama. Many Democrats had a similar attitude when President George W. Bush occupied office. President Obama himself repeatedly assured the public that the health-insurance mandate he proposed was not a tax and then allowed his solicitor general to defend the mandate as a tax in the Supreme Court. Many conservatives call for substantial cuts in domestic spending, yet laud projects that come to their districts; liberals frequently do the same with respect to spending on defense. Intellectual dishonesty runs rampant. Many areas of politics and policy are deeply affected by it.

Back in 2006, Michael Kinsley, a columnist at the *Washington Post*, described the state of American politics this way:

> The conversation in our democracy is dominated by disingenu-ousness. Candidates and partisan commentators strike poses of outrage that they don't really feel, take positions they would not take if the shoe was on the other foot (e.g., criticizing Bush when you would have given Clinton a pass, and vice versa), feel no obligation toward logical consistency. Our democracy occa-sionally punishes outright lies but not brazen insincerity . . .
>
> The biggest flaw in our democracy is the enormous tolerance for intellectual dishonesty. Politicians are held to account for outright lies, but there seems to be no sanction against saying things you obviously don't believe. There is no reward for logical consistency, and no punishment for changing your story depend-ing on the circumstances . . . A few days before the 2000 elec-tion, the Bush team started assembling people to deal with a possible problem: what if Bush won the popular vote but Gore carried the Electoral College. They decided on, and were about

to begin, a big campaign to convince the citizenry that it would be wrong for Gore to take office under those circumstances. And they intended to create a tidal wave of pressure on Gore's electors to vote for Bush, which arguably the electors as free agents have the authority to do. In the event, of course, the result was precisely the opposite, and immediately the Bushies launched into precisely the opposite argument: the Electoral College is a vital part of our Constitution, electors are not free agents, threatening the Electoral College result would be thumbing your nose at the founding fathers . . . It [working to have it both ways] was reported before the election and is uncontested, but no one seems to care, because so much of our politics is like that.[18]

The marginalizing of truth and facts in policy debates was unintentionally revealed several years later when the conservative Senator Jon Kyl of Arizona, a senior member of the Republican leadership team, spoke on the Senate floor in 2011 in support of a motion to strip Planned Parenthood of federal funding. His main reason for supporting the motion, Senator Kyl said, was: "If you want an abortion, you go to Planned Parenthood, and that's well over 90 percent of what Planned Parenthood does." Later, when challenged that the true figure was between 3 and 20 percent, Senator Kyl's office responded: "His remark was not intended to be a factual statement."[19] Apparently, Senator Kyl's office viewed this response to be a satisfactory answer that needed no further explanation.

Today, with the continuous use of the filibuster, power is divided in American government even when a single party controls all three political branches yet without 60 percent of the votes in the Senate. In the context of divided political power, the self-interested win-at-all-costs attitude, which turns intellectual dishonesty into a favored approach, cannot help but lead to political dysfunction and paralysis. Any side that engages in such dishonesty becomes unreachable and unmovable, whether by evidence or by logic, or even by precedent, let alone by goodwill. On top of that, through regular use of the filibuster, the minority can stop the majority in the Senate simply by sticking together, further reducing the incentive to compromise.

Simply put, debate in which some participants are intellectually dishonest is not, by definition, a civil debate. As the Founders warned, a society based upon freedom cannot ultimately succeed if its leaders and citizens abuse freedom by following their self-interests alone and fail to respect the legitimate interests of others, an abuse that would include acting toward others in an intellectually dishonest way.

In the Founders' minds, that's what virtue implied, although as their own political relationships demonstrate, they were not themselves always faithful practitioners of the ideal.

The responsibility we as individual citizens and our leaders have to strive to virtue in a free society arises both because we and our leaders are engaging in activities that will result in coercive decisions on individual citizens through the force of law, and because the collective decision-making upon which freedom relies will ultimately fail—either becoming paralyzed or tyrannical—if self-interest becomes the sole motivating force. The Founders understood that human beings were self-interested. They recognized that virtue, therefore, took great effort and discipline. Above all, though, they knew that in the end freedom required leaders and citizens to be virtuous, and not purely self-interested, in order for freedom itself to succeed.

## A Proposal

How can virtue in our politics be strengthened? Virtue comes most effectively out of firm principle, as a matter of basic belief that it is right and good to act in the proper manner. Absent firm principle, the sole alternative is the clearly inferior one of attempting to appeal, to the extent possible, to people's self-interest.

Political leaders today face few negative political consequences for intellectual dishonesty. They easily deflect charges against them of hypocrisy and intentional falsehoods and exaggerations. Who can challenge them effectively? The opposition itself is so suspect right now, at least to nonsupporters, that it cannot make the other side accountable. The mainstream media generally present different sides of issues as if the sides had equal weight, rarely saying that anything is false, let alone dishonest. They also see distortion as normal and so not especially newsworthy. "The Truth? C'mon, This Is a Political Convention," read a *Washington Post* headline covering the national party conventions in 2012. The article was written by the paper's fact checker, no less.[20]

A variety of independent organizations exist that check assertions against facts, but they get woefully erratic publicity. Moreover, these organizations usually concentrate on random individual speeches. They rarely examine patterns of repeated distortions that officeholders, candidates, and political parties and organizations build up in a variety of areas over time. Intellectual dishonesty that undermines collaboration really has more to do with these patterns of repeated distortions and falsehoods, and how much they account for the totality of a candidate or issue campaign, than with scattered individual instances.

The news media need to step up to the plate. They can no longer view untruths as something everyone engages in and thus unworthy of reporting. A primary mission of good journalism, after all, is supposed to be the search for truth. Fact checking, in the words of columnist Frank Rich, "used to be the very definition of their craft."[21] In that light, the seeming casualness with which the news media treat candidates and elected officeholders when they speak untruths is mystifying.

One way to address this problem would be for the *New York Times* and the *Wall Street Journal*—two of the nation's most eminent papers, and ones perceived as having opposing editorial slants—to collaborate in a joint venture. The aim would be not so much to detect individual untruths but to focus on both numbers and patterns of untruths over a period of time, covering leading elected officeholders, candidates, political parties, and independent organizations. The prominence of the two newspapers would afford their findings the widespread publicity, national attention, and public discussion needed, especially as individual cases of dishonesty were put together in quarterly reports to identify persisting patterns of honesty and dishonesty over time. These reports could establish an "honesty metric" that allowed for easy, plain, and direct comparisons of different elected officials (or candidates, parties, and independent organizations). The fact that the two newspapers have different ideological leanings significantly increases the likelihood that the venture would be regarded as above politics and nonpartisan, so that even people who identify strongly with one ideology or the other would feel the need to take the findings seriously. Such a project would require effective measures to ensure both accuracy and accountability, including a regularized process of independent external review and an easily accessible ombudsman to receive and respond to public feedback.

There are, undeniably, many reasons why such a venture is unlikely to occur, though none that is as compelling as the reasons why it should. Both newspapers have very high news-reporting standards based upon a core mission of truth-telling on matters essential to the public. By establishing such a joint venture, they would be taking a huge stride toward accomplishing this mission, and would make a crucial contribution to the public.

An alternative would be for a privately funded trust, supported by respected eminent figures from both parties, staffed with recognized experts, and armed with rigorous internal and external checks, to engage in the same kind of effort to demonstrate patterns of untruths over time. Such a trust would also require an assured financial endowment of many millions of dollars (there is a long list of philanthropists who could make this happen) that nevertheless allows the trust to remain completely independent of the donors. Income from the endowment would need to be sufficient not simply to produce highly qualified reports that command public confidence because they are expert and above reproach, but also to assure widespread news and advertising publicity for its reports, enabling them to make a serious impact on public debate.

There may be other better and more effective mechanisms for the purpose. What is certain is the need to diminish the level of intellectual dishonesty that both renders collaboration on collective decisions far more difficult to reach and, in its knowing distortions, invades the freedom of every person against whom it operates.

Apart from calling out and broadly publicizing patterns of falsehoods and intellectual dishonesty, another needed step is to ensure that the mechanisms of government themselves don't encourage one-sidedness, but do the reverse. Here, two procedures of government come particularly to mind. One is gerrymandering that makes legislative districts uncompetitive between the two parties, encouraging (even forcing) representatives to pay attention only to their renomination and thus only to their base, rather than to a larger and more diverse general electorate. The practice of gerrymandering not only contributes to extremism in this way, but it also violates the ideal of equal freedom by deliberately arranging elections so that relatively few citizens actually experience competitive contests and officeholders are in effect elected within only their own side. The same can be said for the filibuster in the Senate. Allowing routine use of the filibuster permits the minority party to pay attention only to its own interests, without having to reach out, by enabling it to override the majority as long as it has the support of 41 out of 100 senators. Except for extraordinary kinds of decisions, the Founders believed that majorities should normally decide legislative outcomes, on the principle of equal freedom that every citizen's (and every representative's) vote should have equal weight. The Constitution itself specifies where super majorities are required, and does so only in a small handful of instances. Reform of gerrymandering and the filibuster will help reduce one-sidedness in our politics. The chapter on solutions suggests reforms of these practices that can make a difference.

## MONEY AND DEMOCRATIC GOVERNANCE

Containing intellectual dishonesty and one-sidedness is not enough, however. In a democracy, governmental decisions affect the actions of citizens who live under them on pain of fines or sanctions if they do not comply. This is obviously true even for citizens who disagree with the decisions made by government. Because this is the case, throughout America's history the methods and processes by which these decisions are made have been of paramount concern.

The Founders considered certain features essential to the process, apart from the checks and balances already mentioned. There had to be representation based directly or indirectly upon elections open to all those possessing the right to vote (which as we know was shamefully limited for much of this country's history) and decided by majorities or pluralities of those voting, each person with one vote. Representatives (or, at minimum, the sides they supported) had to have the opportunity for a reasonably equal hearing in discussion and debate within the legislature. As just mentioned, except for extraordinary issues, majority votes of representatives would decide outcomes, and decisions having coercive effects had to get or be rooted in authority from legislative bodies that met these conditions.

The Constitution, in fact, specified such processes of representation not only for the federal government but also for all the states, requiring that each state have a republican form of government.

Writing about the republican ideology of the Founders, the preeminent historian of the Revolution, Gordon Wood, summed up the conclusion of many historians. "Equality lay at the heart of republicanism," he observed, "Republican citizenship implied equality."[22]

There is no doubt that the Founders saw each lawful citizen as being civicly equal. There is no doubt, either, that such equality was essential to the Founders' idea of liberty. Because all of us, as free citizens, must live and abide by the laws, government and lawmaking in a republic had to be accountable to the public with all citizens understood as equals.

The Supreme Court shied away from issuing rulings regarding this area of republican equality for many years, viewing it as an essentially political question beyond the Court's purview. It reversed course toward the middle of the last century in a series of decisions that culminated in *Reynolds v. Sims* in 1964. At the time, elections in many of the states operated under systems that awarded each legislative district a single representative regardless of a district's population. Even though the most highly populated districts might have two, five, or even ten times the population of the least populated, every district had one representative.

*Reynolds v. Sims* had to do with the election system in Alabama, but the claim in the case applied to systems in the majority of states. The contention against Alabama was that the votes of citizens in the most populated districts—one of them having nineteen times the population of the smallest district—were so diluted in weight as to violate the premise of civic equality underlying a republic.

The Court agreed, not only with regard to state legislatures but, in an earlier case, also with regard to the federal House of Representatives. The right to vote, the Court said, "was effectively impaired" if it was "diluted and debased." It went on to say: "To the extent that a citizen's right to vote is debased, he is that much less a citizen." For each citizen to have one vote and one vote only was not enough; each citizen's vote also had to have an equal weight. Even population differences that gave the vote of a citizen in one district twice the weight of the vote of a citizen in another district—let alone five, ten, or twenty times the weight—could not be countenanced. "No right is more precious in a free country," the Court concluded, "than that of having a voice in the election of those who make the laws under which, as good citizens, we must live."[23]

A major study carried out nearly forty years after the *Reynolds* decision found that unequal apportionment in state legislative districts, in violation of the stricture that each person's vote had to have an equal weight, had substantial practical effects on what governments did. State spending prior to *Reynolds v. Sims* and the related cases brought citizens in seriously overrepresented districts about $1,500 more annually per four-person household than in the underrepresented districts, a discrepancy that reapportionment, following the Court decisions, largely eliminated.[24]

Alongside the connection they made between civic and political equality and liberty, the Founders also firmly held that representatives themselves should be independent in the sense that they should not be unduly beholden to particular individuals. The Founders believed representatives who felt beholden to a select few would be less able to act on behalf of the general public good. Propertyholding individuals who were not economically reliant upon others were the most likely to serve in the independent manner that representation in a properly functioning republic required. "I say it again, cultivators of the earth are the most virtuous and independent citizens," Jefferson wrote in his *Notes on the State of Virginia*, expressing a view regarding disinterestedness made possible through ownership of landed property that was widely held among the Founders.[25]

## How the Nation Is Faring

Both in perception and fact, it is hard to imagine any difference bigger than the one separating our current election practices from the Founders' fundamental precepts—first, that there should be civic equality of citizens in government and lawmaking, and, second, that representatives should not be unduly beholden to particular individuals. Seven in ten Americans say that government is run for a few big interests rather than for their benefit, three in five Americans feel that government officials don't care much what people think, and only one in three Americans believes that people have a say in what government does.[26]

How could most ordinary citizens feel that they were civic or political equals in electing representatives, and that representatives were independent, when candidates in elections depend so much upon raising huge amounts of money from a relative few large contributors and from individuals who collect a number of large contributions (called bundlers)? One such wealthy contributor, Ray Tamraz of Texas (who made his fortune through oil), expressed the point bluntly. When a senator asked Tamraz if he was registered to vote, he answered: "Am I registered to vote? No, Senator, I think money is worth a bit more than the vote."[27]

Within the political process, and understandably in the eyes of many ordinary citizens, the weight of one citizen's vote pales in comparison to the weight of campaign contributions in the many thousands or millions of dollars from a large donor or bundler, which enable the sort of publicity and outreach necessary to procure many more votes.

In *Reynolds v. Sims*, the Court had deemed a citizen's vote as unacceptably diluted in the eyes of the Constitution if another citizen's vote had twice the weight. Large financial contributions greatly

dilute each citizen's civic import well beneath half the weight, allowing such donors to gain substantially more heft than an ordinary voter's in an election, even voters who volunteer large amounts of time
to a campaign. It isn't that votes of individual citizens don't count—
they do—but the weight of the influence is distorted beyond recognition. To be clear, the issue here is not necessarily about which
candidate spends more money. In sizable electorates, even victorious
candidates who spend less than their opponents still have to spend
considerable amounts in order to win and thus must depend upon
very large donors.[28]

To win, candidates must mobilize their base of voters and also
attract large contributors. They rarely can win without doing both.
Both groups—the base and large contributors—are of relatively
equal importance to the candidate. The base, however, comprises
hundreds of thousands or millions of voters, while the large financial
backers comprise a few hundred or a few thousand at most. In such
a world, substantial financial contributions bring donors fifty times,
one hundred times, even one thousand times the weight of ordinary
citizens in the eyes of candidates and elected representatives.

As a result, those few voters with heavier standing gain access to
representatives going far beyond what ordinary citizens experience.
If civic equality means anything, it means the right to a reasonably
equal hearing, to reasonably equal consideration. Yet it is universally acknowledged that representatives give much greater access to
the views and concerns of their financial backers than they give to
ordinary voters. *No one—not a single politician, contributor, lobby-
ist, journalist, or analyst—denies it.* And that reality of special access
understandably leaves most ordinary citizens believing that they are
far less than equal in the governing process.

Shaun Breidbart of Pelham, New York, expressed this sentiment
in a letter to the *New York Times* in 2011. Someone had telephoned
Governor Scott Walker of Wisconsin pretending to be the billionaire

David H. Koch, and Governor Walker immediately took the call. The *New York Times* reported the story with a humorous quote from Koch indicating that the prank might hurt his ability to contact senators and members of the House as easily as he was generally able. "If I called up a senator or a congressman to discuss something with them, and they heard 'David Koch is on the line,'" Mr. Koch kidded, "they'd immediately say, 'that's that fraud again—tell him to get lost.'" Shaun Breidbart had a different reaction: the fact that Koch has direct access to politicians in most of the states "while the best I can get from my own representatives is an intern sending me a form letter in response to my inquiries is a perfect example of why we need campaign finance reform."[29]

It is also widely understood that the special access given to large financial backers leads to unequal political influence and that representatives inevitably become unduly beholden to a particular few. Democratic Senator Dick Durbin of Illinois pointedly observed in a 2009 radio interview that despite having caused the 2008 financial crisis, the same financial firms "are still the most powerful lobby on Capitol Hill. And they, frankly, own the place."[30]

The view is bipartisan. On the Republican side, here is the take of former Senator Alan Simpson of Wyoming: "Donations from the tobacco industry to Republicans scuttled tobacco legislation just as contributions from trial lawyers to Democrats stopped tort reform." Or this from Newt Gingrich: "It's hard to be a middle-class candidate . . . We are drifting to a society where millionaires buy Congress."[31]

As recently as 2003, in fact, Alan Simpson's view summed up the Supreme Court's own conclusion. In *McConnell v. Federal Election Commission*, the Court prefaced its decision by stating:

> In addition to "*quid pro quo* arrangements," we have recognized a concern not confined to bribery of public officials but extending to the broader threat from politicians too compliant with the

wishes of large contributors . . . acknowledging that corruption extends beyond explicit cash-for-votes agreements to "undue influence on an officeholder's judgment."

It then ruled in favor of the McCain-Feingold campaign finance reform:

> Plaintiffs argue that without concrete evidence of an instance in which a federal officer has actually switched a vote (or, presumably, evidence of a specific instance where the public believes a vote was switched), Congress has not shown that there exists real or apparent corruption. But the record is to the contrary. The evidence connects soft money [contributions] to manipulations of the legislative calendar, leading to Congress's failure to enact, among other things, generic drug legislation, tort reform, and tobacco legislation.[32]

If the Court itself reached that conclusion, it was surely reasonable for a large majority of Americans to feel that way, as they indeed did and still do: that both in appearance and in practice there was undue access to and undue influence on political officeholders in the way the political process operated under the rules for financial contributions then in place.

Since then, with the notorious *Citizens United v. FEC* ruling in 2010, the Supreme Court has taken a tack that allows even bigger financial contributions to flood the election and political process in the enlarged ability of corporations and unions to make independent contributions. It also reaffirmed and reemphasized the right of individuals and groups to make unrestricted financial contributions to independent campaigns intended to assist candidates—so-called super PACs—on the basis of a 1976 ruling of the Court in *Buckley v. Valeo*. The system is, if anything, now significantly more subject to real and apparent corruption than when the Supreme Court itself agreed it was in 2003, as now independent contributions present a serious problem for civic and political equality as well.[33] This is the case not only for large independent contributions intended to assist individual candidates and likely to make them feel beholden, but even for those contributions that have nothing to do with the election of a candidate, such as donations to finance statewide initiatives or referenda. Just as elections make authoritative decisions in selecting the officeholders who will make the laws by which we will have to live, initiatives and referenda propose directly to voters laws by which everyone in the state must abide if they are adopted. Yet a single wealthy individual, or a few such individuals, can fund an initiative drive, which otherwise would take many thousands of ordinary citizens to organize and finance. And unless a few wealthy individuals or thousands of ordinary citizens organize in opposition, an initiative with financial backing has a decent chance of getting adopted. Thus, with initiatives and referenda, as in the case of the election of candidates, a few wealthy individuals are able to gain the same political importance of many thousands of ordinary citizens.

## A PATH FORWARD

Americans today feel distanced from their government. Once looked upon by many Americans as "us," the government is more likely now to be seen as representing "them." There are many reasons for this attitude, including the growing attempts to restrict voting as well as the gerrymandering of electoral districts; the revolving door between elected representatives leaving office and K Street lobbying firms; and the special treatment too frequently given representatives in such matters as pensions and insider knowledge. No reason is more crucial, however, than the enormous inequalities in access and influence that political contributions bring to large donors both on the debate that takes place during elections and on the elected representatives once in office.

The Court has an avenue enabling it to find robust campaign finance reforms constitutional, including stiff regulations on independent campaigns. That avenue is to reason from *Reynolds v. Sims*.

Because every citizen must live under the laws enacted by the legislature, the Court ruled in *Reynolds*, it is not enough that every citizen have one vote in electing his or her representative. In addition, the vote of each citizen must weigh reasonably equally in determining the composition of the legislature as a whole. It is unconstitutional, the Court said, to give one citizen's vote even twice the weight of another in determining the overall composition of the legislature. From this principle, it would be consistent to reason that large political contributions, direct or independent, can be restricted on grounds that a citizen gains far more weight regarding the terms of the debate in an election campaign and on the elected officials themselves thereafter when that person provides very large financial contributions.

Following the reasoning of *Reynolds v. Sims* and the decisions that preceded it, such inequalities cannot be permitted in a republic in the making of laws under which every citizen must live. The same reasoning would apply equally well to independent campaigns, including campaigns for initiatives and referenda, and to individuals giving large sums to finance their own election campaigns.

Yet if the principle of civic equality applies not simply to the vote but also in some manner to financial contributions, it is legitimate to ask how those contributions would differ, if at all, from other kinds of contributions that might lead to unequal political influence, such as volunteering time to a campaign. Citizens can end up getting greater influence in that way, too. The answer is that while not.everyone has the same amount of time to give to political campaigns, nature does limit anyone from contributing more than, say, fifteen hours a day.

That physical reality imposes a decisive difference between the influences of volunteer work and money, which has no natural limit unless it is legally restricted in some manner. True, the representative of an organization of many people who are volunteering time for a campaign might well gain special treatment and greater influence, but the point here is that such treatment and influence would come about because a great many citizens from the organization were involved as volunteers, thereby relating the special treatment in some measure to numbers of citizens. A large financial contribution from one individual, in contrast, would give the same unequal treatment to that single individual.

No one, including the Court, questions limitations on how much time speakers in court, on the floors of Congress, or in state legislatures have to speak—limitations that are designed to give each speaker or side reasonably equal time. Virtually every American would agree that it is right to have such rules, and that no one side should be permitted to dominate. Only in the case of rules governing the public arena—in elections and in initiatives and referenda—has the Court ruled that this principle of reasonable equality in the presentation of sides violates freedom and is therefore unconstitutional. Such a one-sided individualistic view of freedom fails to consider the freedom of those citizens who then must live and abide by the laws or initiatives that result from the baldly unequal access and influence given to the speech of a special few. This is what turns a government of "us" into a government of "others" and "them."

Large monetary contributors have another insidious effect unlike that of any other resource whose result is to increase an individual's political influence, whether it be volunteer work, personal visibility, intelligence, knowledge, or charisma, all of which can lead to an unequal hearing. None of these other resources is a natural source of political division, whereas, as Madison frequently warned, wealth and economic interests are. Allowing outsized financial contributions in our politics has a likelihood of reinforcing a natural division of interest that, when pressed through the political process, can then be imposed on all—the very meaning of a corrupt process.

There could not be a greater contrast in the Court's rulings. The line of cases culminating in *Reynolds v. Sims* gives constitutional pre-eminence to the reciprocal view of freedom and the conditions such freedom requires, and reflects the beliefs, concerns, and warnings about liberty that the Founders frequently expressed. In contrast, the subsequent line of cases ending with *Citizens United* backs the mistaken individualistic idea of freedom that has increasingly dominated political life in contemporary America, alienating an even greater number of citizens in the process.

## CONCLUSION

In thinking about how to govern ourselves, both as free individuals and as a free people, three insights are particularly crucial, all of them coming from the Founders. First, limited government is not to be measured by its size per se but by whether, however large government is, it is fully large enough to successfully carry out its duties under freedom yet is no larger than that, carefully confining itself to those duties and performing them in the least costly and restrictive way practicable.

Second, we have mutual obligations to each other as free individuals to respect the interests of others in freedom and not simply our own interests, and therefore to care about being open-minded and intellectually honest in our dealings with others. Our leaders have this same obligation. Intellectual honesty—both holding oneself and being held to that standard—is key to the successful operation of a political process carried out by free people. It is a necessary condition for reducing the paralyzing influence of extremism.

Third, since we all must live by the same laws, individuals who are free deserve both a reasonably equal voice in the selection of representatives who will make those laws as well as representatives holding office who are independent and not unduly beholden to a special few. An election process succeeds to the degree that it produces these results, so that election campaigns and government do not in appearance or in fact become an instrument primarily of "others," or "them," but instead can rightly be seen as an instrument of "us."

In all three of these areas, our politics and political process are badly off track today. Building from the Common Credo and its ten core principles laid out in the next chapter, Chapter 7 will outline a series of reforms needed to reverse the gaping discrepancies between the principles that the Founders held and the way the political process currently operates.

## CHAPTER 6

# THE
# COMMON
# CREDO

★ ★ ★ ★ ★

THE PREVIOUS CHAPTERS HAVE demonstrated the need in America for a new political platform, one that supplies a governing philosophy and political process able to unite the nation as well as an effective economic approach to reclaiming prosperity. At the same time, the platform must successfully reconcile conservatism's legitimate goal of setting firm limits on government intervention, so that government does not intrude on citizens' individual freedom, with liberalism's legitimate goal of using government to rectify the sort of economic inequalities that have victimized the average American and undermined the economy. It must do so while avoiding both the self-defeating narrowness that has doomed contemporary conservatism and the self-defeating vagueness that has doomed contemporary liberalism.

The Common Credo is that platform. It overcomes the fatal weaknesses that afflict today's dominating ideologies by recognizing that the tension between conservative and liberal goals is the very same one that the Founders themselves addressed in declaring our independence and designing our republic. The Common Credo thus draws its principles directly from their own. As the Founders did not see these goals as mutually exclusive, neither does the Common Credo. Its central principles, undergirded by the evidence presented in the earlier chapters, form a solid philosophical foundation for the active involvement of government to deal with a wide range of national problems, while simultaneously defining clear limits and boundaries to that involvement—in other words, exactly what a governing philosophy is supposed to do. In accomplishing that, the principles also lay the groundwork for a governing paradigm able to deliver strong, widespread, and sustainable prosperity, reverse debilitating market failures, and work toward a political process that is broadly collaborative and inclusive.

The Common Credo can be summarized by ten principles, as follows:

1. The foundational premise of the Common Credo holds that every individual person has equal and inviolate dignity. All principles of the Common Credo follow from this bedrock premise. As in the Declaration of Independence, the truth of the premise is understood equally well as being self-evident and as being endowed by the Creator.

2. The equal and inviolate dignity of every person means that every person must be free—each person fully as free as every other—to determine and pursue his or her own ends.

3. Freedom, therefore, calls for individual autonomy. Similarly, freedom involves the necessity of placing limits, restrictions, and obligations upon each of us that are required to ensure that the same autonomy is available for

all others. Attaining reciprocal freedom of this kind is the bottom-line focus of the Common Credo.

Many of the obligations that freedom involves have been summarized in earlier chapters. They include the obligations of each individual to be self-reliant to the extent possible through his or her own efforts; to respect the property, person, and health of others; to fulfill contracts and other obligations voluntarily entered into; to respect and follow the law; to take personal responsibility for one's actions; to exercise self-control; to be honest, open-minded, and objective in dealings with others; and to care about protecting the equal freedom of every person as well as to expect and call upon public institutions to do the same. It is appropriate under freedom for government to define and outlaw predatory practices and wrongful harm, whether within or outside market exchanges, and to protect individuals against them.

4.  For self-reliance to be feasible and to comport with freedom, economic opportunities must be sufficient and readily available for individuals to be able to provide a dignified standard of living on the basis of their own efforts and to improve their living by improving their efforts. The same principle describes the widely accepted promise of the American Dream, which calls for an economy in which everybody who is diligent and works hard can make a decent living and get ahead. As a result, equal economic opportunity for all is not enough; there must also be sufficient economic opportunity for all. It is legitimate under freedom for the society to act collectively to attain conditions of equal and sufficient economic opportunity if and to the degree that the market economy fails to accomplish

those ends on its own. The same purposes also define the limits and outer boundaries of the welfare state.

Among the kinds of intervention appropriate for public action to uphold individuals' freedom in this regard are the provision of education enabling individuals to take advantage of opportunity and be effective members of the civic community; job training, temporary job-creation programs, wage subsidies, and a minimum wage focused on a living wage; protection for representative collective bargaining; Social Security retirement pension and time-limited unemployment assistance, both tied to a history of employment and work; time-limited welfare; assistance for access to standard health-care insurance not covered by employment; tax policies related to attaining economic independence through work; equal opportunity regulations; disability insurance; and income-assistance programs based on incapacity. I discuss the legitimacy of these specific actions in Chapter 7, where I examine policy solutions, and public support for them in Chapter 8.

5. Governmental intervention, in the name of freedom, is appropriate in all spheres where individuals, acting separately, cannot effectively or efficiently attain their own goals, but can do so by acting collectively. These are areas that economists often call market failures, so defined because they are dominated by economic incentives leading the market to either inefficient or suboptimal economic outcomes. The means for the involvement of government for this purpose include public regulation of private production, public contracting for private goods or services, and public ownership where necessary. Market failures include matters such as military defense, police protection, basic

research, provision and/or regulation of the infrastructure, control of pollution, provision and/or regulation of various aspects of health care, and the addressing of countercyclical economic conditions.

6. In achieving the objectives just described, freedom requires limited government. Such government does not mean minimalist or small government. Rather, it means a government that is large enough to carry out its responsibilities successfully, but no larger. This is to say, it is government that accomplishes the ends of freedom yet also remains strictly confined within those ends, utilizing the lowest cost and level of coerciveness capable of reaching the ends.

    Limited government must also stay solvent. Debt that government incurs in order to meet obligations we have to each other under freedom must remain financially sustainable over the long run.

7. The objectives of freedom must be national in scope and application. How the objectives are accomplished should be as decentralized as possible—including through state and local governments and devolution to markets—yet consistent with fully attaining the aforementioned ends and achieving them nationwide.

8. In a free and democratic society, leaders and citizens should think and act not simply on the basis of their own self-interest. It is expected that they will also rise above their self-interest to think and act with just as much consideration and concern for the legitimate interests of others in their freedom. The Founders summoned each of us to cultivate and practice such virtue and the obligations

to others it involves, which they considered indispensable both to the morality of freedom and the survival of a free people.

9. Freedom calls for civic equality both in the election of representatives and in the making of laws under which every citizen will have to live. The voices of only a few should not be permitted to dominate debate or otherwise get an undue hearing, and no elected representative making laws that all of us must follow should be unduly beholden to a select few. Likewise, there must be equal treatment of all under the law; no person can be above the law; and, if accused, every person must have the right to a full, fair, open, and timely trial.

The principle of civic equality also means that collective decisions, both in the public and in political bodies, ought ordinarily to be made by the largest number of votes, so that the votes of members of the minority do not count more than the votes of members of the majority. "Super majorities" of greater than 50 percent plus one should be the rule only in exceptional circumstances.[1] Routine use of the filibuster in the Senate runs against this principle. Gerrymandering does, as well, to the degree that it deliberately attempts to remove serious competitive contests in the general election, placing the election and reelection of officeholders effectively in the hands of a subset of the electorate, or deliberately leads to significant differences between the majority of votes cast and the majority of elected officials.

10. Freedom requires the establishment of effective mechanisms to protect every person from governmental decisions

or processes that would wrongfully harm them or that go beyond the legitimate powers of government—for example, procedures protecting the right of the accused to an open and genuinely fair trial, or judicial enforcement of the right to keep our homes and papers safe from government intrusion (barring the issuance of a warrant meeting the criterion of probable cause).

Building on these principles, the Common Credo sets the parameters of government action in a coherent way. Take what is commonly understood as the welfare state. For the able, the limits of the welfare state come when economic opportunities are sufficient that they permit all willing individuals to secure a dignified living through their efforts and to advance on the basis of improvements in productivity. (This sufficiency assumes as well the availability of education and training necessary for individuals to take advantage of such opportunity.) If a market economy were to produce this outcome on its own, then, except for individuals who are incapacitated and those specific areas dominated by market failures, there would no longer be need for a welfare state. Since the market economy has clearly not produced this outcome on its own, whatever least level of government involvment, coupled with the free-market process, that is required to achieve the outcome represents the upper limit on the need for government activity.

Suggested here, too, is a cap on government along another dimension. In intervening to attain satisfactory economic opportunity, as well as in all other spheres, government must remain limited in the sense that it achieves its objectives through the least costly and coercive means practicable. Government must not become either bigger or more powerful than the minimum that is necessary to effectively achieve its legitimate ends.

If these principles are followed, intervention by government is appropriate in all those areas identified in the ten principles of the Common Credo. The previous chapters have shown how the aims of freedom, rooted in the Founders' vision of freedom, justify such interventions in specific contexts.

Of the failures facing the nation today, nothing matches either the collapse of the American economy in 2008, preceded by six years that experienced the slowest growth of any nonrecessionary period since the Great Depression, or the way the economy ignored a solid majority of ordinary Americans for many decades before that. What has happened to the economy is a direct outgrowth of the failure to heed the principles of the Common Credo.

Had the nation been faithful to the principles of the Common Credo, for example, pay for all workers would have provided a living wage or better, and median pay would have kept reasonably in line with overall productivity gains. The next chapter shows how to achieve that result. What happened instead was that over one-third of American workers on average found themselves either in jobs paying less than a living wage or unemployed, while the bulk of all real pay increases went to the top 5 percent, leaving compensation for a clear majority of workers virtually flatlined relative to four decades ago.

The outsized proportion of raises that went to those at the very top, who consume a much lower proportion of their income than do families nearer to or below the median, pulled many hundreds of billions of dollars in consumer demand out of the economy annually during the years preceding the economy's collapse. Demand had consistently weakened over the past forty years.

As we saw in Chapter 3, demand is integral to Adam Smith's "invisible hand" behind a free-market economy. Because producers are motivated by self-interest, the prospect that there will be demand is normally a necessary incentive for them to make new investments, create new jobs, and produce more goods and services.

For many years, the loss of demand was offset by ordinary families' taking on increasingly greater debt and spending well beyond their incomes. That was the only way ordinary families with stagnant real wages could improve their own standard of living.

They did what was necessary for themselves, and for the economy. They lived beyond their means, amply assisted by the increasing deregulation of the financial industry. We all know what happened, and it will take the country and the economy many years to recover.

There is a serious problem here on two different levels. On the moral, philosophical level, there is the problem, even before the collapse, of the ever-widening gap between the economic conditions of freedom in the minds of the Founders and the economic conditions that a majority of Americans have experienced. On the operational level, there is the problem of the serious mismatch between the real-world requirements of a healthy market economy and the way our market economy has actually functioned, which led to its breakdown. Beyond that, too, is the exaserbation of many social illnesses and family dysfunctions, outlined in Chapter 3, that normally accompany huge pay and income disparities.

The economically constrained conditions for most Americans since the early 1970s have also contributed to their growing and justified sense that our economic and political systems have marginalized them, naturally prompting a more defensive posture and self-interested way of thinking. Conservative ideology itself has increasingly lionized people for acting according to their own economic self-interest. Following Adam Smith, conservatives commonly claim that the individual pursuit of self-interest translates into improved conditions for all. "Greed is good" became a byword in the 1980s, and though it is routinely mocked now in pop culture, it has never actually been replaced as a governing ethos. In fact, it has become more widespread than ever for many companies and individuals. Meanwhile, the emphasis of liberals on values like "the common good," "fairness" toward others, and "interdependence" has been weakened and rendered less effective by the lack of any clear definition. As a result, liberals are often at a disadvantage when pitted against a morality that praises the individual pursuit of self-interest as itself delivering the greater common good. The snowballing sentiment of self-interest, transferred into politics and infecting the halls of government, has been essential to producing the continuing political polarization and paralysis of recent years.

The Founders well understood that a free society is not sustainable on a foundation of pure self-interest. Something more is required of both leaders and citizens, which they called virtue. The missing ethic that is needed, however, cannot come from today's conservatism, with individualistic freedom based on self-interest as its core value, or from contemporary liberalism, which has no clearly defined foundational value at all. The Common Credo provides this critical ethic. It spells out a series of obligations we have to each other above and beyond individual self-interest, in the name of individual freedom, and clearly identifies the premise or foundational value from which the obligations come—the equal and inviolate worth of every person. The array of responsibilities we have to one another within this ethic all reflect age-old American values that are grounded firmly in the thinking of the Founders. Many are also biblical injunctions, or derivatives therefrom, with a deep history in Judeo-Christian traditions. They are summarized above in the principles of the Common Credo.

No philosophy, of course, can escape the reality that its principles and obligations are all subject to shadings of disagreement and that differences will also arise over how the individual principles and obligations weigh relative to one another in situations in which they come into conflict.

An example brings the point home. Like the views of the Founders, the Common Credo contains no obligation of economic assistance to help individuals who are able to work yet, in the presence of opportunities to make a decent living, remain idle and unwilling to take responsibility to help themselves. Apart from issues arising over exactly what constitutes sufficient opportunity, idleness, and unwillingness, serious differences will continue to divide people over how to assist the children of such individuals. Most people agree that children are innocents. Even if their parents are no longer eligible for basic public assistance, the children remain deserving of a decent chance in life.

How do we provide those children that decent chance without simultaneously assisting the parents? An answer to this was the 1996 welfare reform. It aimed to make welfare assistance ultimately dependent upon taking up gainful employment, coupled with a renewed emphasis on absent-parent support, thus seeking to place responsibility back on the proper individuals. Simultaneously, in the attempt to make employment pay off better, both the minimum wage and wage subsidies (the Earned Income Tax Credit) were increased.

Even with the increases, however, individuals holding jobs at or near the new minimum wage were still not earning a living wage. Worse, after 2000 the wage-support measures themselves were allowed to atrophy relative to inflation. It is one thing to call upon individuals to work for a living wage or better, and quite another thing to do so outside the realistic availability of such opportunity.

Similarly, the reforms failed to address the well-being of children whose parents had opted not to comply and so became ineligible for welfare assistance.

One possible solution would be to assist such children directly, rather than through their parents, by way of programs carried out in schools from preschool through grade twelve or, where necessary, through community centers. Many material needs of children—including nutrition, clothing, and health care—could be served reasonably effectively in this way, though valid concerns exist about the stigma that often comes in such public settings.

However, children's needs for decent housing clearly cannot be met in this way. Yet providing public housing assistance to the parents for the sake of the children is likely to discourage the parents from taking responsibility. Placing the children in foster care or adoption might be options in place of housing assistance in these cases, but deciding to separate children indefinitely or permanently from their parents puts an awesome power in the hands of public officials. They, like everyone else, are fallible, and so such power should perhaps be reserved only for extreme situations—for example, if the children have actually come to live in a permanent condition of homelessness.

Even this does not seem like a particularly good policy, though. The truth is that there may not be any fully acceptable solutions here; the Common Credo does not provide a definitive answer for every issue.

But that difficulty does not make the principles and values of the Common Credo or the foundational premise from which they flow any less valid. The premise, principles, and mutual obligations contained in the Common Credo all enjoy very broad support among Americans today, just as they did in the vaulted vision of the Founders at the nation's birth. Even with regard to issues for which the Common Credo cannot recommend precise and complete policy answers, its principles provide an effective framework within which elected representatives and the public can debate and discuss the best possible options. And, as we have seen in the earlier chapters and will see in Chapter 7, on many issues the principles of the Common Credo *do* reveal the specific paths, grounded solidly in the American value system, that would enable us to surmount many of the most intractable problems we face today.

In accomplishing these ends, the Common Credo offers something else, too. Individual autonomy and commitment to community are both highly prized values, yet they are obviously also quite different values and in some ways diametrically opposed. The Founders' vision of reciprocal freedom underlying the Common Credo—and particularly the range of mutual obligations we have to one another under it—shows how to bring these two values together into a harmonious whole, by identifying exactly where and how they support each other.[2] In turn, the core idea of reciprocal freedom provides a concrete definition of the larger common good—one that breathes a more precise meaning into the concept than any of the alternative terms used today, such as "fairness," or "equality," or "change," or "progress," or "interdependency," or even "freedom" in its current everyday usage. Put succinctly, the actions of individual citizens and public officials advance the greater common good to the degree that they help bring the nation closer to the conditions of reciprocal freedom spelled out in the Common Credo, itself coming from the Founders' vision and its premise of the equal and inviolate worth of every person. This overarching definition of the common good represents the higher goal toward which the nation ought to aim. With this goal as our guide, we can now explore the specific policies able to get us there and resolve the toughest problems we face as a nation today.

## CHAPTER 7

# SOLUTIONS

★ ★ ★ ★ ★

FOR QUITE A FEW DECADES NOW, great forces, all of them running counter to the Founders' vision, have been marginalizing a majority of Americans both economically and politically. This trend must be reversed if our country is to experience the kind of success that Americans expect and that defined the nearly three decades following World War II. Daunting as the forces are, solutions lie well within our power.

Building upon the previous chapters, the policy recommendations presented here will (1) establish a strong, thriving economy in which prosperity is widespread, sustainable, and able to provide a firm foundation for all American workers and families to live decently and advance; (2) create budgetary discipline that renders projected deficits manageable for the indefinite future; (3) restrain the costs of health care and make them affordable; (4) close the educational opportunity deficits affecting kindergarten through higher education; (5) address carbon emissions that contribute to climate change (the significant reduction of which would also lessen the nation's dependence on oil); and (6) construct a healthier and more inclusive politics and political process.

The proposed solutions are all in line with the principles of the Founders and the Common Credo. They offer specific means for solving our most crucial issues. However, if other ways would be just as likely to accomplish the same ends effectively but do so at less cost or intrusiveness, then I would support them. That is what the national debate should be about—finding policies that will fully achieve the desired ends at the least possible cost and restrictiveness.

Solutions should also be as decentralized and left to local units or individualized markets as possible, so long as they successfully achieve the ultimate ends. As we have seen, however, some of our core problems, such as the disparity in compensation and the widening divergence between workers' pay and productivity, come from the way the market itself operates. Those problems cannot be corrected without some degree of external guidance of the market, even while otherwise building upon and utilizing market forces to the greatest degree possible.

## AN ECONOMY THAT ACCOMPLISHES THE TRIFECTA

To be successful, our economy must ensure the availability of opportunity required for each of us to realize a dignified, customary standard of living or better on the basis of our own efforts and to get ahead as productivity improves. Three elements define this bottom-line definition: first, jobs paying a living wage or better; second, pay that rises in some reasonable fashion with increasing productivity; and, third, a sufficient number of jobs meeting both criteria to be readily available to every willing person.

This economic trifecta identifies the standards necessary to fulfill a core component of the Founders' vision of freedom, in which individuals and families are able to attain independence and self-reliance through their efforts—an economy enabling every willing person who is diligent and works hard to make a decent living and get ahead. The Founders' moral justification for this historic vision, set forth in Chapter 2, was based in the timeless premise of the equal and inviolate dignity of every person. But over the past four decades the economy has fallen so far short of attaining these standards that for two successive generations this quintessentially American vision has eluded a clear majority of American workers and families.

Focusing on the achievement of these standards the Founders held so dear is indispensable to the revival of our economic prosperity. Businesses, whether large or small, can neither produce nor prosper in the absence of a decent prospect of demand. Without customers— or with declining numbers of customers relative to the supply of goods and services that workers produce—such demand cannot emerge. Unless they go into debt, people cannot be customers who do not themselves have work, or who have work but not enough earnings to live on, or whose earnings do not grow as productivity does. Those who go into ever-deeper debt cannot sustain that trajectory, and an economy built upon their backs must eventually collapse. We've seen how this dangerous spiral operates in real life and how it descends into catastrophe. It cannot be allowed to occur again. Directed toward attaining the standards that the Founders' vision of freedom calls for, the trifecta referred to above creates the conditions needed for businesses and the larger economy to thrive in a lasting way.

## Jobs Paying at Least a Living Wage

Family-budget and living-wage studies, along with local living-wage ordinances, have found that the amount of pay needed to deliver a living wage capable of supporting a modest customary living is just below $12 per hour in most locales, plus private or publically assisted health benefits providing access to the customary standard of health care. On that pay, a family of four with one and two-thirds full-time workers and two children would be earning approximately $40,000 annually. Polls of Americans and studies of family spending also find that this income is the minimum amount it takes in most areas of the nation for a family of four to support a modest customary living. The income would be enough for the family of four to own or rent at the borderline of the lowest one-third of house and rental payments, to spend $1.50 per meal per person for food, to operate a single ten-year-old standard car in reliable running condition, to have a telephone, and to go out for fast food every once in a great while, for example. At the same time, the income would be too little to be able to live in a better or safer neighborhood or to spend more than $1.50 per meal per person for food, to own and operate a second car in good running condition, or to go on a family vacation, ever (at least one that requires spending money).[1]

The description above should make it abundantly clear that the living wage the Common Credo seeks to attain does not represent a radical redistribution of luxury in our society, or an enforcement of anything approaching equality of income or wealth. We would be hard-pressed to find anyone who believes the condition just described is more than any working American family is entitled to. Yet more than one-quarter of all American workers in jobs—not to mention those who are out of jobs—receive hourly pay that falls beneath this basic level, that is, beneath a living wage.[2] Among the many occupations they have are security guards, retail sales clerks, construction laborers, preschool teachers, grounds maintenance personnel, cashiers, food processors and preparers, janitors and cleaners, hospital orderlies, office managers, textile workers, child-care workers, and elder-care personnel. And that's just a start. Many workers receive less than a living wage not just for a brief period, or only when young, but for many years.

Two actions can raise earnings to meet the goal pretty much on their own. One action would be to lift the federal minimum wage from $7.25 to $8.75 per hour, adjusting it thereafter so that it retains its level relative to the median wage. At $8.75 per hour, the wage would have a purchasing power still moderately below where it was in the late 1960s. A second action would raise the top benefit of the Earned Income Tax Credit (EITC) from about $5,000 to $8,000. The former strategy is a longstanding liberal project. President Obama, for example, proposed raising the minimum wage as a desirable course of action in his 2013 State of the Union Address. The latter—the EITC—has deep conservative roots going back to the Nixon administration.

The combination of the two would leave the family of four just described (containing one and two-thirds full-time workers) with $38,000 annually, or about 95 percent of the basic income needed to support a modest living. Local arrangements in significantly higher-cost areas would be necessary to close the gap between the higher living costs there and the standard. It is also necessary to assist households whose employment does not cover access to effective health-care insurance, as the 2010 health-care reform act does, and to bring retired individuals on Social Security closer to a living income. Single-parent families, of course, contain only one potential worker at home and not two. They would require appropriate financial contributions from absent working parents or, if unemployed, from the temporary benefits and other assistance they receive. Absent parents already contribute in the case of many such families. For the remainder, efforts to hold such parents accountable for their responsibilities must be redoubled. Even with that, however, a portion of single-parent families will fall short of a basic living income, although the two actions just mentioned will leave them in a considerably better position than they otherwise would be.

Conservatives often argue that raising the minimum wage will have the unintended effect of causing more unemployment through the elimination or slower creation of jobs. Yet the mixed results of studies suggest that the impact is modest at most and that the reduction in employee turnover and other similar effects largely offset the costs.[3] Sizable increases of the minimum wage in the 1990s did not stop the economy from adding substantial numbers of jobs. The zenith of job creation that decade came in 1997, with 2.9 million net new jobs created in that single year, just two years after the minimum wage had been lifted by more than 20 percent.

### Rising Pay with Rising Productivity

Creating conditions in which median hourly pay rises in some reasonable proportion to improved productivity of the labor force is the second major task. Right now, most Americans are unable to get appreciably ahead of where workers were in their parents' or grandparents' generation, despite the enormous increase in worker productivity. The persistence of this gap not only disincentivizes workers but also takes away their freedom and cripples the functioning of the economy as a whole.

When we speak of pay or compensation, of course, we are referring to what employees receive for their work, which is something quite separate and apart from what capital receives as its return on investment through profits, dividends, and interest. As we saw in Chapter 3, compensation for workers in 2010, including all benefits, stood at around three-fifths of GDP.

For about three decades after 1945, the rate of compensation increases for the highest earners stayed pretty much in line with pay gains for workers in the middle. During much of that time, the top tax rate was 91 percent—and never under 70 percent—under Presidents Truman, Eisenhower, and Kennedy. Only when the top tax rate dropped to 50 percent and then well below that, starting in the early 1980s, did compensation begin steeply accelerating in significantly greater proportions to the top 1 percent of earners.[4]

The same trend operated in the relationship between worker compensation and productivity. From the 1940s into the 1970s, compensation for the median American worker kept up with the rise in total compensation for all workers—including those at the top—relative to worker productivity (about 80 percent of productivity gains). During the 1970s, the return for the median worker declined very slightly relative to workers' productivity, and then, starting in the early 1980s, it fell through the floor as gains in compensation began going almost entirely to the top. Not at all coincidentally, the early 1980s were when the tax rates were significantly cut. In those years since the 1970s, up until the Great Recession, the total real-compensation increase for workers remained at approximately 60 percent of productivity gains whereas the returns received by the median American worker dropped to about 13 percent of productivity gains, radically below its level of 80 percent during the years between 1945 and the early 1970s.

The pay disparity of recent decades mirrors what happened in the 1920s before the Great Depression. Then, too, when top tax rates were cut dramatically from 1922 to 1929 (from 73 percent to 25 percent), pay disparities and income inequalities began to rise rapidly.[5]

A high tax rate on very large earnings still leaves room for substantial differences in compensation, including within the top itself. During the 1950s and 1960s, for example, executives earned twenty-five to thirty times as much annually as average workers did. However, the experiences both in the 1920s and over the past four decades indicate that a high top tax rate can help place constraints on how greatly differences in compensation among workers will grow.

This suggests a way to keep the increases in compensation as a percentage of the growth in worker productivity from going too heavily to high-end earners relative to middle- and lower-income working Americans. It is to implement a *temporary* 80 percent tax rate on any form of employment compensation (including grants of stock and stock options) for the highest earners, called an "Eisenhower tax." Tax rates for the top bracket were at that high level—indeed, even higher—during the entire Eisenhower presidency, and it didn't matter whether Republicans or Democrats were in control of Congress. This tax rate would apply only to compensation going to an individual (not to returns on investment, or to other income, or even to a spouse's compensation), and then only to that part of the individual's compensation exceeding a certain multiple of year-round full-time compensation that the median American earns—say, a multiple of fifty. This is still about double the multiple that prevailed during the Eisenhower years, and approximately what top earners receive now in many countries with advanced economies. Implemented in the United States today, this tax would apply only to compensation exceeding $2 million. The tax would be conditional. It is not intended to be permanent or, consequently, to punish. It would remain in force only for as long as the gains in compensation from increased productivity received by the median American worker fall below a certain level. This level would be defined by the *total* compensation gains per worker relative to increased productivity, which is 60 percent today—an acceptable benchmark.

The point of the Eisenhower tax is to create a strong economic incentive among the highest paid to temper how large compensation differences become between themselves and the average worker, and to channel greater worker productivity compensation increases back to the middle, since doing that would then abolish the tax and keep it abolished.[6] Here at last is a tax for which the hope and intention is that it brings in no revenues at all! But if it turns out that the tax, by itself, doesn't reach the benchmark goal of a broader distribution of productivity compensation gains, a second tax—levied on corporations paying any employee more than fifty times what the median worker makes during periods when the goal hasn't been reached—would reinforce the incentive.

In addition to the dramatic change that has taken place in tax policy over the past three decades—slashing tax rates for the highest earners by *half*—the power of organized labor has waned as well, further exacerbating the reduced compensation going to the average American worker. Some studies attribute up to one-third of the widening pay disparity to the single factor of declining worker power.[7] It makes sense that workers who are organized have more weight in negotiations and can press their claims more effectively with employers than can individual workers trying to bargain on their own. Surveys suggest that as many as three times as many workers want to organize collectively as are presently doing so.[8]

Public action can make it easier for workers who so desire to organize—for example, by requiring simple, confidential postcard support for union organizing, administered by an independent third party, as a substitute for the more protracted elections of today, which subject workers to greater possibilities of intimidation. More rigorous enforcement of a wide range of labor regulations and enactment of stiffer penalties against violations are needed as well. Consideration should be given, too, to increasing the input of workers into boards of directors, possibly by way of workers' election of representatives to serve directly on the boards. Likewise, workers who are in employee stock-ownership plans should be afforded greater participation in the proxy matters of the business. All these steps would add pressure for wages to move more into line with productivity.

It would also help low- and middle-income families, as homeowners, if the mortgage interest and real-estate tax deductions for all taxpayers were set at a straight 28 percent write-off of the amounts paid, rather than set according to the taxpayer's tax bracket (10 percent, 15 percent, 25 percent, 28 percent, and more than 30 percent), as it is now. That this form of housing assistance disproportionately helps top-income Americans at a time of galloping income inequality, thereby increasing the inequality even further, is indefensible.

In addition, providing assistance through grants and expanded work-study would enable low- and middle-income students to take advantage of career training and higher education, and possible employment opportunities thereafter, without financially overwhelming their families and themselves. So might new $10,000 four-year college degrees now under experimentation. Connecting community-college technical training programs with projected openings of local businesses would help supply the skill sets needed for jobs now going indefinitely unfilled—approximately one million long-term vacancies as of this writing. There is a shortage of thousands of wind-turbine technicians, for example, whose annual pay averages about $45,000. Public job-training programs that are generally viewed as successful, such as Jobs Corps, along with educational programs within high schools such as Career Academies, also need added support directed to the same purpose.

Improving low-performing schools and educational experiences from prekindergarten through grade twelve is critical as well. A series of proposals is outlined later in this chapter. The proposals include a high-priority effort to develop broadly acceptable measures and procedures for successfully identifying strong and weak teachers, especially at the lowest-performing schools, and to create financial incentives to recruit strong teachers to those schools. The effort should be accompanied with processes for effectively improving or terminating unsatisfactory teachers, with proper teacher protections built in.[9] It should also involve fixing and updating school buildings and supplying low-performing schools with the newest educational technology that is shown to help improve student performance.

### Sufficient Number of Jobs Paying at Least a Living Wage

The third key to the trifecta is generating enough jobs (paying at least a living wage—factoring in the EITC—and with pay increases rising with improved worker productivity) so that such employment will be readily available to all willing seekers. In a strong, healthy economy, economists often consider unemployment at about 4–5 percent to be full employment—the lowest rate of unemployment considered to be compatible with a low and stable rate of inflation. To reach an unemployment level of 4.5 percent, accounting also for workers who have dropped out of the labor market, we need 8 million more jobs above the number of new jobs that are normally created each year in the economy (approximately 1.4 million).[10] Production and job creation in the private sector require demand, in the form of customers. Let's suppose that the strategies outlined above are successful in raising gains in productivity compensation to 60 percent for median workers, from the bare 13 percent that has been the case recently. Given the relative marginal spending patterns of middle- and top-income households, that increase would generate $500 billion *or more* annually in new consumer demand, all of it real, none of it dependent upon a disproportionate (or, indeed, any) expansion of debt.[11] Based on the average consumption needed to create and sustain jobs, $500 billion in added consumer demand would generate nearly 6 million new private-sector jobs on top of normal job creation.[12] That's about three-quarters of the total number of jobs needed right there.

Those jobs would leave unemployment at just below 6 percent, still 2 million Americans above the target rate for full employment. A temporary public jobs program, run and administered through the states, could fill a gap of that size. Such a program would operate competitively in the open labor market and involve no entitlement. It would seem desirable, however, for the program to give priority to veterans and to the long-term unemployed, who are often at a serious disadvantage in private-sector hiring practices.

Admittedly, a program of this type would be expensive, at about $100 billion per year for two or three years. Yet there is certainly no lack of jobs that need doing—rebuilding roads and bridges; replenishing the ranks of teachers, police, and firefighters; modernizing schools; retrofitting buildings and homes to be energy efficient; bringing health care to underserved locales; improving child care and elder care; and so on. There is a nearly endless list.

While the federal government would finance the program, the funds should be devolved to the states. The funds would not be directed to specific projects, but they would be accompanied by clear instructions that the funds be focused on the development of human capital and on renewing or improving the infrastructure, including school buildings, and with careful federal oversight regarding those general instructions. Within the broad areas, states would decide for themselves the most effective places to put the money to create jobs.

Notice, too, that a large majority of the 8 million needed jobs would come from the private market responding to increased demand related to productivity gains, rather than through direct creation of jobs by the government.

In combination, the actions outlined above would take the nation a long way toward the goal of enabling all willing Americans to make a dignified living based on their efforts and to get ahead through improvement. What is more, by permitting hardworking Americans to be independent and get ahead, the actions also ensure the conditions for healthy demand and customer growth that are necessary for businesses to succeed, for the economy to prosper, and for that prosperity to be sustainable. In turn, coupling this dynamic with sound investments in education, in the infrastructure, and in basic research—all areas of broad bipartisan support in the past—would build a strong foundation for a globally competitive economy that can thrive for years into the future.

It is within our power. It depends solely upon our summoning the will.

## IMPORTANT QUESTIONS

### How Do We Reconcile the Hands-off Free-Market Approach Often Attributed to the Founders with the Hands-on Approach Set Forth Here?

The Founders surely would prefer the free market as a solution to the challenge of creating the desired level of opportunity needed for economic freedom if the free market could accomplish that objective on its own. As the chapter on the economy demonstrated, however, achieving such a goal is not the free market's intended aim, let alone its result. Although it has accomplished many good things, the private market has not come near to reaching this crucial condition. Nor, given the evidence of earlier chapters, is there reason to conclude that it will in the future, or that it would come close to doing so even if taxes and regulations were significantly reduced.

In this context, remember Thomas Jefferson's words: "Whenever there is in any country, uncultivated lands and unemployed poor, it is clear that the laws of property have been so far extended as to violate a natural right. The earth is given as a common stock for man to labour and live on. *If, for encouragement of industry we allow it to be appropriated, we must take care that other employment be furnished to those excluded from the appropriation.* If we do not the fundamental right to labour the earth returns to the unemeployed."[13] Society at large has an obligation to ensure that unequal appropriation still leaves ample opportunity available for every person to make a decent living and get ahead through his or her efforts.

In this view, Jefferson, the primary author of the Declaration of Independence, joined the father of the federal Constitution, James Madison. Where economic inequalities were growing unduly great, Madison argued, it was appropriate to turn to government to combat the inequality "by the silent operation of laws, which, without violating rights of property, reduce extreme wealth toward a state of mediocrity, and raise extreme indigence toward a state of comfort." In the same vein, Madison believed that "to provide employment for the poor, and support the indigent, is among the primary and, at the same time, not least difficult cares of the public authority."[14] Both Jefferson and Madison urged that government directly intervene to confront problems of economic disparities that left some citizens with too little.

The principle that a free people required at least a certain level of economic equality was very widely held in both colonial and revolutionary America, and linked the thinking of most leading Founders, including Washington, Jefferson, Madison, Franklin, Adams, and Mason. Recall from Chapter 2 that John Adams and other Founders considered conditions of relative economic equality essential for individuals to be able to attain economic independence and the surest foundation for the success of freedom. These ideas themselves echoed an earlier cry for individual rights embodied in Cato's Letters, written from 1720 to 1723 and often republished and quoted in newspapers across the colonies in the era leading up to the Revolution. The letters were famous for condemning tyranny and advocating the cause of freedom. (For this reason, Cato is the namesake for today's free-market Cato Institute, cofounded by the billionaire Charles Koch, chief executive of Koch Industries and self-declared champion of individual freedom.) Letter 3 said: "A free people can be kept so, by no other means than an equal distribution of property."[15]

Nor do any of the suggested actions lie outside the nation's historical traditions. The strongest of the actions I've proposed is the Eisenhower tax. Very high tax rates, as the Eisenhower tax recommends, are clearly in keeping with American experience. Rates of 70 percent or higher were standard practice for nearly a half century, from 1933 to 1980, under eight different presidents, five of them Democrats and three of them Republicans. And, returning to the views of the Founders, nothing could be more "silent" in operation, to use the aim Madison described, than to have a tax that it is hoped will never need to raise a single penny.

The proposed actions do not deny the value of free exchange and a free market. Their objective instead is to build upon the results that free exchange and the free market can bring. Those positive results are then channeled to reach the end goal of freedom as envisioned by the Founders, rather than simply allowed to accumulate narrowly at the top, failing wildly in this way to meet the Founders' vision in the lives of a significant majority of Americans.

### Where Will the Necessary New Investment Come from If Taxes on Top Compensation Are So High?

Another legitimate concern is how to sustain investment if taxes on top compensation are so high. Who will do the investing?

Remember that the new top rate is on individual compensation (in any form coming from one's employment) and not on other income, such as a second earner's compensation or on dividends or capital gains that are not part of one's compensation. Within the highest-income households, much of the income will escape any additional tax.[16]

Also, as the compensation disparities moderate, we can expect middle-income families to save and invest more. There was certainly plenty of productive investment during the Eisenhower era, when the top tax rate on income was 90 percent and productivity compensation gains were very broadly distributed in the economy. In addition, companies today are sitting on about $1.5 trillion in unspent cash that is available to them for any purpose, including investment. The amount is so vast that, at historic levels, it equals more than a full year of average business investment on its own. The increased consumer demand coming into the economy as compensation gains broaden should add to the incentive individuals and businesses have to invest and produce, helping to pull some or most of that $1.5 trillion in unspent cash off the sidelines. Remember, too, that an individual pays tax only on income coming from a business that isn't reinvested in the business, including for jobs and wages. Thus a business owner actually has greater incentive to leave income in the business and reinvest it there if the tax on his or her compensation is at Eisenhower levels than if it is half or less than half of that.

### Aren't We Encouraging Americans to Become Economically Dependent upon Government Instead of Being Independent and Self-Reliant?

Two actions proposed above, in particular, might raise initial concerns about fostering dependency on government. One is the proposal that a public jobs program create 2 million jobs. Yet both Jefferson and Madison asserted that where there is not enough opportunity, employment needs to be provided to those left out. The proposed public jobs program is intended to last for only a two-to-three-year period, so the jobs created would be temporary. Dependency, by contrast, is usually thought to involve a permanent, or at least an indefinite, condition.

The second action is lifting the Earned Income Tax Credit, which is a form of assistance available indefinitely to low-paid working Americans. Most people do not look upon the EITC as involving dependency of individuals on the government, however, but rather as the opposite: a way of incentivizing work and self-reliance by making work for low wages pay a better return. It was for this reason that President Reagan considered the EITC "one of the best anti-poverty programs this country has ever seen."[17]

Other items calling for governmental help include the proposed increases in aid for higher education and the assistance with housing costs involved in raising the rate of mortgage-interest deduction to 28 percent for low- and moderate-income families. If free public education for K–12 is not looked upon as causing dependency, why should free (or at least significantly less expensive) higher education be? And if proportionately greater mortgage-interest deductions for high-income families have not been seen as producing dependency, and rightly so, why should proportionately lower deductions be viewed that way for families with middle incomes or less?

There remains, however, the larger question of whether receiving benefits from government income and in-kind assistance programs in general is consistent with the ideals of self-reliance and independence espoused by the Founders. How, indeed, can people who depend upon unemployment assistance, Social Security, or public assistance to purchase health insurance, for example, possibly be described as self-reliant and economically independent?

This book has repeatedly demonstrated that all individuals, in order to be self-reliant and independent (that is, free), are due the availability of sufficient economic opportunity enabling them to make a dignified, customary living through their efforts and to advance on the basis of improving their efforts. So far, however, our emphasis has been primarily on people currently employed. The same opportunity, though, applies to individuals who have lost their jobs and are genuinely searching for work, during the limited period in which they are out of work, and to those who have put in lifetimes of work and are now older and in their retirement years. Both of these groups have made the requisite "efforts" and are entitled to the same economic opportunity enabling self-reliance and independence as the currently employed. Few would argue otherwise.

The issue then becomes whether government should be the guarantor of this opportunity to be self-reliant or whether a less centralized, more individualized mechanism would be better. The answer here is plain. Because the provision of such opportunity is not merely optional in the ethic of freedom, private markets, philanthropy, and charity (both local and national) are inappropriate vehicles in and of themselves through which to pursue it: they *by definition* are not obligated to produce any specific set of conditions.

Consider Social Security. Were the system to move in the direction of privatization, it is true that individuals would have more personal control regarding their savings for retirement. In addition, by investing their retirement savings over a lifetime, some individuals would be able to expand their nest egg beyond what Social Security currently provides. But their investments would be vulnerable to the fluctuations of the market, and it is likely that many people's investments would lose some or most of their value or would fail to grow as strongly as needed.

Certainly the performance of the economy in recent years suggests no reason to be confident about a scenario of privatization. Here are excerpts from a couple of letters describing circumstances that have confronted millions of Americans. In September 2008, Deena De Naro of Durham, North Carolina, wrote, "My 74-year-old retired father lost $70,000 of his pension with the banks' collapse."

And according to Thomas Mathews of Auburn, Pennsylvania, "My daughter and her husband have lost a full one-third of their 401(k) in [the] stock market."[18] Imagine what the letters from those who invested with Bernie Madoff or AIG would read like, or from those who invested in any one of the many failed banks and other establishments in the private sector (many of which had perfect AAA ratings when investors threw their lot in with them). Imagine the letters from people whose pension plans through their employers defaulted as thousands of businesses went into a tailspin.

When people are working, or easily able to find work, these sorts of risks in the market are acceptable; they are the inherent chances we take whenever we invest in the private market, and if they don't work out for us, at least we have alternate means of making a decent living and getting ahead: through work. But when people are displaced and lose their jobs when they get older, they may be unable to get new ones or become sidelined for very long periods of time. Or they may no longer have the physical or mental capacity to work effectively. They thus have no alternative means of providing themselves with that decent living. Half of all employed workers have no private pension plans through their jobs to assist them in saving for old age. With real wages flatlined for decades, it has been tough for workers to save very much in any case. And when they are displaced, it is disproportionately difficult for older people to regain employment.

People of advancing age are thus highly vulnerable economically. They, along with those who have lost the capacity to work, may then become dependent on their children or other forms of charity, which of course are not obligated to provide anything, let alone a sufficient amount. The lack of any entity—a job, the market, charity—*guaranteeing* at least a basic economic security grounded in one's efforts deprives these people of access to the economic opportunity that freedom requires. They cannot be said to be independent.

Only government has the capability to ensure the availability of sufficient means to support independence for those who have put in the requisite efforts to qualify for such opportunity. The means for providing Social Security recipients' living have come through the recipients' own past efforts—their past work as employees. The return from those efforts is channeled through Social Security. The recipients are receiving a pension akin to an annuity that they have paid for.[19] It is not a "handout" or "something for nothing." We don't consider individuals receiving annuity coverage from private insurance as dependents; coverage from public insurance in this scenario is no different.

The same logic that governs Social Security can be applied to unemployment insurance benefits, which are also grounded in past work effort. Likewise, public assistance to purchase basic health insurance is appropriate when past and present employment fails to make insurance available or affordable to sizable numbers of employed workers, let alone to the unemployed seeking work and to retirees.

Still, insurance purchased voluntarily may be one thing. It obviously comports with freedom. By contrast, programs such as Social Security and unemployment insurance are compulsory. That distinction would seem to be crucial, if freedom is the aim, yet the distinction is more apparent than real. There is a broad array of compulsory actions individuals undertake in the name of freedom that are needed to protect one's freedom and the freedom of others. Among them are the requirements to pay taxes, to refrain from wrongfully harming others, to do jury duty, to enter military service if there is conscription, and to obey the law. Each of these actions is mandated and in this sense involuntary. Nevertheless, we view all of them as comporting with freedom because we consider each vital to ensuring that one's own freedom as well as the freedom of others is protected and remains secure.

## BRINGING BUDGETARY DEFICITS
## UNDER CONTROL

Of all the concerns raised by the solutions set forth in this chapter, surely the most urgent has to do with the affordability of the proposed actions at a time when budgetary deficits over the long term are already unmanageable, along with the broader question of how to bring the deficits themselves under control. Clearly, a government that rests on an unsustainable financial foundation cannot survive. Though divided on the issue, a number of the key Founders, including both Jefferson and Madison, were extremely wary of running public deficits.[20]

By 2011, the problem of contemporary debt was said to require closing federal deficits by about $5 trillion over a decade—$5.5 trillion including the costs of the health-care reform. The widely touted report from the Bowles-Simpson commission would reduce deficits by approximately $4–5 trillion during the coming decade.

Since then, a combination of actions involving new tax revenues and program cutbacks has reduced the cumulative deficits by about $4 trillion over ten years, leaving approximately $1.5 trillion. But that would only stabilize the debt relative to GDP rather than put the ratio on a downward trajectory. Moreover, it would not account for the costs of the series of actions identified in this and earlier chapters as key to attaining both economic freedom and national economic success.[21] To put the ratio of debt to GDP on a solidly downward trajectory while simultaneously meeting the costs of the combined actions will require an additional $3 trillion of reduced spending and increased revenues on top of the $1.5 trillion, or $4.5 trillion in total over ten years.

The single biggest cause of the projected budgetary deficits is the increasing cost of health care and the need for reform in the area of governmental spending on health care. Expenditures on Medicare *doubled* from 2000 to 2008, climbing from $215 billion in 2000 to $465 billion in 2008, nearly half of it as a result of the effects of medical inflation. That rate of increase projected into the future would spell financial doom for both the government and the nation. Even the slower rate of inflation in medical care during the past few years has continued to exceed general inflation. One estimate finds that $200 billion of total health-care spending annually today goes to paying the costs of overtreatment.[22] Eliminating just one-quarter of that superfluous treatment would save $500 billion over ten years.

Two basic approaches have been suggested to control rising health-care costs. One entails placing Medicare (or an entity similar to Medicare) in competition with private insurance and allowing recipients to choose among them, using a subsidy (or voucher) from the government to defray all or part of the price. A plan put forth by Democratic Senator Ron Wyden and Republican Representative Paul Ryan in 2011 would have set the government subsidy high enough to pay for the cost of the second-lowest insurance plan meeting the equivalent of Medicare's coverage of medical-care benefits.[23] Presumably, participants in that plan would have continued to pay an amount out of pocket, including approximately the same deductibles that Medicare recipients were currently projected to pay for a similar level of coverage. Presumably also, insurance competitors would have been obliged to accept all recipients in the same manner as Medicare accepts all recipients—that is, there could be no self-selection of the least costly customers while refusing the more costly ones.

The rationale of the approach is that it would significantly reduce the costs to government. Advocates say that the competition among all the different plans vying for customers, including Medicare (which everyone would continue to be eligible for and able to choose), should constrain costs and reduce inflation. The approach would also provide room for experimenting with insurance plans that might reduce spending in other ways, too—for example, plans that, unlike Medicare, have no monthly premium, but instead have a high deductible, which would give recipients more of their own money in the game when they choose individual services and might prompt them to pay more attention to the relative costs of their own health-care choices and to treatments that are unnecessary.

The second approach to containing costs would systematically implement a broader application of evidence-based medicine, along with other cost-saving reforms involving the way health care is organized. It involves emphasizing what works and de-emphasizing treatments and procedures that compelling evidence shows to be no more (or even less) effective than other less costly treatments, always keeping in mind the unique medical situations of individual patients. In addition, this approach focuses on coordinating medical services from different sources now carried out largely independently from one another so that they can be more effective and efficient in treating diseases and preventing duplication—with the possibility, too, of organizing payments so as to base them on successful outcomes rather than simply on the number of treatments. This approach also promotes efficiency by legislatively capping total administrative costs as a proportion of overall insurance expenditures.

The goal of both approaches is to reduce health-care inflation to something closer to the normal consumer rate of inflation and to curtail the overuse that occurs in the system. The Congressional Budget Office estimates that the 2010 health reform will cut approximately $500 billion, mostly through avenues described in the second approach.[24] If that reform fails to bring and keep medical inflation more into line with general inflation, as projected, we can then bolster it by either enforcing evidence-based medicine through regulation or implementing the more competitive approach to Medicare, presuming, again, that the subsidy retains its same defined-benefit character and that insurance competitors cannot exclude less healthy customers.

Medicare accounts for only a portion of federal spending on health care. Another large health-care program, Medicaid, is currently slated for reductions that cumulatively total $500 billion over the coming decade, lowering its projected rate of inflation by about 3 percent a year. The cost-reducing actions contained in the 2010 health reforms, to the extent that they succeed, will help achieve this result.

These estimates for Medicare and Medicaid of $1 trillion total in reduced costs over ten years have been included in the $4 trillion figure for deficit cuts already begun that I referred to at the start. A further $200 billion could be trimmed over ten years by permitting Medicare to negotiate drug prescription prices with pharmaceutical companies the way that the Veterans Health Administration now does. Yet another $200 billion could be saved across governmental health-care programs by instituting a safe-harbor rule in malpractice cases, which would reduce the need for and costs attendant to defensive medicine. While not limiting malpractice awards, a safe-harbor rule would protect against malpractice judgments physicians who have given care meeting the standards that normal medical practice has established as reasonable. Up to an additional $100 billion could be cut from the Medicare deficit by modestly increasing the cost-sharing that now applies to high-income households.

There are also many other program areas where reductions are feasible. Consider the myriad federal payments to contractors not now subject to competitive bidding or effective oversight as well as the many federal grants to states and localities with no systematic congressional review. Together they amount to $800 billion outside of health care.[25] Shaving just 5 percent off them would save $400 billion over a decade.

Additionally, the heightened economic activity generated by sustained increases in demand and tax revenues following from the revised policies will bring $500 billion more in revenues into the Treasury over a decade.[26] Another $600 billion will come naturally from the effects of the policies in lowering other costs of government. Expanding the availability of jobs, raising the return from them, and cutting the size of the projected debt itself will reduce the costs of a wide range of other activities of government, such as unemployment benefits, SNAP expenditures (formerly food stamps), housing as well as health-care assistance, and interest we would otherwise have to pay on the debt.

Suppose we were also to launch an all-out effort to reign in tax cheaters, capturing one-third of the taxes on income now owed but unpaid each year. Tax cheating involves so much money that capturing merely one-third of unpaid taxes would amount to a $1.3 trillion growth in revenues over the coming decade, most of it coming from underreported income.[27]

The aforementioned actions, in combination, raise $3.3 trillion of the $4.5 trillion required. That leaves $1.2 trillion. Other actions can easily come up with that amount and more. Consider six tax reforms that would raise $2.7 trillion in new revenues over ten years—and do so without increasing individual income-tax brackets by one penny.

The six actions on taxes are:

1. Taxing capital gains left in estates that now go untaxed and have never been taxed
2. Establishing a tax of $50 per $10,000 transacted on speculative financial transactions, similar to a levy already in place in Great Britain

3. Closing offshore tax havens

4. Raising the highest salary level under which the Social
   Security tax applies to 90–91 percent of total wages and
   salaries, close to its historical level, from the current 84
   percent (this step alone would go far in closing Social
   Security's own projected long-term deficit)[28]

5. Ending corporate tax exemptions for contributions made to
   very high-end pension plans

6. Capping all deductions on individual tax returns other than
   for charity at 28 percent and, for the portion of incomes
   surpassing $3 million, at 15 percent

Are these and the other actions proposed earlier in this chapter
radical? The most "radical" of the proposals, the Eisenhower tax,
mirrors policies implemented under a Republican president when
Republicans formed a majority in both houses of Congress. Indeed,
the tax policies under Eisenhower were actually stiffer on the top
income bracket than the temporary rate I propose here. The combination of actions seeks nothing more than to enable the majority
of Americans who for four decades have been left outside on the
fringes to come back inside the economic tent, and thus to enjoy the
same kind of freedom that the Founders fervently espoused.

The point (and ultimate result) of these reforms is not to pun-
ish high earners or to prevent individuals from making many times
more than average Americans; rather, by re-empowering the median
worker and the middle class, everyone—including business owners
and those at the very top, who would now have an expanded base
of real and stable consumer demand from which to draw a larger
profit—would benefit. By facilitating a significant expansion of
customers based on workers' improved productivity, the Common
Credo reestablishes the foundations necessary for *everyone* to prosper within a strong economy capable of sustaining itself.

## Overview

The policies that have been proposed will bring about many needed changes:

- ★ Economic growth that is more powerful and more widely distributed
- ★ Reduction of unemployment to 4 percent
- ★ Access of all workers to a living wage or better
- ★ Increased pay of middle-American workers at rates more closely aligned with productivity gains of the labor force
- ★ Elimination of the need for households to take on escalating debt in order to be able to get ahead
- ★ Reductions in poverty
- ★ Curbing of the many family and societal dysfunctions that accompany wage stagnation and economic insecurity among working families
- ★ An economy capable of meeting global competition head-on, advantaged by improved education, pay in line with productivity, an updated infrastructure, and innovation generated from worldwide leadership in basic research
- ★ A reduction of budgetary deficits to manageable levels for the foreseeable future

Imagine how Founders such as Jefferson, Adams, Madison, Franklin, Mason, or Washington would greet such an outlook.

Many of the proposed policies have had significant support within both the Democratic and the Republican parties, either now or in the recent past. The same is the case for the areas of education and climate change, discussed next. There are exceptions. For example, Republicans have never broadly accepted raising the minimum wage (although 2012 presidential candidate Mitt Romney did in the past), strengthening worker bargaining, or directly creating public jobs. And as of this writing, a proposal such as the 2011 Ryan/Wyden Medicare reform plan, as well as the use of broadly accepted educational performance measures in decisions regarding teacher retention and pay, has not gained substantial Democratic support. Only the Common Credo is currently able to welcome both types of approaches within its philosophy, and both may be needed to get us back on the right path.

## EDUCATION

Improved education is closely tied to opportunity and to the future success of the nation's economy. Public debate on education tends to focus on grades K–12, yet higher education, both four-year and community college, also requires quite a bit of attention. The United States once led the world, by far, in the proportion of adults who had completed a college education. We no longer do.

It is true that the pay for college-educated Americans as a group, over the past forty years, has fallen behind the overall productivity gains of the workforce by nearly as much as it has for Americans who have not completed college. Even so, college educated Americans have remained able to take advantage of the economic opportunities that were available and to get ahead far better than less-educated Americans. Further, Americans with college or postgraduate educations will be crucial to the economy's competitive success in the coming years.

Regaining the global lead in higher education must be a national goal because of its importance both for individual economic opportunity and for the nation's future economic success. An important part of the problem is the increasing unaffordability of higher education. Lower-income students who have scored near the top of college-entrance exams are *less* likely to graduate from college than high-income students who have scored lowest on the exams.[29] Making a four-year-college education affordable to low- and middle-income students without burdening them unduly with large loans should be a goal both on grounds of educational opportunity and on the grounds that it is a crucial national resource. A combination of raising income-based assistance and experimenting with increasing the availability of affordable $10K college degrees can help reach this goal.[30]

There must also be viable alternatives to four-year college through bolstered community-college trade and vocational programs; for example, we should orient skills training leading to associates' degrees more closely toward well-paying occupational openings in local markets, and expand access to those programs.

Obviously, education before college is indispensable, as well. About half of the variation in K–12 educational performance in both the United States and elsewhere is related to variation in child-poverty rates.[31] With poverty come problems of inadequate nutrition and health care, fewer books and other educational advantages in the home, fewer educational activities both after school and during the summer, and greater stress related to neighborhood crime and violence, all of which diminish educational performance.

Poverty rates in the United States are substantially higher than in any other major western nation. Reducing rates of poverty in the United States, as the proposals in this chapter will do, will likely improve our educational performance relative to other nations. So will expanding and strengthening preschool education along with identifying and recruiting the strongest teachers to locales with poorer-performing students while improving or removing the weakest teachers.

There is also much to learn from programs that have already demonstrated the capacity to close or even eliminate the learning gap between low- and higher-income students, such as Kipp and the

Uncommon Schools. Along the same line, more attention can be paid to instituting programs emphasizing noncognitive deportment skills, such as ambition, self-control, and persistence. Such an initiative, coupled with providing teachers and students with the newest educational technology, will raise still further the number of students able to attend college. We spoke earlier, as well, of the importance of enhancing career academies within high schools. The combination of all these actions has the potential to lift the nation's performance appreciably in international comparisons of students' abilities from kindergarten through grade twelve, and to make a strong start toward restoring the nation's world lead in higher-educated adults.

## CLIMATE CHANGE

One more challenge that has bedeviled the nation is reducing the carbon emissions that contribute to climate change, which would also serve to remove the nation's dependency on oil. As pointed out in Chapter 4, this problem arises from a market failure that only a collective societal response can correct. The evidence about climate warming, and the human contribution to it, underpins a nearly universal consensus among knowledgeable scientists about the threat that climate change poses for the future.[32] Even if we agree only that mounting human carbon emissions have an effect merely on the margins, accelerating the trend, it is surely prudent to protect ourselves against a possible substantial threat, just as we do in purchasing insurance. The question then arises, how do we respond effectively to the threat in a way that is affordable and involves the least governmental expense and restrictiveness necessary?

The problem we need to tackle is that transactions in the private market do not include the costs that pollution generates, leading to poorer health, shorter life, and damage to property. Because the costs are not internalized, those costs are not part of the prices charged in the market. As a result, market forces do not—and cannot— restrain the amount of pollution. Changing that scenario in the least restrictive way possible would involve placing a price on polluting emissions that approximates their understood costs (which is exactly what the free market *would* do if it could). If a metric ton of carbon emissions involves, say, $80 in measured costs of life, health, and property, then putting an $80-per-ton price on carbon emissions into market transactions, increased in steps over a number of years from zero to $80, would restrain emissions because the real-world costs would now be added in. It would also give the relative price of energy alternatives emitting less carbon and carbon-capture products a competitive boost to the degree that the alternatives don't involve such costs.[33] Except for setting the price on carbon emissions to hold producers accountable, this approach would leave private-market transactions otherwise untouched.

While this is about as surgically unrestrictive an intervention as possible, can the substantial cost to the public at large, as a result of paying the price of carbon emissions, be similarly minimized? With the price at $80 per ton, the total cost would slightly exceed $400 billion annually, about 3 percent of GDP, dropping off sharply thereafter as use of new energy sources replaced the old. Suppose the price were set by putting a monetary charge in the form of a public fee on energy-per-ton-of-carbon emissions. Also, suppose the legislation required that the revenues from the public fee (except for 2 percent for administration costs) would then be returned in its entirety to all individual citizens and a restricted set of companies as a refund. The refund to companies would be determined by the nature of a company's foreign trade and global competition; companies for which the new fee threatens to undercut their global trading position (because most of their foreign competitors pay no such fee) would get a commensurate refund, to counteract this threat. Unaffected companies would receive no refund.

The refund to individual citizens would come half on a per-capita basis and half on a basis related to income, with the refund of the latter part rising proportionately with income. The refunds would come as checks sent straight from the Treasury that never become part of the government's operating budget. The median family of four would receive a refund of approximately $2,500 annually.

For a strictly limited period of, say, five years, an extra share of the revenues might be directed to industries, communities, and individuals that become dislocated because they engage in producing high-carbon energy supplies such as coal and oil, to help them transition to the new marketplace—in the same spirit as we now do for trade dislocation.[34] In addition, also for a restricted period, a portion of the refund to individuals might be limited to paying the up-front costs of retrofitting homes and other major energy-saving purchases whose cost-savings on the use of energy will themselves provide the money needed, or more, to finance the purchases, therefore ending up costing the buyer nothing or leaving the buyer with a profit. Apart from those specific shares, all revenues would be returned directly to individuals with no restrictions on their use.

This combination of actions would significantly reduce carbon emissions by doing what a market is supposed to do but is incapable of doing in the case of pollution—that is, by putting a price on pollution. At the same time, the reduction would come at a modest overall financial cost to individual consumers and to taxpayers, and would involve no other long-term restrictions.

In British Columbia, a carbon tax has been in place since 2008. Pollution has been significantly reduced, and rebates to individuals and businesses now make income and corporate tax rates in British Columbia the lowest in Canada.[35]

## CHANGING OUR POLITICS

As it currently operates, our political process has failed to resolve every problem described in this chapter. In many cases the problems have simply continued to grow. It doesn't help that the ideology that regularly invokes the Founders and the ideal of freedom (contemporary conservatism) casts public action through government as the problem, and that the other ideology, which sees the possibilities and potential of public action (contemporary liberalism), seems rarely able to invoke either the Founders or the ideal of freedom in relation to most of these problems.

Viewing the role of government within the framework of the Founders and the ideal of freedom that they promoted can provide a means to bridge the two ideologies while identifying key places that are necessary to make both our politics and our government operate better.

A central principle of the Common Credo holds that government must attain its legitimate aims at the lowest possible financial cost with the least possible coercion or restrictiveness. In the public's eyes (and in fact), that principle is not now honored in government, with the result that government spending is widely seen to (and in places does) involve considerable amounts of waste.

Chapter 5 contained proposals to respond to this concern. They involved establishing an entity devoted to examining all proposed programs and reauthorizations of existing programs with an eye to whether these programs are designed to achieve their purposes at the lowest practicable level of cost and restrictiveness. This organization would play a role similar to that of the Congressional Budget Office, and its conclusions would be accorded a legislative weight similar to that now given to CBO analyses of revenues and costs. A formal annual report delivered orally to the public by the president, based upon these analyses and also including a comprehensive plan for examining the cost and restrictiveness of programs that do not come up for reauthorization, would underline the high priority the government places on operating efficiently and with the smallest possible footprint in attaining its proper aims.

In addition to this effort, our political process needs to moderate the polarization presently afflicting it. It could make a start by focusing on the Common Credo, which integrates the main philosophical concerns and aims of both the left and the right. Invoking the Common Credo would also reduce the intellectual dishonesty that has become rife today, dishonesty that entrenches the polarization by making it difficult (if not outright impossible) to instill accountability in our leaders and political pundits for what they say—accountability necessary to have real discussions that lead to compromise. Here, reference to the Common Credo reminds us about the great importance the Founders attached to virtue, and the imperative need for each of us to rise above self-interest to respect the legitimate interests of others in order for freedom itself to succeed, including its mandate for intellectual honesty. It would also serve the nation well to establish a highly respected trust (as described in Chapter 5) to identify and widely publicize continuing patterns of intellectual dishonesty in politics. Equally valuable in reducing one-sidedness would be legal action to reverse gerrymandering and make congressional districts more competitive, inducing representatives to focus on the broader general electorate rather than appealing solely to the narrow partisan base they need in order to survive the primary election for nomination or renomination.[36] Placing the power to redistrict in the hands of an independent commission rather than the legislature (as some states have done) and making competitiveness a main criterion, while far from perfect, is likely to moderate abuses.

Reducing polarization is essential, yet even success in that endeavor will not make better government possible if the minority has a surefire way to block decision-making. Routine use of the filibuster today effectively gives the Senate minority this power, nullifying the principle of giving each member's vote equal weight. The filibuster is a valuable tool that the minority ought to have as a means to stop extreme decisions, but its overuse has led to minority-party control of governance on many issues. To end this sort of abuse, and assuming that both sides are permitted to propose a manageable number of amendments for debate on the floor, we should restore the original rule that required those engaging in a filibuster to actually keep it going by their continuous presence and continuous speaking on the floor of the Senate, and also require that those filibusters respond to periodic motions on the Senate floor to show that they have the forty-one votes needed to sustain a filibuster. This would ostensibly limit the use of the filibuster as a purely political tool, inspiring opponents of a decision to utilize it only in severe cases. Further, as a way to emphasize even more strongly that the sole legitimate purpose of the filibuster is to avert extreme decisions, the rule might add that after one day a certain number of senators (say, twenty) must identify and affirm that a specific constitutional violation is at stake in the proposed action on the floor in order for the filibuster to continue.

Successful politics depends as well upon the ability of citizens to see the political process as their own. For most Americans, government no longer seems to be "of the people, by the people, and for the people." The view has grown instead that government is "them" rather than "us." The feeling is realistic because a relative few citizens often *do* have a greatly exaggerated influence during the elections themselves and on the elected officeholders thereafter. One analysis of the U.S. Senate found that "the opinions of constituents in the bottom third of the income distribution have *no* apparent statistical effect on their senators' roll call votes," and that in nearly every area of policy senators were substantially more responsive to the opinions of their affluent constituents than to middle-class constituents. The latest major study involves a comprehensive examination of the policy responsiveness of the entire political system since 1981. It came to a similar conclusion: that the system has been highly responsive to top-income Americans but generally unresponsive to middle-income or low-income Americans. As Princeton University political scientist Martin Gilens, the study's author, put it, "The policy preferences of affluent Americans are strong predictors of whether potential policy changes are adopted." With regard to middle-income and low-income Americans, he concluded that "the preferences of less well-off Americans are essentially unrelated to policy outcomes." The only exception—an erratic one—was for very abbreviated periods next to presidential elections.[37]

The Founders would have found this condition profoundly disturbing. They would have questioned it on two grounds: first, on the grounds that the proper operation of a republic requires representatives to remain independent and not become unduly beholden to any particular subset of the public or to any relatively few individuals; and second, on the grounds that individual citizens have been deprived of the basic civic equality essential to freedom, leaving them forced to live by laws over which other individuals were able to have substantially greater influence than they in shaping. Up through the late 1960s, the Supreme Court recognized these same two principles as ones central to the Constitution.

If the principles just mentioned were followed—principles of freedom and republicanism that were widely held at the time of the founding—strict campaign finance limitations would surely follow. True, Madison believed that the proliferation of many opposing interests would allow all these interests to act as checks on one another, resulting in a more freewheeling kind of politics with less need for other rules. But he would still agree that interests are unable to check one another if some of them are permitted to dominate. No matter how it is approached, whether by pure republicanism or its Madisonian variant, elections require rules enabling different sides to have their respective views heard without either side or a relative few dominating the debate or making individual representatives unduly beholden to them thereafter.

Recently, the Supreme Court has taken a very different course. Over the past four decades, its opinions have given little consideration to these bedrock principles, and none to the way in which independent campaigns and super PACs, as well as bundlers' contributions to individual candidates, threaten them. Similarly, the Court now allows few restrictions on either candidates' personal contributions to their own campaigns (even into the tens of millions of dollars) or on the total spending of candidates' campaigns. That line of thinking, again, ignores concerns about civic equality and about debates being unduly dominated by one side or a relative few.[38]

The Court nevertheless still accepts the principle that while money is speech (and thus financial contributions to campaigns are considered to be speech), money contributions as speech can be limited when they impede other interests of freedom.[39] For example, limitations are justifiable if such contributions of money would plausibly result in political corruption or even a reasonable appearance of such corruption.

Averting the corruption of officials is not the only interest of freedom worth guarding, however. Another interest of freedom—and thus another reason to limit financial contributions as speech—is assuring that every citizen has a reasonable degree of civic equality in the process of choosing representatives who will make the laws under which all of us must live and in influencing the decisions representatives make when in office. In 2003, the Court ruled in *McConnell v. Federal Election Commission*:

In addition to *"quid pro quo* arrangements," we have recognized
a concern not confined to bribery of public officials but extend-
ing to the broader threat from politicians too compliant with the
wishes of large contributors . . . , acknowledging that corruption
extends beyond explicit cash-for-votes agreements to "undue
influence on an officeholder's judgment." Of almost equal
importance has been the Government's interest in combating
the appearance or perception of corruption engendered by large
campaign contributions.[40]

What is "undue influence on an officeholder's judgment"? If the
answer is a weight made possible through money contributions
of more than twice the weight of the ordinary citizen, or just the
appearance of such an imbalance, then it is starkly obvious that the
present system is rife with undue influence. That is exactly what
the largest campaign donations buy: greater access to and influence
on the candidates. In this context, recall what the Court decided in
*Reynolds v. Sims* in 1964. It ruled that a voting system that ended
up giving citizens of one district twice the weight it gave citizens of
another district in determining the composition of the legislature
violated the Constitution. Is gaining twice the weight or more of an
ordinary voter (and, in the case of large financial contributions, it is
more likely ten, a hundred, or even a thousand times the weight) in
actually influencing who gets elected and/or how they act once in
office, which routinely happens in our political system today, similar
to one's vote's being counted twice in tabulating the overall results
of an election? Is it sufficiently similar to qualify as unconstitutional
under the very same principle? I certainly believe so, and I believe
that most Americans would say the same.

The principles of equal civic weight for every citizen and independence in elected representatives must be reasserted in our political
system. Reasserting them calls for serious campaign finance reforms,

many of which have already been tested at the national, state, and local levels. Such reforms also need to be extended to apply both to independent campaigns and to individuals using disproportionate amounts of money to finance their own campaigns. Reforms that have been explored include public financing of campaigns, to largely substitute for private contributions; strict limitations on individual and group financial contributions; and, when the spending of a campaign exceeds a defined maximum, public funding of the opposing campaign to match the privately resourced campaign. There has also been discussion of the possibility of using regulation of the public airways to provide substantial free advertising time for candidates on television.

Let me suggest an additional approach involving public funding that has not yet been part of the discussion. It is inspired by the tax check-off mechanism used in presidential elections, applied more widely to encompass not only presidential but also congressional and independent campaigns. It would involve granting every registered voter an account based on a tax credit worth, say, $40 or $50 in a presidential year (less in off years), administered publicly, possibly in the manner of a PayPal account. Using the $40 or $50 credit, each recipient could contribute up to $20 to any individual federal presidential and/or congressional candidate, party organization, or independent campaign that has met matching private financing rules similar to those that are now required under public funding for presidential candidates. The $20 limit would cover both the primary and the general election. Either no further private financial contributions to candidates would be allowed (including from the candidate him- or herself), as is currently the case for public funding of presidential candidates, or only strictly limited additional contributions would be allowed.

Such a reform would ensure a level of equality among voters and prevent elected representative from becoming unduly beholden to a particular few. At the same time, just as in the case of vouchers, the reform would permit every individual to decide on his or her own what and whom to support. If one-half of all registered voters participate and use the credits, approximately $4–5 billion will be available for federal campaigns during a presidential year. If a disproportionate amount of that money goes to one candidate, it would speak to the candidate's ability to appeal to the greater number of voters, not their ability to appeal simply to the greater number of millionaires.

Many will surely object that such restrictions on private financial contributions constitute unacceptable limitations on free speech, if candidates have no opt-out provision to fund their own campaigns in a private manner. But for all the reasons described in Chapter 5, money is a uniquely insidious political resource whose invasiveness extends far beyond speech itself. Moreover, if the restrictions on private financial contributions do involve speech at all (and this begs the question of whether money really is the same as speech), the limitations are being placed on the amount and volume of an individual's speech *relative to that of others* and not on free speech per se. We accept this distinction all the time, without reservation, in the rules that operate in federal and state legislative bodies and in county boards and city councils, in governing bodies both large and very small—rules that limit the time allotted to individual sides, officeholders, and individual members of the public to present their views, so that no side dominates.

More important, as noted earlier, even the current Supreme Court has agreed that money contributions as speech can be regulated when they impede other important interests of freedom. That is why contributions, even when viewed as speech, can be restricted, constitutionally, if such contributions could plausibly lead to the corruption, or appearance of corruption, of officials. Ensuring a reasonable degree of civic equality in the making of decisions that all of us must live under, and ensuring that no one side or particular few individuals will be able to dominate debate in elections or unduly influence those occupying office thereafter, are key interests of freedom and, as such, follow that same logic.

## RETHINKING WHAT WE MEASURE

The policies and reforms outlined in the previous pages would be incomplete if not accompanied by a change in the economic measures we value and emphasize. To measure prosperity today, we focus on how much GDP is growing. By doing so, we miss—and have missed for many years—the fact that the growth of GDP is becoming ever more narrowly distributed, largely bypassing most Americans. Middle Americans have struggled economically for four decades, working today for real hourly compensation that is nearly the same as in their grandparents' generation. Yet GDP has more than *doubled per person* over the same period, even after adjustment for inflation. What kind of prosperity is that?

Growth of GDP in and of itself is not what we should be paying most attention to. Instead, we should be concentrating on measures that tell us more about prosperity as felt by average Americans: for example, trends in the median real compensation of workers as well as trends in the growth of median real compensation relative to gains in the productivity of the workforce. Measures such as these should be given far greater emphasis and priority than is the case now. Also, in reporting them, public officials and news outlets should include not just the last month's figure, but also trends over longer periods of time.

Unemployment figures can be equally misleading as to how well or poorly American workers are doing. Consider an alternative, one focusing on what we might call "distressed workers." Distressed workers are those who either are paid less than a living wage per hour or are unemployed.[41] Jobs are supposed to enable people to live minimally decently. If distressed workers were factored into unemployment figures, the latter would provide a more accurate measure of American economic reality. In 2007, the unemployment rate stood at 4.6 percent, a pretty rosy picture. It is near to what economists consider to be a condition of full employment in a healthy economy. Yet the share of distressed workers in 2007 exceeded 30 percent of all workers, or seven times as many as were counted jobless, a vastly different picture. The measure does have some error in it, to be sure, because there is a small minority of people working below a living wage who have another member in the family unit whose pay is far higher. Nevertheless, even including that small minority, it is a considerably more accurate measure of the economic conditions workers face than is the present unemployment rate.

And instead of the poverty line, we should be focusing on the share of families earning less than a basic living income. The current poverty line calculates in today's inflated prices the level of what was considered a living income *in 1955*, which was the reference year for the family budget data used in the early 1960s in first establishing the poverty line. Because it is more than a half-century out of date, the poverty line is a meaningless measure for today.[42]

Being so outdated profoundly affects the way the measure makes the world look. Families falling beneath the present-day official poverty line, using the wage data available for 2008, contained fewer than 3 million year-round full-time workers, whereas families that earned less than a living income contained more than 12 million year-round full-time workers—in effect, 12 percent of all year-round full-time workers (approximately one in eight) versus 3 percent (one in thirty-three). Compared to the number of adults then on welfare, nearly six times as many workers were employed *year-round full-time* yet were still unable to attain a living income. Year-round full-time employment might be counted to enable nearly all families to get above the meaningless calculation of poverty we have right now. However, by no means does year-round full-time employment in America today allow nearly all families to reach a basic living income.

Imagine during times of strong growth for GDP if it were broadly reported that about 30–35 percent of American workers were in economic distress, a lot of them for many years, instead of focusing primarily on the 4–5 percent who are unemployed. Or imagine if it were regularly and widely publicized that the real hourly pay for a majority of American workers had risen hardly at all in nearly forty years, despite the enormous productivity gains of the workforce, even while the real GDP had more than doubled. Which figures do you think would catch the attention of individual Americans or tell us most about what is actually happening in their economic lives?

One more measure worth developing would trend the amount of consumer demand lost or gained in the economy during the past year relative to the year earlier, as well as the aggregate gain or loss in consumer demand per year from five, ten, fifteen, and twenty-five years earlier, resulting from changes in the distribution of compensation that have taken place in the economy.[13] Because businesses are less likely to invest, hire, and produce when they have fewer customers—that is, when consumer demand is reduced—this measure would be a very helpful tool for businesses, policymakers, and the public at large in determining our economic policies.

This leads to a final observation. We are prone to regard the American Dream as a value or a hope. It is—or should be—far more than that. Actual realization of the American Dream is, in truth, a powerful economic model. The American Dream is built upon individual entrepreneurship and striving. In turn, actually realizing the American Dream for all establishes the setting necessary for the success of entrepreneurship and striving. Entrepreneurial success requires the availability of good customers, which is exactly what results when opportunity is genuinely available for everyone to make a decent living through their efforts and get ahead through improvement. This condition is the very essence of the American Dream. Policy today focuses on economic growth, measured by GDP, yet growth in GDP does not necessarily lead toward this condition. It has not, in fact, for much of the past forty years.

## Conclusion

If the proposals set forth in this chapter were implemented, the nation would enjoy economic conditions enabling all willing individuals to be self-reliant and get ahead. Individuals and families would no longer have to take on escalating debt to improve their standard of living. The number of Americans facing poverty would be significantly reduced. Economic conditions that lead to and worsen family dysfunctions would be mitigated. We would have built a more competitive global economy by bolstering consumer demand, improving our infrastructure, lifting our world position in education, and fostering innovation by protecting our lead in basic research, among other actions. Carbon pollution would be substantially cut. Budgetary deficits would be reduced to manageable levels. Beyond that, government would become continuously concerned about the efficiency and restrictiveness of its activities. Grounds for collaboration across political aisles would expand, intellectual dishonesty in our politics would be moderated, and a political process that citizens can feel is theirs would become a possibility.

Such a nation would come far closer to reaching the Founders' high aims, the principles of the Common Credo, and most Americans' fervent hopes. We can create that nation or keep going the way we are now. It is entirely up to us.

## CHAPTER 8

# ATTITUDES ABOUT GOVERNMENT

★ ★ ★ ★ ★

MANY OF THE SOLUTIONS REQUIRED for the nation to get back on track call for government action, typically in partnership with private markets and the private sector. The solutions depend upon greater governmental activism in the needed areas and upon the willingness of the public to use government thusly.

Yet we know that many Americans today have deep misgivings about government. As mentioned back in Chapter 1, 89 percent of Americans polled in 2011 said that they distrusted government to do the right thing.[1] It's hard to find anything else, anywhere, able to unite 89 percent of Americans.

Political leaders opposing a large activist government often invoke the Founders. They beseech listeners to return to the fundamental teachings of the Founders, certain that doing so supports their opposition to engaging the government. Meanwhile, supporters of an activist government generally talk past this argument, hardly ever directly confronting or answering it. Instead, they emphasize how the context and requirements of the modern day have changed since the time of the Founders in ways that require new and different answers.

What this book has sought to do, in part, is provide a greater understanding of how the Founders *actually* viewed government. It has aimed to recover the distinction between limited government— that is, a government fully powerful and active enough to attain its duly constituted ends, but no stronger (which was a central aim of the Founders)—and *small* government as an end unto itself, which was not an aim of the Founders. This book has also sought to provide a better understanding of the Founders' beliefs regarding freedom— particularly the range of obligations we have to each other as part of freedom and the many kinds of contributions that they believed needed to come from governmental action in order for individual freedom to flourish. It has illustrated the vast gulf that now exists between the Founders' idea of freedom as reciprocal and the idea of freedom that dominates our thinking and politics today: freedom as mere personal volition or choice within the unconstrained operation of a free market.

My hope is that these discussions will help answer the claims of critics and take a step in reshaping popular attitudes about the proper role and boundaries of government in a free society. But beyond the points already made, there are two others very much worth exploring. The first is that, despite the public's view of government now residing at an all-time low, citizens are actually far more supportive of government than even they may realize. There are many areas of great public importance in which we take for granted not only extensive government involvement, but government proficiency. The second is that there are several crucial facts about government that too few Americans know. If made more visible, those facts could help upend popular myths that today wrongfully diminish government.

I certainly don't mean to suggest that our government needs no serious change or increased accountability for its activities—surely the previous pages have made clear that it does. My purpose in this chapter is only to demonstrate that, despite its current failings, our government as an actor in citizens' lives works better (and even more cost-effectively) than many of its critics give it credit for, a conclusion that, underneath the surface, most Americans themselves already understand and accept.

## POSITIVE PUBLIC VIEWS ABOUT GOVERNMENT

Americans' attitudes about government are, in many ways, much more positive than is commonly supposed. For one thing, virtually no Americans are opposed to government, or anything close to it, as a matter of general principle.

In spite of their objections to governmental interference in the free market, even many conservatives are very strong proponents of government when it comes to a wide range of other activities: military defense, provision of health care for veterans, police powers, protection of contracts, immigration control, building and maintenance of much of the infrastructure, funding of public and higher education, and upholding marriage and protecting the fetus, to name just a few. In these and other sectors, a large majority of conservatives do in fact turn to government and feel it is a valuable asset.

Critics often portray government as ineffective and incompetent by its very nature. But were that true, how could that same defective entity hope to be successful in defending the nation, which is a highly complicated task involving enormous coordination of a multiplicity of actions? How could it succeed in performing police powers, or in doing any of the long list of things that critics of activist government in the economy *do* believe government can handle effectively? There is a basic contradiction between the claims that government is naturally incompetent and ineffective and the many areas in which even the harshest critics trust that government can be successful. If government can do such tasks ably, which nearly all agree it can, it cannot be inherently ineffective and incompetent.

There is a saying that Americans are conservative about government philosophically or in theory, supporting small government in the abstract, and liberal about government in practice, advocating governmental activism when it comes to specifics. Yet in both theory and practice, even many conservatives who think of themselves as proponents of small government feel comfortable with big government in quite a few individual areas.

Given this reality, it is no surprise that, despite misgivings Americans might have about government in the abstract, they actually support, often by large majorities, government involvement to deal with a great number of problems. Beyond matters like defense, police powers, the infrastructure, and education, solid majorities of Americans support government programs in economically related areas like Social Security, Medicare and Medicaid, unemployment benefits, workers' compensation and disability, and veterans' programs. Solid majorities of Americans also back government regulation in areas such as food and drug safety, consumer safety, worker safety, and the control of environmental pollution. There is likewise strong support for government involvement in the preservation of national parks, the space program, disaster assistance, and even activities as small in scale as national public radio. Indeed, the public broadly supports government involvement in the large majority of areas in which it currently operates, including most Americans who identify as Republicans and conservative.[2]

Clearly, then, in seeking popular support for activist government, there is much to draw on: the Founders' own views about the need for government involvement in a wide range of activities; the reality that virtually all Americans trust government to deal with a number of highly sensitive, complicated, and hugely important matters; and positive public support for governmental engagement in the great majority of areas in which the government currently actually operates.

## HIDDEN TRUTHS

Yet Americans still have several serious concerns about government that make such support fragile. One of these is the sense that government knows no bounds—that it spends recklessly, that it just keeps growing, that it will ultimately bleed away the vital energies needed for the nation to succeed. The fear is that government can't be kept limited and under control. Many critics label it a "beast." As Fox News host Greg Gutfeld put it, "The more you feed the beast, the beast will never go on a diet. The beast will keep eating."[3] Give it an inch, and it will take a mile.

Notwithstanding this popular, often unquestioned picture of government, the facts reveal a very different reality. True, total spending at all levels of government—federal, state, and local—has indeed grown by quite a bit over the past half-century: from 28.7 percent of GDP in 1960 to 35.2 percent in 2007. That trajectory fits the "beast" moniker perfectly.

However, government spending has grown mostly because of insurance programs with high public support that are separately taxed and funded (principally Social Security, Medicare, and unemployment benefits) and public-employee retirement, including the military. Subtract them from the equation, and the entire remainder of government spending—covering all the bureaus and agencies at all levels of government, including national security and foreign aid, the police and law enforcement, public education and student assistance, highways, Medicaid, all other public assistance programs such as SNAP and housing assistance, agriculture and farm extension programs, energy and the environment, the postal service, com-

TABLE 1

TOTAL GOVERNMENT EXPENDITURES EXCLUDING
SOCIAL SECURITY, MEDICARE, UNEMPLOYMENT, AND
PUBLIC-EMPLOYEE RETIREMENT, AS A PERCENTAGE OF GDP,
1960–2007 (IN BILLIONS OF DOLLARS)

| Year | GDP | Governmental expenditures | % of GDP |
|------|------|------|------|
| 1960 | 527 | 132 | 25.1 |
| 1970 | 1,040 | 266 | 25.6 |
| 1980 | 2,796 | 719 | 25.7 |
| 1990 | 5,803 | 1,610 | 27.7 |
| 2000 | 9,825 | 2,425 | 24.7 |
| 2007 | 14,078 | 3,674 | 26.1 |

merce, research, regulatory programs, and *everything else*—rose from 25.1 percent of GDP in 1960 to 26.1 percent of GDP in 2007 (see Table 1), the last year before the Great Recession. That's an increase of less than one-twentieth in the size of the entire expanse of government relative to GDP, save for the four separately taxed and funded programs mentioned above, over a period exceeding half a century. In the process, large numbers of individual programs were cut and scaled back in terms of money and personnel—by one estimate by at least 15 percent of federal programs per year on average.[4]

A closer look at Table 1 shows that total government spending actually would have diminished by a about 1.5 percent of GDP from 1960 to 2007 except for two unusual periods when the government did grow. Those periods were 1980 to 1990 (under the presidencies of Ronald Reagan and George H. W. Bush) and 2000 to 2007 (under the presidency of George W. Bush). Aside from those two periods, the constant trend over forty years was for government to remain steady in size relative to GDP or, if anything, to shrink.

Clearly, the great majority of government in the United States does not just keep expanding inexorably; to the contrary, it has typically remained firmly disciplined and under control.

Given this evidence about the growth of government, what explains the widespread public misperception? One explanation is a social-scientific theory of government that seems so sensible that it has become common wisdom. It is called public choice theory. Its premise is that politicians and bureaucrats do what is in their own interests. Since politicians get reelected by bringing projects and programs back to their districts and bureaucrats attain more power by expanding projects and programs within their agencies, government naturally grows because the government's enlargement is in the direct interests of both politicians and bureaucrats. This is not to mention the role of interest groups back home: the concentrated benefits they seek and receive in the form of government projects in their districts far outweigh the costs of those projects as felt by the public at large, since the costs are dispersed among all individual taxpayers.

The theory makes intuitive sense. The only problem is that it's not generally true. And currently there is no countertheory among proponents of activist government to explain why we *should* expect government to remain under control. Liberal thinking promotes activist government pragmatically, but it has not offered a compelling theory as to why our government does not naturally grow. Nor, as I've argued in this book, has liberalism supplied a concrete, straightforward, or principled basis for placing limits on government involvement.

Adding to the sense that government grows inexorably is the widespread impression that government is inefficient. Given a choice between government and the private sector in executing a task, many Americans tend to believe that private-sector performance will be substantially more cost-efficient. There are stories about the Justice Department's $16 breakfast muffins or the Pentagon's $500 hammers, and popular comparisons between the postal service and FedEx or UPS. Indeed, Chapter 5 identified a number of areas, involving billions of dollars, where government could and should become more efficient.

Of course, some of the alleged examples of government waste are outright false.[5] Moreover, there are also plenty of examples of failure and inefficiency in the private market. When it came to light in 2012 that quite a few of the factories that Mitt Romney's former company, Bain Capital, had invested in had been closed, his defenders argued that participating in the free market is inherently chancy and that not everything succeeds.[6]

There's no question about the risk of failure involved in the free market. About 50 percent of all businesses that form and find investors are no longer in operation at the end of five years.[7] Additionally, many scores of businesses go bankrupt each year but continue under the same name, many of their financial obligations having been forgiven. A trip to an establishment nicknamed the Museum of Failed Products, outside Ann Arbor, Michigan, acquaints the visitor with thousands of products from highly regarded companies in the private sector that failed miserably, many of them almost overnight. Examples include "A Touch of Yogurt" shampoo from Clairol, "For Oily Hair Only" from Gillette, and "AM Breakfast Cola" from Pepsi. According to some estimates, the failure rate of new commercial products is as high as 90 percent.[8]

Of late, critics of government have emphasized the lush pay and benefits enjoyed by public officials relative to workers in the private sector. That was Governor Scott Walker's rallying cry in Wisconsin in 2010–11 when he sought to reduce the power and role of public unions. How big is the problem? Referring to an analysis by the Federal Office of Personnel Management in 2011, Congressman Dennis Ross, a Republican from Florida, told a congressional hearing that the average worker in the public sector receives over 60 percent more in total compensation annually than does the average private-sector worker—$101,628 versus $60,000.[9] That's a substantial difference.

Of course, some of this difference might also come from comparing apples with oranges. More federal workers than private-sector workers have advanced or professional degrees and hold professional or administrative jobs. Lawyers, for example, received $127,500 on average working for the federal government in 2009. They got $137,540 on average working in the private sector.[10]

When all is said and done, though, it likely is the case that government does pay its workers somewhat more than the private sector does. Taking a wide array of factors into account (education, occupation, experience, and location), a Congressional Budget Office analysis covering 2005 to 2010 suggests that overall compensation was 16 percent higher on average for federal government workers than for workers in the private sector. However, nearly the whole difference was due to benefits. Salaries and wages per hour were almost exactly the same for workers in federal government and the private sector.[11]

Moreover, while the federal government did pay a higher amount, the difference in compensation occurred primarily at the middle and lower levels of pay. That's the exact population whose compensation has stagnated in the private market over the past four decades. "We . . . live in a society," Governor Walker said, "where the public employees are the haves and taxpayers who foot the bills are the have-nots."[12] Governor Walker is correct that taxpayers at the middle and lower levels have indeed been "have-nots" in the private sector for decades, but that would seem to say more about the occurrence of a serious problem in the private sector than about what government pays its employees.

It is noteworthy, too, that those who say that pay in the public sector concerns them seem generally untroubled by the more drastic reverse situation: that top executives in the private sector, who average $10 million per year in compensation, receive far, far more than do top executives in government. To my knowledge, not a single one of the critics of government pay has ever said, "Look at the money the public sector saves taxpayers in pay for its top executives" or "Look at how much the private sector is wasting in the pay its top executives receive."

A favorite example of my own about government inefficiency, here about one hand not knowing what the other hand is doing, was headlined on the front page of the *New York Times* in 2010: "While Warning about Fat, U.S. Pushes Cheese Sales."[13] The nutritional side of the Department of Agriculture was trying to induce Americans to eat less fat while the marketing side of the very same Department of Agriculture was trying, among other things, to increase the amount of cheese used in commercially sold pizzas. It seemed laughably irrational to me. Then I remembered the number of times at baseball and basketball games I noticed fans devouring hot dogs and french fries from one hand while gulping down various diet drinks with the other. I'm not saying that what the government does makes sense simply because many individual Americans do something similar in their own private lives. I'm saying only that government and the private sector may have more similarities than at first meets the eye.

A fascinating study relevant to the question about pay for public-sector versus private-sector employees examined the personnel costs to government when it contracts out services versus the costs government would have incurred had it performed the same services through its own personnel. Undertaken by the nonpartisan Project on Government Oversight in 2011, the study found that, on average, government paid nearly twice as much to hire private contractors as it would have paid to have public officials perform the same services. In thirty-three of the thirty-five service areas the analysis examined, it cost government more for private contractors than it would have paid to public employees.[14]

This is not to condemn the private sector. Indeed, government may be not be doing an effective job in hiring private contractors. It is to say that, seeking to maximize profit, private-sector enterprise will take advantage if it can and charge a good bit more than public employees are in a position to do.

The bottom-line question, really, is whether private for-profit enterprise can deliver services of government more effectively or efficiently than bureaus and public officials can. The popular premise is that the private sector, wanting to realize a profit in a competitive world, is more efficient and therefore delivers services at lower cost than government. Yet the evidence from direct comparisons of private-sector enterprises and government producing the very same services is so mixed as to suggest that there is no conclusive answer. It is not clear that private enterprise does perform consistently better or more efficiently than the public sector in providing public services.[15] In open bidding for contracts, private contractors and public agencies each win competitions about half of the time, adding evidence to the conclusion that private contractors are by no means consistently more cost-effective than public entities.[16]

## What to Do

So we know that the public broadly believes that government is capable of carrying out highly complicated tasks and that it positively backs the engagement of government in the great majority of areas in which government is presently involved. We also know that the vast bulk of what the public sector does has not demonstrated any inherent tendency to grow incessantly or to expand out of control, and that the private sector does not dependably outperform the public sector in the delivery of services. Assume, too, that the budget deficits in relation to GDP are reduced and made manageable. Will all this be enough to gain the public's full support for the stronger activist role needed from government? Not entirely, I believe, because Americans still will not have any logical reason to believe government won't then continue to grow relentlessly thereafter. In addition, many Americans also feel they are marginalized by government. They believe they have little say in a government that is distant from them and their needs. Their trust needs to be earned back. If we are going to ask the public to feel more comfortable with greater government activism in critical areas, then we must implement the reforms to the internal processes of government that have been called for in earlier chapters.

First, limited government—in the sense of a government that costs and restricts as little as possible (while remaining able to achieve its legitimate aims)—must be viewed and treated as a basic, unconditional principle in itself. This goal cannot simply be thought of as a pragmatic aim or second-tier consideration—a nice ideal. Both at a philisophical and at a practical level, it must be regarded by politicians, *and witnessed by the public*, as a bedrock goal of government, continuously and assiduously pursued, rather than as an afterthought or merely a means for achieving other more important goals.

Second, methods to ensure the least possible cost and restrictiveness possible, like the ones suggested in Chapter 5, must be set in place, enforced, and emphasized publicly by both the president and Congress. Third the reforms of campaign finance practices, also discussed in Chapter 5, designed to bring those practices into line with the principles of civic equality espoused by the Founders, must be implemented, so that campaigns and elected officials are not unduly influenced by a particular moneyed few, and government can again be viewed as being of and by "all of us."

All these steps follow the Common Credo. All of them are in keeping with the views of the Founders and the widely shared values of the American public. While political leaders can gain a good measure of public support for the use of government without taking these steps, the task will be easier and the forthcoming support far stronger and more lasting if they do. That holy grail of governance— a truly national mandate—awaits those candidates willing to try.

CHAPTER 9

---

# MOVING FORWARD CONFIDENTLY

★ ★ ★ ★ ★

SO HERE WE ARE. Very few would deny that America faces serious problems today. Yet, absent an urgent crisis—real or manufactured—that would hurl the nation into the abyss and thus force political action, our political process is often stalemated. Americans do not feel that the government represents them. The term "dysfunctional" may be the most oft-used descriptor of our current politics, and it is hard to argue with its accuracy. The favorability rating of Congress has fallen to levels it would seem impossible for political institutions to reach, at one point hitting 11 percent, the lowest level ever recorded. Cynicism is sky-high.

As for the economy, tens of millions of Americans experience unemployment or underemployment while pay beneath a living wage hits tens of millions more. On top of that, earnings for the average American worker have been flat for decades. Even as a large majority of American workers and families have suffered economically in the process, their plight has gone untreated by a political system that marginalizes them. It's tempting to think that these disconcerting conditions have occurred mostly as a result of the economy's collapse in

2008. The reality, though, is the opposite: these conditions have been building unattended for the past forty years. The increasing ascendancy over that time of an individualistic view of freedom, rather than of the reciprocal ideal held by the Founders, has led to policies that have simply reinforced the problems and made them worse.

Beyond this, we face budget deficits that are unmanageable over the long term. Unless health-care costs are brought under control, those costs will bankrupt increasing numbers of families and businesses and ultimately the government itself. Our worldwide lead in public education disappeared a couple of decades ago. We are now well down the list of nations on educational measures of all kinds, and with each passing day our lead in basic research gets less certain. Our aging infrastructure is falling behind that of other developed countries. Despite many years of talking about it, we have yet to come firmly to grips with issues concerning either pollution related to climate change or the dependency of our economy upon oil whose wildly fluctuating price, governed by global forces, lies outside our control.

Taken together, it's an ugly and even terrifying picture. And it's not just the political process that has failed. The ideologies of contemporary conservatism and liberalism, which now serve as the only viable political platforms we have to address these challenges, have failed as well. They do not provide effective answers to our most basic and pressing questions. Both of them, in their way, alienate vast segments of the population. Both, in their way, fail to follow the ideal of freedom upon which this country was founded, with the result that we are left with a nation in which a solid majority of Americans find themselves on the margins of the economic and political systems, such that neither system can function effectively.

Consider the people I worked alongside all those years ago at the bakery and the electroplating plant, and so many other American workers like them. For many of them, substantial increases in workers' productivity over the past four decades have brought little or no return in real pay increases. Average workers like them are hardly better off than their counterparts were two generations ago. For a clear majority of Americans, the American Dream has gone on life support. Meanwhile, top earners, who used to make 20 to 30 times more than the average worker, now make 150 to 250 times more.

It's been a rough experience for everyday Americans. Moreover, it has left the economy with steadily fewer customers relative to the increase taking place in production, damaging businesses both large and small. This discrepancy was papered over for years by most Americans entering into greatly accelerating debt as the main remaining way to lift their living standards, a condition that was predisposed at some point to end in reduced growth and ultimately the collapse of the economy itself, which is what happened.

The wheels have come off the political system, too. Intellectual dishonesty has grown rife in everyday politics, making a meeting of minds nearly impossible. And while all Americans do have a vote, most of them do not have the millions of dollars necessary to be true political equals with vastly weathy individuals and campaign bundlers. Average Americans are merely being realistic in feeling that the federal government does not truly represent them. In fact, it has not done so for a long time. Not surprisingly, after being treated in this way, few Americans today express a high level of trust in government.

We have, quite simply, lost our bearings as a nation and gone badly off course, becoming increasingly divided and acrimonious in the process.

We have not, however, lost the power to turn matters around. An effective remedy, in the Common Credo, is available. At one level, the Common Credo might be seen as simply good old practical American common sense. At another level, it can be equally understood as a deep, fundamental moral faith and full-fledged comprehensive governing philosophy.

There are three principal advantages the Common Credo brings to the table. First, it provides answers that have great potential to alleviate and surmount many of the most difficult national challenges described in the previous pages, reversing the trends of the past four decades, during which the problems simply festered or became worse.

Second, the reasoning of the Common Credo eliminates and corrects for the limitations, misunderstandings, and lapses found in contemporary conservatism and liberalism that have been so debilitating and steered the nation off course for so long.

Combining the first two advantages, the Common Credo provides not only a correct diagnosis of grave problems the nation faces but also an effective prescription for attacking and reversing those problems.

Third, the Common Credo is a body of moral precepts built upon a single root premise going back to the thinking of the Founders, which they understood to be at once self-evident and divinely given: that all men are created equal and endowed with equal rights, including life, liberty, and the pursuit of happiness. Practically all Americans subscribe both to this basic premise and the many subsidiary principles shown in this book to follow from it. As a result, even as it reconnects us with our historical roots, the Common Credo also establishes a much-needed foundation in the present for gathering broader public consensus on crucial political and economic issues. This consensus is cemented further by the way the Common Credo aligns viscerally with the key economic interests and longstanding economic concerns of a large majority of Americans and their families, not to mention the core needs of the economy as a whole. The simultaneous appeal to the deepest economic interests and bedrock moral values of a large majority of Americans gives every reason to believe that the Common Credo, if activated, has the potential to inspire the breadth of public support essential for effective governance. Neither of our current ideologies can make that claim.

As it works toward these ends, the Common Credo identifies the obligations we have to one another under freedom that join us together into an organic, collaborative community, not simply a cluster of disparate individuals. It describes how and why we are involved in a common enterprise. At the same time, as it should, the Common Credo delineates the limits and boundaries of those same mutual obligations.

A valuable lesson suggested by the weaknesses of our current ideologies is that if the Founders' vision of reciprocal freedom is not taken as the starting point, it becomes very difficult to construct any coherent and effective governing philosophy, at least one that can be helpful to most Americans. For example, contemporary free-market conservatism, with its thin individualistic rather than reciprocal view of freedom, ends up with no philosophic minimum, or lower limit, for the proper role of government as regards either social insurance or public aid. Contemporary liberalism suffers from the opposite flaw: having no clearly defined bottom-line principle, it sets forth no philosophic upper limit for the role of government in people's economic lives. Building from the Founders' vision of reciprocal freedom removes this elemental deficiency of each current approach.

In the same way, neither of the current ideologies provides a useful approach for the ordinary running of the economy at large. Contemporary conservatism's near-total emphasis on today's free-market model permits disparities in pay that have resulted in meager economic progress for a substantial majority of the public over a very long period. Bad enough in itself, this snail's pace of progress for ordinary Americans contributed decisively to the economy's ultimate breakdown. Responding to free-market conservatism, liberalism's answer has typically been a laundry-list approach to the everyday running of the economy that has failed to offer the public a clear overarching alternative model.

By contrast, we have seen that the Founders' vision of reciprocal freedom does map out a coherent alternate economic model. Though grounded in voluntary exchange, entrepreneurial initiative, and fierce private-sector competition, this model averts the serious limitations of today's free-market approach and creates the conditions that competitive businesses and the private sector absolutely require in order to thrive. This model focuses not directly on economic growth per se, but on the realization of the American Dream for all, defined by the Founders' reciprocal idea of freedom, which in turn sets up immensely fruitful conditions required to fuel entrepreneurial striving and the healthy, sustainable growth of the economy, what we may someday call "the new prosperity."

Possibly the most exceptional asset of the Founders' thinking and the source of its undying power, reflected also in the Common Credo, is the way it joins disparate, contending values. We have seen how the Founders' thinking identifies where the great yet often conflicting ideals of freedom and equality intersect and come together. Where they intersect, the two ideals no longer oppose one another. Rather, they support each other with the result that both ideals can be secured together—furthering one of them simultaneously furthers the other, safeguarding one of them simultaneously safeguards the other. Similarly, the place where freedom and equality intersect and become the same identifies the point where equality and economic efficiency, or growth, no longer involve a tradeoff. Instead, the intersection marks the place where promoting equality is itself indispensable to increasing and sustaining the economy's growth. The same thinking of the Founders, as well, demarcates the intersection between freedom and the range of obligations we have to one another, where individual freedom and commitment to community support and reinforce rather than oppose each other. The thinking of the Founders and Common Credo, that is, bring together the majestic ideals of freedom, equality, community, and prosperity into a magnificent harmony.

Ultimately, the Common Credo demonstrates that, beneath the surface, America does not have to be the fractured nation that today's political divisions would seem to suggest it is. Underneath all the sound and fury there lies a deeper common purpose and a comprehensive set of firm principles for governing that we all share. This set of principles connects the core truths and strengths of both conservatism and liberalism, both Smithian and Keynesian economics, and both individual self-interest and the transcendent common good.

A public philosophy derived from the Founders and agreed upon by nearly all Americans; one that has the potential to produce solid governing majorities, overcome the serious mistakes of the contemporary ideologies, and help solve many of the major problems facing the nation today: this is what the Common Credo offers. By activating the Common Credo, we can rediscover our compass as a nation, regain our better instincts, inspire hope, and put the nation back on the only path to its success.

# NOTES

## CHAPTER I
### HOW WE GOT HERE

1. Regarding the measure of a living wage, over the past several decades Gallup and Roper polls have found that Americans believe the smallest amount of money it takes for a family of four "just to get by" ranges from 150 to 180 percent of the government-established poverty line, or up to $40,000 per year for a family of four. (See Jeffrey M. Jones, "Public: Family of Four Needs to Earn Average of $52,000 to Get By," Gallup News Service, February 9, 2007, at www.gallup.com/poll/26467public-family-four-needs-earn-average-52000-get .aspx [accessed January 7, 2013]; and John E. Schwarz, *Illusions of Opportunity: The American Dream in Question* [W. W. Norton, 1997], pp. 60–64 and table 1.) Studies of family budgets also show that $40,000 for a family of four in most areas of the country is enough to own or rent only the cheapest one-third of two-bedroom housing, to have about $1.50 per meal per day per person, to operate a single ten-year-old car in running condition, to have a telephone, and to go out very occasionally to a movie. It is too little, however, to live in a better neighborhood or a safer neighborhood, to have more than $1.50 per meal per day per person for food, to own and operate a second car in reliable running condition, or to go away on any vacation, even for a weekend. Expenditures of families recorded in the U.S. Department of Labor's *Consumer Expenditure Survey* show that low-income households actually have to and do spend about 150 percent

to 180 percent of the poverty line to make ends meet. The official poverty line itself, if its formula were updated using the same method as the original, would come to more than 170 percent of the present measure. With one and two-thirds full-time workers in a family, a wage of about $11.70 per hour would amount to $40,000 annually. (More than one and two-thirds full-time workers is an uneconomical proposition for families with children who need and have to pay for the costs for child care.) See John E. Schwarz, *Freedom Reclaimed: Rediscovering the American Vision* (Baltimore: Johns Hopkins University Press, 2005), pp. 48–61 and accompanying notes.

It is important to make clear that the living wage identified here is a social standard—a modest and frugal minimum standard understood in terms of the customary living of the day—and not an absolute standard of sheer survival. The official poverty line, too, was designed and meant to measure a social standard relative to the budgets of average families in 1955, the data for its base year (see Schwarz, *Freedom Reclaimed*, pp. 49–50). Since then, it has been updated only for inflation so that, today, it simply measures the cost in today's dollars to purchase the standard considered appropriate to 1955.

Lawrence Mishel, Jared Bernstein, and Heidi Shierholz, *The State of Working America, 2008–2009* (Ithaca, N.Y.: Cornell University Press, 2009), p.140, table 3.8, shows that in every year since 1973 at least 25 percent of all employed workers have earned less than $11.25 per hour, adjusted by my calculation to 2012 dollars. When those who are unemployed and looking for jobs are added in, 30 percent or more of the American workforce consistently earned less than $11.25 per hour—a living wage—or were unemployed.

2. Mishel, Bernstein, and Shierholz, *The State of Working America*, p. 161, figure 30, for trends in both median compensation and workforce productivity from 1973 to 2007. Data are for the nonfarm sector and those who are not self-employed.

3. John E. Schwarz, *The Forgotten Americans: Thirty Million Working Poor in the Land of Opportunity* (New York: W. W. Norton, 1992); idem, *Illusions of Opportunity: The American Dream in Question* (New York: W. W. Norton, 1997); idem, *Freedom Reclaimed: Rediscovering the American Vision* (Baltimore: Johns Hopkins University Press, 2005).

4. Quoted in Jared A. Favole, "Obama: Jobs Plan Could Help Jump-Start the Economy," Dow Jones Newswire, September 26, 2011.

5. See "Elizabeth Warren Blasts GOP 'Class Warfare' Charge, Tax Cuts for the Rich," *Huffington Post*, www.huffingtonpost.com, first posted on September 22, 2011 (accessed July 17, 2012).

6. Ryan quoted in Ryan Lizza, "Fussbudget: How Paul Ryan Captured the G.O.P.," *New Yorker*, August 6, 2012, p. 27; Obama, speech in Delray Beach, Fla., October 28, 2012, broadcast on *All Things Considered*, National Public Radio, October 31, 2012.

7. Jeff Zeleny and Megan Thee-Brenan, "New Poll Finds Deep Distrust in Government," *New York Times*, October 25, 2011, from a New York Times/CBS News poll.

## CHAPTER 2
## FREEDOM AND EQUALITY

1. Quoted in Eric Foner, *The Story of American Freedom* (New York: W. W. Norton, 1998), p. 22.

2. At first glance, it may seem that defining the wrongful harms that are out of bounds is a fairly simple and straightforward matter, but it is not. What is negligence, for example, and what isn't it? What kinds of information can a corporation or business keep secret, and what information must it make public? Are there circumstances in which one individual can kill another without violating the proscription against murder? Should every car owner have to purchase and carry automobile insurance, and, if so, how much? What kinds of safety rules must mines and factories adhere to, or oil and gas companies, in the drilling of wells and the construction of pipelines? Are there situations in which one party can unilaterally nullify a binding contract?

There are a million questions just like these about what does and doesn't constitute wrongful harm. Freedom depends upon public institutions not merely to help protect against wrongful harm—through the police, regulatory agencies, courts, and an effective law enforcement system—but also, just as importantly, to define exactly what wrongful harm is.

3. George Will, "West Ignores Loss of Faith at Its Peril," *Arizona Daily Star*, April 17, 2005, p. H2. Will speaks in the same tradition as numerous philosophers and economists of individualistic freedom. Some of the leading voices among them are Robert Nozick, *Anarchy, State, and Utopia* (New York: Basic Books, 1974); Friedrich Hayek, *The Road to Serfdom* (Chicago: University of Chicago Press, 1944) and *The Constitution of Liberty* (Chicago: University of Chicago Press, 1960); Milton Friedman, *Capitalism and Freedom* (Chicago: University of Chicago Press, 1962); and Milton Friedman and Rose Friedman, *Freedom to Choose: A Personal Statement* (New York: Avon, 1980). A popular fictional

account is Ayn Rand, *Atlas Shrugged* (New York: Signet, 1996). For a philosophical treatment of freedom from a broader view, see Gerald Gaus, *The Order of Public Reason: A Theory of Freedom and Morality in a Diverse and Bounded World* (Cambridge: Cambridge University Press, 2012).

4. "About Us," FreedomWorks website, www.freedomworks.org (accessed March 8, 2012).

5. For the Virginia Declaration of Rights, see A. E. Dick Howard, "For the Common Benefit: The Virginia Declaration of Rights of 1776," appendix to *The George Mason Lectures: Honoring the Two Hundredth Anniversary of the Virginia Declaration of Rights, Williamsburg, June 12, 1776* (Williamsburg, VA: The Colonial Williamsburg Foundation, 1976), pp. 20–21. For Jefferson's quote, see Hugh Howard, *Houses of the Founding Fathers: The Men Who Made America and Where They Lived* (New York: Artisan, 2007), p. 226.

6. For John Adams' philosophy regarding economic independence, relative economic equality, and freedom, see R. Carter Pittman, "George Mason: The Architect of American Liberty," *Vital Speeches of the Day*, 21 (December 15, 1954), 926; George A. Peck Jr., ed., *The Political Writings of John Adams* (New York: Liberal Arts Press, 1954), p. 96; W. Cleon Skousen, *The Five Thousand Year Leap* (Washington, D.C.: National Center for Constitutional Studies, 1981), pp. 126–128; Foner, *The Story of American Freedom*, pp. 19–22; Gordon S. Wood, *The Radicalism of the American Revolution* (New York: Alfred A. Knopf, 1992), pp. 232–235; and Drew McCoy, *The Elusive Republic: Political Economy in Jeffersonian America* (Chapel Hill: University of North Carolina Press, 1980), pp. 64–69. For James Madison, see Saul K. Padover, *The Complete Madison: His Basic Writings* (New York: Harper and Brothers, 1973), p. 324. For Madison and Washington, as well as Jefferson and Mason, in their understanding of liberty in both economic and political terms and the relevance of independence, see Bruce A. Ragsdale, *A Planters' Republic* (New York: Rowman and Littlefield, 1996). For Benjamin Franklin's thinking regarding economic independence and freedom, see McCoy, *The Elusive Republic* pp. 46–68; Skousen, *The Five Thousand Year Leap*, pp. 126–128; and Pittman, "George Mason," p. 925.

7. For Jefferson's likely original draft of the Declaration of Independence, see Julian R. Boyd, *The Declaration of Independence: The Evolution of the Text as Shown in Facsimiles of Various Drafts by Its Author, Thomas Jefferson* (Princeton: Princeton University Press, 1945), pp. 19–21.

8. Pauline Maier, *American Scripture: Making the Declaration of Independence* (New York: Alfred A. Knopf, 1987), pp. 133–136.

9. It is clear that during the years surrounding the writing of the Declaration of Independence, Thomas Jefferson hoped the nation would someday abolish slavery. In 1774 he wrote: "The abolition of domestic slavery is the great object of desire in those colonies where it was unhappily introduced in their infant state." From the mid-1770s onward he advanced a plan of gradual emancipation whereby any person born into slavery after a defined date (December 31, 1800, in one version) would be declared free. In his draft of the Virginia Constitution, in 1776, he proposed: "No person hereafter coming into this country shall be held within the same in slavery under any pretext whatever." In 1778 he authored a bill prohibiting the importation of slaves to Virginia (it did not pass). In *Notes on the State of Virginia*, in 1781, he wrote about a law regulating slavery adopted in Virginia: "This will in some measure stop the increase of this great political and moral evil, while the minds of our citizens may be ripening for a complete emancipation of human nature." See Julian R. Boyd, ed., *The Papers of Thomas Jefferson*, 21 vols. (Princeton: Princeton University Press, 1950–1984), 1: 130, 363; 2: 87; 6: 298. It is indeed difficult to reconcile Jefferson's numerous attempts to limit and end the practice of slavery in his home state of Virginia with his own ownership of hundreds of slaves throughout his life, even at death failing to free them. It is among the greatest ironies in American history.

10. Smith quoted in Foner, *The Story of American Freedom*, p. 10; Webster quoted in ibid., pp. 19–20. On Washington, see "George Washington and Micah's Vine and Fig Tree Vision," vftonline.org/VFTINC/history/Washington.htm (accessed November 20, 2012); and Daniel L. Dreisbach, "The 'Vine and Fig Tree' in George Washington's Letters," www.questia.com/library/IP3-1336846211/the-vine-and-fig-tree-in-george-washington-s-letters (accessed November 20, 2012).

11. Adam Smith, *Wealth of Nations* (New York: Modern Library, 1937), bk. 1, chap. 8, p. 79.

12. Kenneth Shank, a security analyst for the Northern Trust Company in Chicago, served briefly in a line job at a McDonald's in order to learn about innovations taking place there. Describing his experience, he said: "This is stressful. The work's much harder than sitting and thinking about things in my office." Quoted in Dave Carpenter, "Stock Analysts Get inside McDonald's," *Arizona Daily Star*, September 30, 1999, p. B4.

13. Letter from Jefferson to Madison, October 28, 1785, quoted in Jennifer Nedelsky, *Private Property and the Limits of American Constitutionalism: The Madisonian Framework and Its Legacy* (Chicago: University of Chicago Press, 1990), p. 33.

14. Fifty acres was within the range of acreage typical for farms of the day (see Allan Kalikoff, *The Agrarian Origins of American Capitalism* [Charlottesville: University Press of Virginia, 1992], p. 46). For a description of life on a fifty-acre farm during the second half of the eighteenth century, see Daniel Vickers, "Competency and Competition: Economic Culture in Early America," *William and Mary Quarterly*, 47 (January 1990), 3–12. From diaries, Vickers shows that through a fifty-acre farm, along with commercial exchange that the farm made possible, a family was able, among other things, to build and support a new house with nine rooms, twenty-four windows, and six fireplaces.

15. Thomas Jefferson, "First Inaugural Address," March 4, 1801, in *A Compilation of Messages and Papers of the Presidents*, vol. 1 (New York: Bureau of National Literature, 1897), p. 323; Jefferson quote in John F. Manley, "American Liberalism and the Democratic Dream: Transcending the American Dream," *Policy Studies Review*, 10 (Fall 1990), 96.

16. Quoted in Foner, *The Story of American Freedom*, p. 102.

17. Quoted in David Leonhardt, "A Free-Market-Loving, Big-Spending, Fiscally Conservative, Wealth Redistributionist Barack Obama," *New York Times*, August 24, 2008, p. 54.

18. N. Gregory Mankiw, "How to Break Bread with Republicans," *New York Times*, January 2, 2011, Sunday Business, p. 6.

19. For Jefferson's view regarding a living standard customary to the day, well above subsistence, following from his proposal to grant individuals fifty acres of public land, see page 37 and note 14 of this chapter. James Madison, as well, spoke of bringing individuals up to a threshold of modest comfort. For Madison's view, see Jennifer Nedelsky, *Private Property and the Limits of American Constitutionalism: The Madisonian Framework and Its Legacy* (Chicago: University of Chicago Press, 1990), p. 33. In Chapter 1, note 1, I show that a living wage as used in this book also adheres to measuring a modest and frugal minimum living in terms customary to the day.

20. Franklin Roosevelt, "State of the Union Address," January 11, 1944, in "The America Presidency Project," at www.presidency.ucsb.edu/ws/index .php?pid=16518; idem, "Inaugural Address," January 20, 1937, ibid., at pid=15349 (both accessed on January 22, 2012).

21. For the relationship between the minimum wage and a living wage, see John E. Schwarz, *Illusions of Opportunity: The American Dream in Question* (New York: W. W. Norton, 1997), p. 68, table 2. For the progress of average Americans from 1947 to the 1970s versus thereafter, see Robert B. Reich, "The Limping

Middle Class," *New York Times*, Sunday Review, September 3, 2011. Income for each 20 percent of the public approximately doubled, or did slightly better, from 1947 to the 1970s.

22. Friedman and Friedman, *Free to Choose*.

23. For some entrepreneurs' ways of making this same point, see Chapter 3, note 28.

24. Jefferson's original draft of the Declaration said: ". . . that all men are created equal and independent, and from that equal creation they derive rights inherent and inalienable . . ." The final Declaration said: ". . . that all men are created equal, that they are endowed by their Creator with certain unalienable Rights . . ."

25. Nozick, *Anarchy, State and Utopia*, p. 331; and Hayek, *The Constitution of Liberty*, p. 137. As Hayek said earlier in *The Road to Serfdom*, freedom is "The recognition of [the individual's] own views and tastes as supreme in his own sphere, however narrowly that may be circumscribed." All that must be on offer is "the minimum of food, shelter, and clothing, sufficient to preserve health and the capacity to work." See F. A. Hayek, *The Road Serfdom: Text and Documents, The Definitive Edition*, ed. Bruce Caldwell (Chicago: University of Chicago Press, 2007), pp. 68, 148.

William J. Voegeli, *Never Enough: America's Limitless Welfare State* (City Encounter Books, 2011); and Stephen F. Hayward, "Modernizing Conservatism," *Breakthrough*, Fall 2011, argue that conservatism must accept the welfare state at some level, not continue to reject it philosophically; but they give only politically pragmatic reasons for doing so rather than principled reasons, let alone principled reasons that follow from individualistic freedom and free-market conservatism.

26. Friedman, *Capitalism and Freedom*, p. 191. A more general discussion of market failures is found in Chapter 4.

## CHAPTER 3
## THE ECONOMY

1. Regarding the need for a basic retirement as related to an individual's ability to retain a condition of independence, see pages 181–184. Regarding access to standard health care, surely such access would be included within the meaning of the minimally decent standard of living in terms customary to the day that

independence involves. The need for societal collaboration to assure affordable access to standard health care is considered on pages 92–104.

2. Regarding measurement of a living wage, see Chapter 1, note 1.

3. See Chapter 1, note 1. For evidence on full-time workers and continuous years beneath a living wage, see John E. Schwarz, *Illusions of Opportunity: The American Dream in Question* (New York: W. W. Norton, 1997), pp. 76–77. For evidence regarding the comparatively low levels of intergenerational economic mobility in the United States relative to other industrial nations, see Isabel V. Sawhill, Scott Winship, and Kerry Searle Grannis, "Pathways to the Middle Class: Balancing Personal and Public Responsibilities," Brookings Institution, Social Genome Project Research, no. 47, September 20, 2012; Miles Corak, "Do Poor Children Become Poor Adults? Lessons from a Cross Country Study of Intergenerational Mobility," Institute for the Study of Labor (Bonn), Discussion Paper No. 1993, 2006; and Markus Jantti et al., "Economic Inequality through the Prisms of Income and Consumption," *Monthly Labor Review*, April 2005.

4. For 2007 and 2008, for example, see U.S. Department of Commerce, *Statistical Abstract of the United States*, 2011–2012 (New York: Skyhorse Publishing, 2011), p. 435, table 666, for GDP; p. 443, table 677, for compensation. According to the estimates of Nobel laureate economist Gary Becker, human capital involving the education, information, skills, and ideas of workers, relative to capital factors such as factories and machinery, accounts for more than 70 percent of the productive capital of today's economy. See Gary Becker, "The Age of Human Capital," in *Education in the Twenty-first Century*, ed. Edward P. Lazear (Stanford, Calif.: Hoover Institution Press, 2001), p. 3. At the turn of the millennium and for the prior half-century in manufacturing, the productivity of workers far exceeded the productivity growth attributable to capital and other factors. See U.S. Bureau of Labor Statistics, "Multifactor Productivity Trends in Manufacturing, 2000," August 29, 2002, table 1, www.bls.gov/mfp (accessed October 26, 2011).

5. For comparison of the two periods, see Robert B. Reich, "The Limping Middle Class," *New York Times*, Sunday Review, September 3, 2011, graphs titled "The Great Prosperity" and "The Great Regression."

6. Lawrence Mishel, Jared Bernstein and Heidi Shierholz, *The State of Working America, 2008–2009* (Ithaca, N.Y.: Cornell University Press, 2009), p. 140, table 3.8, shows that 30.5 percent of employed workers in 1989 earned less than $11.25 per hour (in 2012 dollars by my calculation; $6.10 per hour in 1989 dollars). An additional 6 percent of workers were unemployed in 1989. For the

growth of compensation relative to productivity increases in the 1980s, see ibid., p. 161, fig. 30.

7. Schwarz, *Illusions of Opportunity*, p. 76.

8. Mishel Bernstein, and Shierholz, *The State of Working America*, p. 161, fig. 30. The data are for the nonfarm sector and those who are not self-employed. Another analysis by Mishel for the entire economy, including the farm sector and the self-employed, found a slightly lower average hourly compensation increase of about 41 percent between 1973 and 2007. See Lawrence Mishel, "The Wedges between Productivity and Median Compensation Growth," Economic Policy Institute, Issue Brief No. 330, April 26, 2012, fig. B.

9. Natasha Singer, "A Rich Game of Thrones," *New York Times*, Sunday Business, April 8, 2012, p. 4. For prior years, see Mishel, Bernstein, and Shierholz, *The State of Working America*, p. 221. fig. 3A–E.

10. Mishel, Bernstein, and Shierholz, *The State of Working America*, p. 146, table 3.10.

11. James B. Stewart, "Rewarding C.E.O.s Who Fail," *New York Times*, October 1, 2011, pp. B1–2.

12. Again, the analysis here refers to all workers in the nonfarm sector who are employed, not to the self-employed.

13. Claudia Golden and Lawrence F. Katz, *The Race between Education and Technology* (Cambridge, Mass.: Belknap Press of Harvard University Press, 2010).

14. See Mishel, Bernstein, and Shierholz, *The State of Working Amercia*, p. 163, table 3.15, for wage-level changes by education from 1973 to 2007.

15. Edward H. Crane and David Boaz, *Cato Handbook for Congress*, 1995 (Washington, D.C.: Cato Institute, 1995), chap. 1, p. 6.

16. Quoted in Kevin Sack, "Republicans Rise to Power, with Enmity for Health Law," *New York Times*, November 19, 2010, p. A19.

17. Top federal tax rates on income were 72 percent in 1970 and 35 percent in 2012.

18. See David Brooks, "The Wonky Liberal," *New York Times*, December 6, 2011, p. A23; and Charles Babington, "G.O.P. Proposals' Viability Disputed," *Arizona Daily Star*, October 31, 2011, p. A16.

19. See Brooks, "The Wonky Liberal"; and the results in the National Federation of Independent Business, "Small Business Economic Trends," June 20, at www .nfib.com/research-foundation/small-business-economic-trends-sbet-archive (accessed January 22, 2012)

20. See Kevin G. Hall, "Regulations, Taxes Aren't Killing Small Business, Owners Say," September 1, 2011, www.mcclatchydc.com/2011/09/01/122865/regulations-taxes-arent-killing.html (accessed January 20, 2012).

21. Quoted from an interview of Nick Hanauer by Lawrence O'Donnell and accompanying video on *The Last Word*, MSNBC, May 17, 2012.

22. Mishel, Bernstein, and Shierholz, *The State of Working America*, pp. 92–93, tables 1.21 and 1.22, shows trends in work hours and family income for 1979–2000 for married couples aged 25–54 with children.

23. For household debt in the United States from 1990 to 2008, see U.S. Department of Commerce, *Statistical Abstract of the United States, 2011–2012*, p. 470, table 721.

24. Regarding the amount of consumer demand pulled out of the economy as a result of the disparity in compensation, the Bureau of Labor Statistics' *Consumer Expenditure Survey*, September 2011, table 2301, shows that household units with more than $150,000 in income annually, averaging $240,000 per year, spend about 55 percent of their aftertax income on consumer items, including housing, as opposed to savings, called "implied savings" in the report. Households with a median income (calculated at about $55,000 per year) spend an estimated 85–90 percent of their incomes on consumer items and 10–15 percent on savings. That is, the difference between the household units in spending on consumer items is approximately 33 percent of income. By 2007 the amount required to finance the disparate raises in compensation to the top 10 percent was $1.2 trillion. Thirty-three percent of that was $400 billion in lower consumer demand in 2007, and nearly $500 billion with a multiplier factored in. The figure for lower consumer demand would be still greater (as much as $900 billion) if it were calculated on the basis of marginal dollars, that is, on how the last dollars were expended, rather than on overall dollars. In line with the difference in spending between low- and high-income households, Mark Zandi, chief economist for Moody's Analytics and economic advisor to Republican presidential candidate John McCain, found that increased federal spending and tax breaks when focused on higher-income Americans has about one-fifth the economic impact that increased federal spending and tax breaks do when focused on lower-income Americans. See Mark Zandi, "Perspectives on the Economy," testimony before the House of Representatives Budget Committee, July 1, 2010, p. 6, table titled "Fiscal Stimulus Bang for the Buck."

Say's law in economics—from the French economist J. B. Say (1767–1832)—argues that production or supply creates its own demand. Adam Smith held a similar view. Because economics dealt with a world of scarcity, it was a basic rule of classical economics that a deficit of demand for the supply produced by competitive enterprises could not exist. Supply-side economics has this same presumption today. It is clear, however, that production or supply will not create its own consumer demand if disparities in compensation continuously reduce the proportion of total income spent on consumer demand. In that situation, the only way to replace the lessened consumer demand by way of the private market, other than through continuously rising debt, is through increased investment demand—yet, demand from investment cannot be expected to increase by much in a private market, if at all, and certainly not by enough, when consumption demand is itself diminishing.

Much of the income that high-income households do not spend on consumption goods and services presumably is either invested or kept on the sidelines for investment. Even for the part that is invested, however, an economy with low consumer demand relative to its production may not be as attractive a place for investors as would investments in other economies elsewhere around the world, or in tax havens in Switzerland or the Cayman Islands, or in art masterpieces expected to increase in value, or in manipulative financial instruments, or in the actual relocation of American industries.

25. For productivity increases and pay for the average worker after 2000, see Mishel, Bernstein, and Shierholz, *The State of Working America*, p. 134, table 3.5, and p. 161, fig.30. On family income after 2000, see ibid., p. 62, table 1.8.

26. Survey results and commentary in National Federation of Independent Business, *Economic Trends*, June 2011.

27. Quoted in Steven Greenhouse and Reed Abelson, "The Cost of Change: Small Employers Weigh Impact of Providing Health Insurance," *New York Times*, Business Day, December 1, 2012, p. B3.

28. Nick Hanauer former board member of Amazon.com, in the MSNBC interview with Lawrence O'Donnell, May 16, 2012, described it this way: "Hiring more people is a course of last resort for capitalists, what we do if and only if rising demand requires it. The measure of the quality of a business, how profitable it is, is largely the difference between how few workers we hire per unit of sales versus our competitors. The fewer jobs I create per unit of sales, the more profitable I become." See also the observation of former commercial banker and later columnist Colbert I. King: "True, a majority of Americans work in the private sector. But General Motors, Food Giant, the TV networks and others don't exist to employ Americans. General Motors sells cars, Food Giant sells food and the networks sell entertainment to make a profit for their owners and investors. Without question, a payroll is a necessary ingredient in building and selling

vehicles, groceries, and entertainment. But owners, regardless of industries, are obligated to cut costs. The fewer workers they employ, the better." Colbert I. King, "Romney Runs from His Talent—Generating Profits," *Arizona Daily Star*, June 10, 2012, p. A14.

29. Andrew G. Berg and Jonathan D. Ostry, "Equality and Efficiency," in International Monetary Fund, *Finance and Development*, September 2011, p. 14. See also Joseph E. Stiglitz, *The Price of Inequality: How Today's Divided Society Endangers Our Future* (New York: W. W. Norton, 2012).

30. For a similar conclusion, see David Madland, "Growth and the Middle Class," *Democracy: A Journal of Ideas*, Spring 2011.

31. See note 24, above. For a supporting argument in reply to objections from classical and supply-side economists, see the penultimate paragraph of note 24.

32. Data and sources concluding that the economy was losing $500 billion or more in demand yearly are found in note 24, above.

33. See Arthur M. Okun, *Equality and Efficiency: The Big Tradeoff* (Washington D.C.: Brookings Institution, 1975).

34. Richard Wilkinson and Kate Pickett, *The Spirit Level: Why Equality Is Better for Everyone* (London: Penguin, 2010). Further evidence on the relationship between downward wage trends and violent crime can be found in Eric D. Gould, Bruce A. Weinberg, and David B. Mustard, "Crime Rates and Local Labor Market Opportunities in the United States, 1979–1997," *Review of Economics and Statistics*, 84 (February 2000); and "Higher Youth Wages Mean Lower Crime Rates," National Bureau of Economic Research, at www.nber.org/digest/nov97/w5983.html (accessed January 7, 2013).

35. W. Bradford Wilcox, "When Marriage Disappears: The New Middle America," Institute for American Values, State of Our Nation Project, Charlottesville, Va., December 2010, pp. 13–62.

## CHAPTER 4
## COLLECTIVE ACTION
## VERSUS INDIVIDUAL FREEDOM

1. Roy P. Basler, ed., *The Collected Works of Abraham Lincoln*, vol. 2 (New Brunswick, N.J.: Rutgers University Press, 1953), pp. 220–221. A similar argument is made in *Federalist No. 23*, by Alexander Hamilton, "The Necessity of a Government as Energetic as the One Proposed to the Preservation of the Union."

2. Milton Friedman, *Capitalism and Freedom* (Chicago: University of Chicago Press, 1962), p. 2.

3. Importantly, too, the provision of education is required to enable individuals to join in and be effective members of the civic community.

4. Ezekiel J. Emanuel, "Spending More Doesn't Make Us Healthier," *New York Times*, Sunday Review, October 30, 2011, p. 5.

5. "The Money Traps in U.S. Health Care," *New York Times*, Sunday Review, January 21, 2012, p. 12.

6. Ibid.

7. Simon Johnson and James Kwak, *The White House Burning: The Founding Fathers, Our National Debt, and Why It Matters to You* (New York: Pantheon, 2012), p. 177.

8. Tara Parker-Pope, "Overtreatment Is Taking Harmful Toll," *New York Times*, "Science Times," August 28, 2012, p. 1.

9. Quoted in Kevin Sack, "Judges Weigh Limits of Health Law's Powers," *New York Times*, June 8, 2011.

10. Quoted in Kendra Marr, "Newt Gingrich Walks Back Health Care Mandate Support," Politico.com, May 16, 2011, www.politico.com/news/stories/0511/55051.html (accessed August 29, 2012).

11. Mitt Romney, "Health Care for Everyone? We Found a Way." *Wall Street Journal*, April 16, 2006, http://online.wsj.com/article/SB114472206077422547.html (accessed August 29, 2012).

12. In the case involving the Affordable Care Act, the majority opinion concluded: "Allowing Congress to justify federal regulation by pointing to the effect of inaction on commerce would bring countless decisions an individual could potentially make within the scope of federal regulation and—under the government's theory—empower Congress to make those decisions for him . . . Everyone will likely participate in the markets for food, clothing, transportation, shelter or energy; that does not authorize Congress to direct them to purchase particular products in those or other markets today. The commerce clause is not a general license to regulate an individual from cradle to grave, simply because he will predictably engage in particular transactions . . . Under the government's theory, Congress could address the diet problem by ordering everyone to buy vegetables. That is not the country the framers of our Constitution envisioned." Quoted in "It Is Not Our Role to Forbid It, or to Pass upon Its Wisdom: From the Majority Opinion," *New York Times*, June 29, 2012, p. A15; and James B. Stewart, "In Obama's Victory, a Loss for Congress," *New York Times*, June 30, 2012, p. B1.

13. *National Federation of Independent Business v. Sebelius,* 567 U.S.—(2012), Syllabus, p.3.

14. Paul Krugman, "Medicaid on the Ballot," *New York Times,* October 29, 2012, p. A27.

15. A wide array of examples within the United States and globally is cited in Paul Krugman, "The Medicare Killers," *New York Times,* August 30, 2012, www.nytimes.com/2012/08/31/opinion/Krugman.html (accessed September 10, 2012).

16. Stuart A. Ludsin et al., "Life after Death in Lake Erie," in Ecological Society of America, *Ecological Applications,* June 2001, pp. 731–746. Comparisons of lung cancer to the effects of air pollution and smoking cigarettes are found in Bertram W. Carnow, "The Urban Factor and Lung Cancer: Cigarette Smoking or Air Pollution," *Environmental Health Perspective,* 22 (February 1978), 17–21. Having been the poster child for ecosystem recovery, now fifty years later Lake Erie is again under threat from agricultural pollution.

17. Quoted in U.S. Department of Health and Human Services, *Prevention Report,* 16, no. 3 (2002), 1.

18. For the period up to 1980, see U.S. Environmental Protection Agency, *Trends in the Quality of the Nation's Air* (Washington, D.C.: U.S. Government Printing Office, 1980), pp. 5–12; Council on Environmental Quality, *Environmental Quality, 1981* (Washington, D.C.: U.S. Government Printing Office, 1982), pp. 244–245; and Lester B. Lave and Gilbert S. Omenn, *Cleaning the Air: Reforming the Clean Air Act* (Washington, D.C.: Brookings Institution, 1981), p. 21.

19. Very few respected scientists remain skeptics about global warming as a phenomenon. Recently, when he was a skeptic, Richard Muller, a physicist at the University of California at Berkeley, led an extensive study to examine and correct for weaknesses in prior measures of temperature change, and thus thoroughly test climate change from a skeptic's perspective. Muller and his research team found that climate change exists even according to the corrected measures. Richard Muller, "The Conversion of a Climate-Change Skeptic," *New York Times,* July 30, 2012, p.A17; and idem, "The Case against Global-Warming Skepticism," *Wall Street Journal,* October 21, 2011, http://online.wsj.com/article/SB1000142 4052970204422404576594972796327348.html (accessed October 30, 2011).

20. Rick Perry quoted in "Where the Republican Candidates Stand on Key Issues," *New York Times,* December 31, 2011, p. A1.

21. Gingrich quoted in ibid.

22. The Battelle Memorial Institute estimates that the Human Genome Project

has helped generate nearly $800 billion in economic activity. Neal F. Lane, "Science Is the Key to Growth," *New York Times*, October 29, 2012, p. A27.

23. Richard R. Nelson, *High Technology Policies: A Five Nation Comparison* (Washington, D.C.: American Enterprise Institute, 1984), p. 43.

24. Adam Davidson, "When the Idea Machine Stops," *New York Times Magazine,* June 1, 2012, p. 12.

25. The government might, however, mandate insurance companies to charge higher health-insurance premiums connected to specified health-related characteristics, strictly in line with their true actuarial costs, as long as the characteristics are physically controllable, such as smoking, physical activity, and, in many cases, weight.

## CHAPTER 5
## RULES FOR GOVERNMENT

*First epigraph:* Attributed to Thomas Jefferson, *The Jefferson Monticello*, at www .monticello.org/site/jefferson/government-best-which-governs-least-quotation (accessed January 26, 2012).

1. The Founders' generation likewise both instituted a national bank and implemented the Louisiana Purchase.

2. James Madison, *Federalist No. 10*, November 22, 1787, at www.constitution .org/fed/federa10.htm (accessed March 8, 2012).

3. Quoted in Anna Fifield, "Obama Declares War on Mouse Pads," *Financial Times*, November 12–13, 2011, p. 7.

4. Quoted in Harlene Cooper, "The Biden Assignment," *New York Times*, September 15, 2011, p. A22.

5. Brian Friel, "Where Will the G.O.P. Go Digging?" *New York Times*, November 14, 2010, p. 9.

6. At present, cost/benefit analyses are carried out for most programs and regulations and presumably would continue. Such analyses generally focus, however, on determining whether the measured benefits from the program or regulation exceed the measured costs of operating the program or regulation, not on whether the program or regulation is being carried out at the lowest practicable cost. They also generally assume the level of restrictiveness involved in a program or regulation rather than looking into whether there are reasonable ways to achieve the same ends through less restrictive means.

7. Quoted in Eric Lipton, "Support Is Mutual for Senator and Makers of Nutritional Supplements," *New York Times*, June 21, 2011, p. A18.

8. Robert Dreyfuss, "Grover Norquist: 'Field Marshal' of the Bush Plan," *The Nation*, April 26, 2001, www.thenation.com/article/grover-norquist-field-marshal-bush-plan (accessed November 20, 2011).

9. Thomas E. Mann and Norman J. Ornstein, *It's Even Worse than It Looks: How the American Constitutional System Collided with the New Politics of Extremism* (New York: Basic Books, 2012), p. 118.

10. Quoted at The Jacobs Report, www.vernonjacobs.com/tax-questions.htm (accessed November 20, 2011). Judge Hand's statement is quoted by scores of tax preparers and tax opponents.

11. Jason Brennon, *The Ethics of Voting* (Princeton: Princeton University Press, 2011).

12. Quoted in Eric Foner, *The Story of American Freedom* (New York: W. W. Norton, 1998), p. 8.

13. Quoted in University of Chicago, *The Founders Constitution*, vol. 1, chap. 13, doc. 36, at http://press-pubs.uchicago.edu/founders/documents/v1ch13s36.html (accessed May 20, 2012); and W. Cleon Skousen, *The 5,000 Year Leap* (Washington, D.C.: National Center for Constitutional Studies, 1981), p. 54.

14. Quoted in Drew McCoy, *The Elusive Republic: Political Economy in Jeffersonian America* (Chapel Hill: University of North Carolina Press, 1980), p. 69.

15. Foner, *The Story of American Freedom*, p. 8.

16. Lipton, "Support Is Mutual."

17. Ibid.

18. Michael Kinsley, "Election Day," *New York Times Book Review*, November 5, 2006, pp. 13, 14.

19. Alexandri Petri, "After Jon Kyl, This Is Not Intended to Be Factual Statement," *Washington Post*, April 12, 2011, at www.washingtonpost.com/blogs/compost/post/after-jon-kyl-this-is-not-intended-to-be-a-factual-statement/2011/03/03/AFltUdSD_blog.html (accessed January 22, 2012).

20. Glenn Kessler, "The Truth? C'mon This Is a Political Convention," *Washington Post*, August 31, 2012, at www.washingtonpost.com.blogs/fact-checker/post/the-truth-cmon-this-is-a-political-convention/2012/08/31/88550120-f3c0-11e1-892d-bc92fee603a7_t (accessed September 5, 2012). Kessler characterized falsehoods as "par for the course."

21. Frank Rich, "Fantasyland: Denial Has Poisoned the G.O.P. and Threatens the Rest of the Country, Too," *Huffington Post*, November 9, 2012, www.huffingtonpost.com (accessed November 9, 2012).

22. Gordon Wood, *The Radicalism of the American Revolution* (New York: Alfred A. Knopf, 1992), p. 233.

23. *Reynolds v. Sims*, 377 U.S. 533 (1964) at 556, 567, 562, and 560.

24. Stephen Ansolabehere, Alan Gerber and James M. Snyder Jr., "Equal Votes, Equal Money: Court-ordered Redistricting and Public Expenditures in the American States," *American Political Science Review*, 96 (December 2002), 767–777.

25. Thomas Jefferson, "Public Revenue and Expenses," *Notes on the State of Virginia* query 22, at etext.virginia.edu/toc/modeng/public/jefVirg.html (accessed April 6, 2012). The importance that Jefferson, Madison, and other Founders ascribed to "disinterestedness" in public officials, and to its relationship to ownership of landed property, is recounted in Gordon Wood, "Interests and Disinterestedness in the Making of the Constitution," in *Beyond Confederation: Origins of the Constitution and American National Identity*, ed. Richard Beeman et al. (Chapel Hill: University of North Carolina Press, 1987), pp. 69–93. Wood concludes (p. 91): "These values, this need for disinterestedness in public officials, were very much on the minds of the founding fathers at the Philadelphia Convention, especially James Madison's."

26. American National Election Studies, *The ANES Guide to Public Opinion and Electoral Behavior*, "Public Officials Don't Care What People Think, 1952–2008," at www.electionstudies.org/nesguide/toptable/tab5b_3.htm.

27. Quoted in John E. Schwarz, *Freedom Reclaimed: Rediscovering the American Vision* (Baltimore: Johns Hopkins University Press, 2005), p. 143.

28. Including super PACs, the Obama side spent considerably less than the Romney side and also received far more in small donations, but still depended greatly upon very large contributors. See Nicolas Confessore, "Result Won't Limit Campaign Money Any More than Ruling Did," *New York Times*, November 11, 2012, www.nytimes.com/2012/11/12/us/politics/a-vote-for-unlimited-campaign-financing.html?pagewanted=all&-r=0 (accessed November 12, 2012).

29. Shaun Breidbart, Letter to the editor, *New York Times*, March 13, 2011, Sunday

30. Quoted in Thomas Friedman, "Did You Hear the One about the Bankers?" *New York Times*, Sunday Review, October 30, 2011, p. 11.

31. Senator Simpson quoted in Richard A. Oppel and Neil A. Lewis, "Campaign Law Set for a Big Test in a Courtroom," *New York Times*, December 3, 2002, p. A29. Newt Gingrich, video appearance on *Jansing and Co.*, MSNBC, January 10, 2012.

32. *McConnell v. Federal Election Commission*, 540 U.S. 93 (2003) at 40.

33. Journalist Nicolas Confessore wrote following the 2012 presidential election: "In virtually every respect, the growth of unlimited fund-raising and the move of outside groups to the mainstream of politics have magnified the already outsize role of money in political campaigns. They have changed how incumbents and challengers alike campaign and raise money, altered how voters experience politics, and expanded the influence of a small group of large donors on the policies and messages espoused by the candidates." "Result Won't Limit Campaign Money Any More than Ruling Did."

## CHAPTER 6
## THE COMMON CREDO

1. The presidential veto, which requires a two-thirds vote by both houses of Congress to override, does not violate the general principle, because the president is in office as a result of an election by the whole public, just as each house of Congress is. By contrast, constant use of the Senate filibuster does violate the principle.
2. An examination of the ancient (communal) and modern (individualist) ways of understanding freedom is found in Alan Ryan, *On Politics* (New York. W. W. Norton, 2012).

## CHAPTER 7
## SOLUTIONS

1. Living costs do differ by region across the nation. However, most Americans residing in locales that differ significantly (by more than 20 percent) from the standard cost-of-living estimate experience substantially higher rather than lower costs of living. They are urban areas such as Boston, New York City, and the major coastal cities in California. Such locations would need to supplement the actions proposed to enable earnings to reach the level of a living income.
2. On a living wage and the proportion of working Americans in jobs paying less, or unemployed, see Chapter 1, note 1, and Chapter 3, pages 56–58.
3. Results from the wide variety of studies on the effects of raising the minimum wage are so mixed as to suggest that it is not clear at all that raising the minimum wage does cause any job loss, and, certainly, it does not *necessarily* cause a loss of jobs. Intervening effects from raising the minimum wage that lead to the main-

tenance of jobs and even the creation of new jobs include reduced employee
turnover (thus relieving employers of the burdensome costs that turnover usually involves) and increases in consumer demand leading to stronger sales. For
a comprehensive review of the results of studies, see Arindrajit Dube, T. William Lester, and Michael Reich, "Minimum Wage Effects across State Borders:
Estimates Using Contiguous Counties," *Review of Economics and Statistics*, 4
(November 2010), 946–948, 961–962.

4. Compensation growth for the top 1 percent has been rising more than for other
groups since 1973, but the trajectory of the disparity shifted sharply higher in
1982–83, leveled off for a few years in the late 1980s and early 1990s, and then
began another surge in the mid-1990s. See Lawrence Mishel, Jared Bernstein,
and Heidi Shierholz, *The State of Working America, 2008–2009* (Washington,
D.C.: Economic Policy Institute, 2009), p. 147, fig. 3H. Tax figures are from the
Tax Foundation, "U.S. Federal Individual Marginal Income Tax Rates History,
1913–2011," at taxfoundation.org/articles/us-federal-income-tax-rates-history-
1913-2011-nominal-and-inflation-adjusted-brackets (accessed March 8, 2012).

5. For tax rates, see Tax Foundation, "Federal Individual Marginal Tax Rates."
For changes in income disparity since 1913, see "Two French Economists Say
the Richest Ought to Pay More than the Buffett Rule, "*New York Times*, April
17, 2012, chart titled "Income Earned by the Wealthiest," at www.nytimes
.com/2012/04/17/business/for-economists-saez-and-piketty-the-buffett-rule-is-
just-a-start.html?pagewanted=all (accessed April 19, 2012).

6. The close inverse relationship between steep changes in the tax rates and
income inequality in the United States from 1913 to 2008 is described in Liam
C. Malloy and John Case, "What Would Pigou Do?" *American Prospect*, November 2012, pp. 88–92.

7. Bruce Western and Jake Rosenfeld, "Unions, Norms, and the Rise in U.S.
Wage Inequality," *American Sociological Review*, 76 (August 2011).

8. Richard B. Freeman, "Do Workers Still Want Unions? More than Ever," Economic Policy Institute Briefing Paper No. 182, February 22, 2007.

9. For an analysis of the impact of high-value-added teachers on students, see Raj
Chetty, John N. Friedman, and Jonah E. Rockoff, "The Long-Term Impacts of
Teachers: Teacher Value-Added and Student Outcomes in Adulthood," National
Bureau of Economic Research, Working Paper No. 17699, December 2011.

10. The figures for needed jobs are based on the need for jobs given 14.3 million
American workers who were either unemployed or discouraged as of September
2012 to reduce unemployment to 4.5 percent.

11. For the $500 billion figure, see Chapter 3, note 24. Based on last dollars

households spend, a total approaching $1 trillion is likely more accurate. I am working with the *smallest* figure possible, not what is likely the most accurate figure.

12. In 2007, the year before the recession, total consumption expenditures (including government consumption expenditures) of $12.5 trillion supported 146 million jobs, requiring approximately $86,000 in consumer demand per job. Divided by $86,000 per job, the $500 billion in increased consumer demand per year should support just under 6 million continuing jobs.

13. Quoted in Jennifer Nedelsky, *Private Property and the Limits of American Constitutionalism: The Madisonian Framework and Its Legacy* (Chicago: University of Chicago Press, 1990), p. 33, emphasis added.

14. For the first Madison quote, see ibid., p. 45; for the second quote, see Philip R. Fendell, ed., *Letters and Other Writings of James Madison*, vol. 3 (Philadelphia: Lippincott, 1865), p. 162.

15. Cato's Letter, Number 3, Thomas Gordon, "The Pestilent Conduct of South-Sea Directors, with the Reasonable Prospect of Publick Justice," November 19, 1720, at classicliberal.tripod.com/cato/letter003.html (accessed April 5, 2012).

16. As a result, any incentive those persons with top compensations might have to move out of the country will be considerably moderated since they will face higher rates of tax on much of their other income in many foreign locations than they do here, not to mention that the Eisenhower tax rate itself is intended to be and hopefully will be very temporary.

17. Quoted in Annie Lowrey and Michael Cooper, "Romney's Anxiety over 'Takers' Conflicts with Longtime G.O.P. Stands," *New York Times*, September 19, 2012, p. A16.

18. Letters quoted from Mark Greif, "Dear Bankers: Thanks for Wrecking Our Lives," *New York Times*, Sunday Review, September 16, 2012, p. 6.

19. On the basis of today's minimum wage and Social Security tax, a worker who has been paid the minimum wage while employed full-time over a period of forty years would receive a Social Security benefit of approximately $10,000 annually in real dollars for a lifetime. That worker would have paid in enough to support a lifetime annuity of that amount based upon the contributions themselves (including from employers) during a forty-year work career and a return on the contributions averaging a real 2 percent per year over the period. The worker, of course, should have been earning a living wage, not the minimum wage, and be receiving an annuity and return justified by a living wage.

20. Simon Johnson and James Kwak, *White House Burning: The Founding*

*Fathers, Our National Debt, and Why It Matters to You* (New York: Pantheon, 2012), pp. 15–27.

21. The additional actions include adjusting the Earned Income Tax Credit and housing tax deductions, creating public jobs, investing both in pre-K–12 and college education as well as basic research, expanding job training, improving the infrastructure, and raising Social Security benefits at the bottom end. There would also be enough funds to bolster other programs identified as underfunded in this and earlier chapters, including legal aid, the National Labor Relations Board, the Food and Drug Administration, the Internal Revenue Service, and assistance to those who are physically or mentally incapable of employment. Finally, the figure takes into account the reduced tax revenue resulting from the broader distribution of compensation gains and a shift to households in lower tax brackets.

22. Tara Parker-Pope, "Overtreatment Is Taking a Harmful Toll," *New York Times*, Science Times, August 28, 2012, p. 1.

23. Wyden withdrew his support for the plan in 2012, when Ryan reduced the rate at which the subsidies for health insurance would rise, thereby breaching the principles behind the program.

24. Brian Friel, "Where Will the G.O.P. Go Digging?" *New York Times*, November 4, 2010, p. 9.

25. A Congressional Budget Office estimate in early 2013, in fact, found that the reduction in medical inflation since 2010, if it lasts, is enough to shave $500 billion from Medicare spending over the period to 2020, by itself. See Sarah Kliff, "Graph of the Day," February 20, 2013, at www.washington post.com/wonkblog (accessed February 22, 2013).

26. Averaging just $5,000 yearly in federal income and Social Security taxes (including employers' contributions), an additional 8 million employed as a result of the policies outlined on pages 167–177 alone, would generate nearly $500 billion in revenues over a decade, including the multiplier effects from their spending.

27. Adam Davidson, Jacob Goldstein, Catlin Kennedy, and Dan Kedmey, "What's the Easiest Way to Cheat on Your Taxes," *New York Times Magazine*, April 8, 2012, p. 17, calculates that $385 billion is lost to the IRS per year from what is actually owed, mostly as a result of underreporting of income.

28. For the percentage of earnings covered by Social Security historically and now, see Johnson and Kwak, *White House Burning*, p. 130.

29. Paul Krugman, "American's Unlevel Field," *New York Times*, January 9, 2012, p. A17.

30. What are called $10K college degrees are accredited four-year degrees that can be earned at a total four-year tuition cost of $10,000 or less. On $10K college degrees, see Thomas K. Lindsay, "Anatomy of a Revolution? The Rise of the $10,000 Bachelor's Degree," Texas Public Policy Foundation, Austin, Texas, September 2012. There may also be ways through the allocation of student loans to penalize higher educational institutions that fail to keep tuition costs under control relative to others and reward institutions that do better relative to others.

31. Helen F. Ladd and Edward B. Fiske, "Class Matters, Why Won't We Admit It?" *New York Times*, December 12, 2011, p. A21. The educational testing gap today in the United States between low-income and affluent students "has grown by about 40 percent since the 1960s, and is now double the testing gap between blacks and whites." By contrast, in the 1950s and 1960s, race was a stronger factor in testing results than family income. See Sabrina Tavernise, "Education Gap Grows between Rich and Poor, Studies Say," *New York Times*, citing the results of research by Stanford University sociologist Sean F. Reardon. Accessed February 11, 2012, at www.nytimes.com/2012/02/10/education/education-gap-grows-between-rich-and-poor-studies-show.html?pagewanted=all.

32. See Chapter 4, note 19.

33. If carbon-capture technologies become economical, for example, that would then allow new coal-fired power plants to comport with emission reductions, helping coal producers to adapt successfully.

34. The reciprocity character of freedom suggests that individuals and industries acting in good faith under a policy in place should be cushioned from damage to some degree or assisted to readjust when circumstances call for a change in policy. That protection would apply to industries producing high-carbon energy supplies during the period when public policies are revised to put a price on carbon emissions. It would apply as well to providing assistance to industries most of whose foreign competitors do not have to abide by such policies.

35. Shi-Ling Hsu, *The Case for the Carbon Tax* (Washington, D.C.: Island Press, 2011); and Yoram Bauman and Shi-Ling Hsu, "The Most Sensible Tax of All," *New York Times*, July 5, 2012, p. A17.

36. To the degree that gerrymandering in a nation, state, or city ends up electing a solid majority of representatives by a minority of voters, it is also noteworthy that gerrymandering violates the basic precept of freedom that majority rule should be the norm, while doing so for no good reason that benefits freedom. Other actions that can help temper partisanship are found in Thomas Mann

and Norman Ornstein, *It's Even Worse Than It Looks: How the American Constitutional System Collided With the New Politics of Extremism* (New York: Basic Books, 2012); and the No Labels website, "12 Ways to Make Congress Work," www.nolabels.org.

37. The first quote and Senate results are from Larry Bartels, "Economic Inequality and Political Representation," August 2005, cover page, republished in Lawrence Jacobs and Desmond King, eds., *The Unsustainable State* (Oxford: Oxford University Press, 2009), p. 174. Regarding the undue influence given to large financial donors in Congress, the Supreme Court agreed in 2003 that ample evidence justified such a conclusion, in *McConnell v. Federal Election Commission*, 540 U.S. 93 (2003) at 40. Results from the more comprehensive examination of policy responsiveness to different income groups of Americans and the accompanying quote are contained in Martin Gilens, *Affluence and Influence: Economic Inequality and Political Power in America* (Princeton: Princeton University Press, 2012), chap. 3 and p. 87. Gilens found that policy responsiveness to top-income Americans remained high at all points in time, significantly higher than to other income groups. Policy responsiveness to the other income groups gained strength only during the years of presidential elections; yet even that responsiveness was diluted in the following years as the programs were cut far more sharply than the programs that were adopted in other years.

An important study covering the period 1935–1979 found greater congruence between public opinion and policy. See Benjamin I. Page and Robert Y. Shapiro, "Effects of Public Opinion on Policy," *American Political Science Review*, 77 (March 1983), 175–190.

38. See Chapter 5, note 33.

39. The Court regarded money contributions and expenditures as speech in *Buckley v. Valeo*, 424 U.S. 1 (1976).

40. *McConnell v. Federal Election Commision*, 540 U.S. 93 at 34.

41. See Chapter 1, note 1, for information on the measurement of a living wage, which is currently at just below $12 per hour.

42. The Bureau of the Census now has another supplemental poverty formula that does partly correct the problem with the present measure but remains mostly based on that measure. It comes no more than about one-quarter of the way further toward measuring an actual living income and thus fixing the problem.

43. A measure we have, called "potential GDP," does not address the loss of demand arising from trends in pay inequality. Potential GDP tells us how far GDP falls below the full utilization of resources, but says nothing about how the distribution of compensation affects demand or the effect of that loss of

demand on other economic considerations such as investment, production, and job creation.

CHAPTER 8

**ATTITUDES ABOUT GOVERNMENT**

1. Jeff Zeleny, "Distrust of Government Grows," *New York Times*, October 26, 2011, p. A20.

2. For polling evidence regarding Republican identifiers concerning support for government programs, see Amitai Etzioni, "Gridlock," *Forum*, 14, no. 3 (2011), article 9, 31–33. According to the Pew Research Center, a majority of Republican identifiers supported keeping spending the same amount on or increasing the amount of spending for seventeen of the nineteen program areas that were examined. See "As Sequester Deadline Looms, Little Support for Cutting Most Programs," Pew Research Center, February 22, 2013, at www.people-press .org/2013/02/22/as-sequester-deadline-looms-little-support-for-cutting-most -programs/ (accessed March 4, 2013).

3. Greg Gutfeld, "The O'Reilly Factor," Fox News, November 16, 2012.

4. See Bryan Jones, Frank L. Baumgartner, and James L. True, "Policy Punctuations: U.S. Budget Authority, 1947–1995," *Journal of Politics*, 60 (February 1998), p. 8, fig. 1, and p. 16, table 2.

5. The $16 breakfast muffins, for example, were found to be the cost for the whole breakfast, including rental of the facilities. On $500 hammers, see James Q. Wilson, *Bureaucracy: What Government Agencies Do and Why They Do It* (New York: Basic Books, 1989), pp. 319–320.

6. Dustin Hawkins, "The Business Successes of Mitt Romney and Bain Capital," *US Conservative Politics: News and Issues*, August 28, 2012, part 1, at usconser vatives.about.com (accessed September 19, 2012).

7. Small Business Administration, Advocacy Small Business Statistics and Research, "Frequently Asked Questions," answer to Question 7, from U.S. Bureau of the Census and Bureau of Labor Statistics data, web.sba.gov/faqs/ faqIndexAll.cfm?areaid=24 (accessed December 20, 2012).

8. The material on the museum, products, and estimates of product failure are from Oliver Burkeman, "Happiness Is a Glass Half Empty," *Guardian Weekend*, June 16, 2012, pp. 24–27.

9. Associated Press, "Who's Right in Debate over Federal Workers' Pay?" *Arizona Daily Star*, April 8, 2011, p. A16.

10. Ibid.

11. Justin Falk, "Comparing the Compensation of Federal and Private-Sector Employees," Congressional Budget Office, January 30, 2012.

12. William Finnegan, "The Storm," *New Yorker*, March 5, 2012, p. 34.

13. "While Warning about Fat, U.S. Pushes Cheese Sales," *New York Times*, November 7, 2010, p. A1.

14. Project on Government Oversight, "Bad Business: Billions of Taxpayer Dollars Wasted on Hiring Contractors," September 13, 2011, at www.pogo.org/pogo -files/reports/contract-oversight/bad-business/co-gp-2011913.html (accessed September 19, 2012).

15. Brinton Milward and Keith G. Provan, "Governing the Hollow State," *Journal of Public Administration and Theory*, April 2000, pp. 359–379; George W. Downes and Patrick D. Larkey, *The Search for Government Efficiency* (New York: Random House, 1986), pp. 30–40; Eyal Press and Jennifer Washburn, "Neglect for Sale," *American Prospect*, May 2000, pp. 22–29. The United States Energy Information Administration found that in thirty-two of forty-eight states where both municipal and private electric utilities exist, municipal utilities delivered cheaper residential electricity than did private utilities. See Diane Cardwell, "Power to the People: More Cities Weigh Taking Electricity Business from Private Utilities," *New York Times*, March 14, 2013, p. B4.

16. Derek Bok, *The Trouble with Government* (Cambridge, Mass.: Harvard University Press, 2001), pp. 230–231; Richard W. Stevenson, "Government May Make Private up to 800,000 Jobs," *New York Times*, November 15, 2002, pp. 1, 21.

# ACKNOWLEDGMENTS

I HAVE BENEFITED INVALUABLY throughout the book from the advice and assistance of numerous people from many different fields, spanning political science, economics, philosophy, history, and the law. From within the academy, they are Alberta Charney, Tom Christiano, Chris Freiman, Amy Gutmann, Benjamin Irvin, Jack Marietta, Brinton Milward, Catherine Ruetchlin, David Schmidtz, Deborah Stone, and Gerry Swanson. From outside the academy, they are Rich Benjamin, Clint Bolick, David Callahan, Lew Daly, Phil Lopes, Erica Payne, David Safier, Barbara Warren, and Jim Woodbrey. Longtime friends also gave indispensable help on sections of the book: Joan Kaye Cauthorn, Frank Dobson, Janet Dobson, John Jenkin, Joe Hawkins, David Lasker, and Glenda Wilkes. The contributions of editors were decisive. I especially thank my main editor, Jake Schindel, with whom it has been a privilege and true pleasure to work; my copyeditor, Ann Hawthorne; longtime friend and former editor of mine at W. W. Norton, Roby Harrington; Bob Weil at Liveright; and Linda Cashdan. My name may be on the book's cover as its author, but this was a thoroughly collaborative project in every sense of the word. I am deeply grateful to every one of these individuals, all of whom contributed out of their sheer care for the subject matter of the book and for me. Whatever errors remain are mine alone. Finally, the book is dedicated to my family, both here and gone—to Judi, Maria, Jodi, Kaz, Laurie, Rick, Eli, and the grandchildren, and to my parents and my brother and sister. The book originated from serious concerns that Judi, my late wife, expressed in her last years about the kinds of divisions that were taking place in America. She was more frightened than I had ever seen her before. Following a research stage, I began writing the book as a result of the enthusiasm and near insistence of my present wife, Maria. No words can express how much I owe and how thankful I am for my family.

# INDEX

abortion issue, 130

absent parents, 169

acid rain, 105

Adams, John, 15, 34, 35, 178, 238n
  Massachusetts Declaration of
    Rights composed by, 33
  on virtue, 127

Affordable Care Act (2010), 22, 99,
  169, 187, 247n

agriculture and farm extension programs, 215

Agriculture Department, U.S., 220

airline industry, 109

air pollution, 104–7
  *see also* carbon emissions

Alabama, 136

American Dream, 7, 16, 28, 40, 41,
  56, 76, 151, 229
  as economic model, 207–8, 232

American Lung Association, 104

Ann Arbor, Mich., 218

Apotheker, Leo, 63

Apple, 65

Arizona, 22–23, 130

Articles of Confederation, 120

automated diagnostic systems, 110

autonomy, of individuals, 28–29, 30,
  36–37, 44, 150–51, 161

Bain Capital, 218

bankruptcies, 93, 95, 218, 228

banks, 7, 249n
  failures of, 182–83
  greedy practices of, 13

basic research, 13, 17, 152–53, 177,
  191, 208, 216, 228
  collective action and, 108–11,
    114, 115
  free-giving in, 92

Battelle Memorial Institute, 248n–
  49n

Becker, Gary, 242n

Biden, Joe, 122
blue-collar workers, 3–5, 228–29
BMW, 65
Bowles-Simpson commission, 185
Breidbart, Shaun, 139–40
brewery equipment, 65
bridges, aging, 21
British Columbia, 196
*Buckley v. Valeo*, 141
budget deficits, xii, 13, 17, 83, 95,
    122, 191, 208, 228
  health-care costs in, 185–89
  in policy solutions, 165, 185–90
  reduction of, 21–22
Bureau of Labor Statistics (BLS), 69,
    243n
Bush, George H. W., 216
Bush, George W., 21–22, 39, 74, 79,
    125, 216
  in 2000 election, 48–49, 129–30
businesses, 7, 167, 174, 183, 190,
    207, 228, 229, 232
  failure of, 218
  health-care costs of, 95, 103
  unspent cash accumulation of,
    180

campaign finance, *see* election cam-
    paign finance
Canada, 84, 196
cap-and-trade systems, 106, 107
capital, human, 176, 242n
capital gains, 68, 73, 74, 170, 189
carbon-capture products, 195, 256n
carbon emissions, 90, 105–7, 114,
    208
  in policy solutions, 165–66, 194–96

*see also* global warming
carbon tax, 196
Career Academies, 174
career training, 174, 194
car loans, 71
Cato Institute, 68, 178–79
Cato's Letters, 178–79
center, philosophy of, 17
charitable services, 50, 183
cheese marketing, 220
chief executive officers (CEOs),
    61–64
China, 65
  projected product innovation of,
    111
*Citizens United v. Federal Election
    Commission*, 141, 145
civic equality, 134, 135, 136–37,
    138–40, 142–45, 146, 154,
    200–205, 222
civic involvement, 92, 112, 152, 161
civic virtue, 126–35, 153–54, 158
civil rights, 121
civil rights movement, 43–44
Clairol, 218
climate change, *see* global warming
Clinton, Bill, 39, 55
Clinton, Hillary, 10
collective bargaining, 43, 64, 70, 73,
    75, 152, 173
collective public action, 87–116, 126,
    131, 134, 151–52
  American public support of, 114
  basic research fostered by, 108–
    11, 114, 115
  in Common Credo, 151–52, 154
  controlling environmental pollu-

tion and, 92, 104–7, 114, 115,
194–96, 208, 214, 215, 228
of criminal laws, 111–12
freedom and, 89, 94, 95, 97–104,
106, 107, 111–15
free market as, 89–90
infrastructure and, 91, 113, 115
limits to, 112–13, 115
market failures addressed by, *see*
market failures
in military defense, 22, 91, 113,
114, 115, 129, 152, 184, 213,
215
opponents of, 113–15
police forces and, 11, 91, 114,
115, 152, 176, 213, 215
in preventing wrongful harm,
89–90, 104–7, 112
in providing education, 90, 92,
112, 114, 152, 181, 213, 215,
247*n*
right and left benefited by, 115–16
socialism and, 113
*see also* government
command-and-control regulations,
106
Common Credo, xii–xiii, 15, 56, 78,
79, 86, 113, 116, 147–61, 208,
223, 229–33
advantages of, 230–31
appropriate governmental intervention in, 152–53, 155–56
civic equality in, 154
civic virtue in, 153–54, 158
collective action in, 151–52, 154
decentralized national objectives
in, 19, 153

economic opportunities in, 151–
52, 155, 158–60
foundational premise of, 150, 158,
160, 161, 167
freedom in, 150–51, 161
as fundamental to American thinking, 17–20
goals of, 149–50
individual autonomy with reciprocity in, 150–51
limited government in, 18–19,
150, 151, 153, 155, 197
market failures addressed in, 150,
152–53
policy solutions and, 166, 190,
197, 198
preventing wrongful harm in,
154–55
self-reliance in, 151
ten principles of, 17, 150–55,
158
community centers, 159–60
community colleges, 174, 192, 193
"compassionate" conservatism, 48–49
compensation, *see* wages and salaries
competition, 19, 75, 91, 94, 103–4,
108, 195, 232
global, 7, 60, 64–66, 70, 191,
195–96, 208
computers, 108, 109–10
Confessore, Nicolas, 252*n*
Congress, U.S., 75, 123, 144, 190,
218–19, 222, 252*n*
corruption of, 138–42, 145, 201–
2, 204
debt ceiling debate in, 21, 22–23
favorability rating of, 227

Congress, U.S. (*continued*)
  and federal spending relative to
    GDP, 125
  free-ridership issue and, 100–102
  Homestead Act (1862) of, 37–38
  interstate commerce powers of,
    101–2
  lobbying of, 140, 142
  polarized partisan warfare in, 6,
    20–23, 158, 198–99
  taxation power of, 124–25
  2010 health-care reform bill in,
    22, 187
  2012 transportation bill in, 20–21
  *see also* House of Representatives,
    U.S.; representatives, elected;
    Senate, U.S.
Congressional Budget Office (CBO),
    123, 187, 197–98, 219, 255*n*
"Congress on Your Corner" sessions,
    22
conservatism, xi, xii, 1–23, 44, 80,
    82–83, 129, 170, 197, 233,
    241*n*
  collective action's benefits for,
    115–16
  "compassionate," 48–49
  economic goals of, 38–40
  EITC and, 169
  as failed ideology, 9–13, 228, 230
  foundational principles of, 11–12
  freedom defined by, 11
  free-market economy advocated
    by, 11–13, 231–32
  fundamental dilemmas faced by,
    47–51
  goal of, 149

  government activism supported by,
    213–15
  "greed is good" motto of, 157
  income distribution as viewed by,
    39–40
  limited government in, 121–25
  self-contradictory nature of, 12
  small government model of, 11,
    12–13
Constitution, U.S., 120, 125, 130,
    135, 136, 138, 178, 200, 202
Consumer Financial Protection
    Bureau, 10
consumer safety, 124, 127–28, 214
Continental Congress, Committee of
    Five of, 32, 34
contracts, 90, 126, 151, 213
countercyclical economic conditions,
    153
credit card debt, 71

data- (evidence-)based medicine, 96,
    187–88
Davidson, Adam, 111
debt, 8, 21, 22–23, 83, 153, 185,
    191, 208
  demand based on, 13, 71–72,
    74–75, 77, 78, 79, 80, 81, 157,
    167, 175, 191, 229
  income ratio to, 70, 71
  *see also* budget deficits
Declaration of Independence, 16,
    27–38, 119, 178
  "All men are created equal" in,
    18, 27, 28, 31, 34–35, 46, 230,
    241*n*
  Committee of Five and, 32, 34

"Creator" in, 27, 46–47, 150, 241n

freedom in, 28–31

government in, 119, 120, 121, 125

historical background of, 31–34

ideal conveyed by, 35

Jefferson's original draft of, 27–28, 30, 32, 34, 239n, 241n

meaning of, 34–38

"self-evident truths" in, 27, 46, 150

slavery and, 35

and states' declarations of rights, 32–33, 34

"unalienable rights" in, 27, 31, 241n

defense, national, 22, 91, 113, 114, 115, 129, 152, 184, 213, 215

Defense Department, U.S., 110

demand, 13, 77–81, 90, 176–77, 189

consumer, 71–72, 74–75, 77–78, 79–81, 156–57, 167, 175, 180, 190, 207–8, 244n, 245n, 246n, 254n

as created by supply, 244n–45n

debt-based, 13, 71–72, 74–75, 77, 78, 79, 80, 81, 157, 167, 175, 191, 229

as economic measure, 207–8

government as source of, 109–10

investment, 245n

job creation by, 75, 156, 175, 245n

loss of, 13, 69, 79, 93, 156–57, 229, 244n, 246n

perverse economic incentives in, 93

for product innovations, 109

supply and, 78, 167, 244n–45n

Democratic National Convention (1996), 10

Democratic Party, xi, 38–40, 122, 129, 140, 179, 191

identified narrative of, 38–49

in 2012 election, 20

De Naro, Deena, 182

Depression era, 5, 42–43, 156, 171

dietary health supplements, 124, 127–28

disaster assistance, 214

distressed workers, 205–7

dividends, 58, 68, 170, 179

DNA, 109

Du Pont, 110

Durbin, Dick, 140

Earned Income Tax Credit (EITC), 159, 169, 175, 181

Earth, as common stock, 33, 36–37, 177–78

economic efficiency, 75, 80, 95, 232

economic growth, 13, 22, 43, 44, 47–48, 55–56, 66, 79, 191

consumer demand required by, 71–72, 80–81

equality and, 80–81

income inequalities required by, 80

sustainable, 15, 17, 45, 75, 77, 81, 86, 232

see also gross domestic product

economic independence, 32–42, 82, 178

economic independence (*continued*)
  getting ahead in, 6, 7, 31, 33, 38,
    41, 55–56, 70, 72, 76, 79, 81,
    83, 85, 166, 167, 176–77, 183,
    191, 192, 208
  individually controlled means of,
    38, 56
  moral force of, 35–37
  as natural right, 35–37
  New Deal and, 42–43
  reaping return of one's own labor
    in, 35–36, 38, 44, 58, 76
  time for nonlaboring aspects of life
    in, 38, 42, 57
economic measures, 205–8
  *see also* gross domestic product
economic opportunity, 30–31, 35,
    36–41, 44–45, 76, 99, 166, 177,
    181–84, 207–8
  available, 36–38, 40–41, 44, 47,
    50, 56, 79, 92, 151, 159, 192,
    240n
  charitable services vs., 50
  collective action in support of, 90,
    92
  in Common Credo, 151–52, 155,
    158–60
  distribution of, 45
  sufficient, 30–34, 41, 44, 50, 85,
    90, 112, 113, 151, 155
  *see also* standard of living, decent
economy, xi, xii, 5–6, 7, 31, 36,
    51, 53–86, 149, 156, 227–28,
    230–32
  American Dream as model of,
    207–8, 232
  collapse of, *see* Great Recession

  consumer demand pulled from,
    79, 156, 244n, 246n
  countercyclical conditions in, 153
  freedom and, 56–59
  GDP and, 55–56, 57, 59
  goals of, 38–40, 76–77
  industrial market, 42–45
  Keynes vs. Smith models of, 80
  land-based, 42
  market, 38–40
  policy solutions of, 165, 166–67
  successful, definition of, 76
  supply-side, 78, 244n–45n
  *see also* free-market economy
educational technology, 175, 194
education and skills, xii, 3, 4, 13, 17,
    56, 155, 165, 208, 228
  affordability of, 192–93
  collective provision of, 70, 92,
    112, 114, 152, 181, 213, 215,
    247n
  college degree in, 6, 58, 59, 63,
    66, 67, 85, 174, 181, 192–94,
    213
  free-giving in, 92
  high-school degree in, 66, 85, 174
  in income inequalities, 58, 59, 60,
    63, 66–67, 70
  noncognitive deportment skills
    programs in, 194
  in policy solutions, 174–75, 177,
    181, 191, 192–94
  preschool, 193
  professional degrees in, 219
  student assistance in, 174, 215
  technical training programs in,
    174, 193

$10,000 college degrees in, 174, 193, 256n
Eisenhower, Dwight D., 171, 172, 180
Eisenhower tax, 172–73, 179, 180, 190, 254n
election campaign finance, 14, 17, 138–45, 146
  corporate, 141
  of initiatives and referenda, 142, 143, 144
  large contributors to, 138–48, 202–5, 222, 229, 251n
  money as speech in, 201, 204
  public funding of, 203–4
  reform of, 140–41, 143, 200–205, 222
  Supreme Court rulings on, 140–42, 143–45, 204
  tax check-off mechanism in, 203–4
  volunteer work vs., 143–44
  in winning, 139
elections, 17, 135, 154, 200, 202, 252n
  of 1996, 10
  of 2000, xi, 48–49, 129–30
  of 2008, 38–39
  of 2010, 68, 79
  of 2012, 10–11, 19–20, 132, 192, 252n
  see also representatives, elected
elections, state, 136–37
Electoral College, 129–30
electoral districts:
  gerrymandering of, 134, 135, 142, 154, 198, 256n
  unequal apportionment of, 136–37
employment, 42–43, 152, 159, 182, 183, 184
  full, 64, 175, 206
  Jefferson's view of, 36–37, 177–78, 180
  see also unemployment
energy-saving purchases, 196
Enlarged Homestead Act (1909), 37–38
entrepreneurs, 13, 77–78, 80, 207–8, 232
environmental pollution, 17, 92, 104–7, 114, 115, 153, 194–96, 208, 214, 215, 228
  see also carbon emissions
equality, xiii, 1, 10, 25–51, 178
  civic, 134, 135, 136–37, 138–40, 142–45, 146, 154, 200–205, 222
  independence and, 32–34
  liberal view of, 10, 43–44, 83
  merging of freedom with, 40–51, 80, 81, 232
  in natural law, 33
  in republicanism, 136
  see also Declaration of Independence
equal opportunity, 27, 113, 151
equal rights, 27, 230
Erie, Lake, 104
evidence- (data-)based medicine, 96, 187–88
externalities, 104–6

factory owners, 10–11
fair trial, 154, 155

family dysfunctions, 85, 86, 157, 191, 208

farms, 42, 215

fifty-acre, 37, 240n

federalism, 121

Federalist Papers, The, 29, 121, 246n

Federal Office of Personnel Management, 218–19

fee-for-service payment basis, 93, 96

fetus, protection of, 213

filibusters, 130–31, 134–35, 154, 199, 252n

financial industry, 7, 93, 140, 157, 182–83

firefighters, 91, 176

Foner, Eric, 127

Food and Drug Administration (FDA), 124, 127–28

food and drug safety, 92, 114, 214

food stamps (Supplemental Nutrition Assistance Program), 12, 189, 215

forced labor, 100–101

Founding Fathers, xii–xiii, 15, 18, 21–51, 56, 59, 78–79, 81, 82, 85–86, 89, 101, 131, 137, 149–50, 156, 222, 228, 230, 232–33

on civic virtue, 126–27, 131, 153–54, 158

freedom as defined by, 15–16

goals of, 31, 76–77

government and, 119, 120–21, 125, 126–27, 131, 135, 137, 145–46, 211–12, 214

policy solutions and, 166, 167, 178, 179, 185, 191, 197, 198, 208

public deficits deplored by, 185

see also Declaration of Independence; freedom; specific Founding Fathers

Foxconn, 56

Fox News, 215

France, 65, 84

health care in, 94, 103

Franklin, Benjamin, 15, 35, 126, 178

on freedom and independence, 34

Frazier, Rev. Garrison, 38

freedom, 7–8, 11, 15, 21–51, 56–59, 76–77, 78–79, 82–83, 85–86, 94, 156, 167, 178–79, 197, 198

as "anything goes," 89, 99, 101

appropriate inequalities of income and wealth in, 41, 76, 80

civil rights movement and, 43–44

collective action and, 89, 94, 95, 97–104, 106, 107, 111–15

in Common Credo, 150–51, 161

compulsory actions in name of, 184

Founders' definition of, 15–16

free market as not equivalent of, 41–45, 95

government and, 119, 120–21, 124, 126–31, 134, 135, 145–46

government regulation vs., 30, 39

independence in, 32–42; see also economic independence

individual autonomy in, 28–29, 30, 36–37, 44, 150–51, 161

individualistic definition of, 20, 29–31, 39, 44, 48–49, 100, 144, 158, 228, 231, 237n–38n, 241n as individual right, 28–31

merging of equality with, 40–51, 80, 81, 232

moral absolutism of, 45–47

in natural law, 28, 32, 33, 34, 35–36

preventing free-riders in, 98–99

reciprocal duty to others in, 29–31, 36, 44, 47, 51, 58, 79, 89, 101, 107, 126–31, 145–46, 150–51, 161, 212, 228, 231, 232

religious, 29, 46

self-reliance and, 31, 37, 40, 41, 42, 44, 45, 75, 76, 82, 90, 151, 167, 180–84, 208

slavery vs., 35, 38

see also Declaration of Independence; economic opportunity; wrongful harms

Freedom's Lighthouse, 29

Freedom Works, 29–30

free-giving, 91–92

free-market economy, 16, 41–51, 68, 73–86, 116, 155, 212, 218, 241n

alternative paradigm to, 75–86

as ascendant paradigm, 73–75

as cause of economic problems, 64

competition in, 19, 75, 91, 94, 103–4, 108, 195, 232

conservatism's advocacy of, 11–13, 231–32

consumer coercion by, 91

demand in, see demand

economic efficiency as goal of, 75, 80

employers' objectives in, 44

entrepreneurs in, 13, 77–78, 80, 207–8, 232

externalities of, 104–6

freedom as not equivalent of, 41–45, 95

government regulation of, 73, 74–75, 81, 82, 89–90, 91, 126

in health care, 94, 97, 99–100, 102, 103

incentives of, 73, 74, 75, 83, 108, 109, 156–57

marginal product and, 63

obligatory sharing in, 47–50, 76–80

policy solutions and, 177–79

pollution unrestrained by, 104–5, 106, 194–96

price mechanism of, 91, 104, 105, 194

public guidance of, 45, 75, 166

right goals of, 76–77

risk of failure in, 218

self-interest in, 75, 77–78, 80, 92–93, 156–58

taxation and, 73–74

theory of, 73, 75

voluntary choices as basis of, 42, 44, 45, 47, 48–49, 94

free-market socialism, 113

free-riding, 92, 97–102

free speech, 29, 121

money as, 201, 204

Free to Choose (Friedman and Friedman), 44

Friedman, Milton, 44, 49

on purpose of government, 89

Friedman, Thomas, 65
Frontiers of Freedom, 29

General Accounting Office (GAO),
    122–23, 124
General Motors, 95
generic drug legislation, 141
genomic science, 109, 248n–49n
George III, King of England, 119,
    121
Germany, 64, 65, 84
    health care in, 94, 103
gerrymandering, 134, 135, 142, 154,
    198, 256n
getting ahead, 6, 7, 16, 31, 33, 38,
    41, 55–56, 70, 72, 76, 79, 81,
    83–84, 85, 166, 167, 176–77,
    183, 191, 192, 208
Giffords, Gabrielle, 22–23
Gilens, Martin, 200
Gillette, 218
Gingrich, Newt, 98–99, 107, 140
global competition, 7, 60, 64–66, 70,
    191, 195–96, 208
global warming (climate change),
    105, 114, 165–66, 194–96, 228,
    248n
    scientists' alleged conspiracy
    about, 106–7
God, 27, 46–47, 150, 241n
Gore, Al, 129–30
government, xii, 7, 69, 117–46, 208
    accountability of, 14–15, 50–51,
    122–23, 136, 198, 212
    bureaucrats of, 217
    checks and balances of, 121,
    126–27, 135

coercive power of, 90, 119, 126,
    128, 131, 135, 153
corrupt, 138–42, 145, 201–2,
    204
in Declaration of Independence,
    119, 120, 121, 125
developing dependency on, 180–
    84
dysfunction of, 128–29, 130–31
efficiency of, 121, 217–21
expansion of, 11, 120
goals of, 28, 120
growth periods of, 216
inadequate funding of, 124–25
income inequalities attributed to
    cost of, 60, 67–70
insufficient resources provided to,
    124–25
majorities in, 128–29, 134–35,
    154
as naturally incompetent and inef-
    fective, 213–14
product innovation supported by,
    108–11
public choice theory of, 217
public opinion on, 138
purpose of, 89, 90, 93, 103
representative, see representatives,
    elected
services contracted by, 152, 188–
    89, 220–22
as source of demand, 109–10
state, 136–37, 153, 176, 198
subsidies by, 92, 106, 152, 159,
    186–88
tyranny of, 128–29
as "us," 142, 146, 199, 222

# INDEX

*see also* Congress, U.S.; House of
Representatives, U.S.; Senate,
U.S.

government, attitudes about, 209–23
    fears of uncontrolled expansion in,
        215–17, 221, 222
    federal vs. private-sector workers'
        compensation in, 218–21
    perception of incompetence and
        inefficiency in, 213–14, 217–21
    positive, 212, 213–15, 221
    private sector and, 217–22
    trust issues in, 21, 211, 212, 214–
        15, 221, 222, 229
government, limited, 18, 101–2,
        120–35, 155–56
    activist, 211–15, 217, 222
    civic virtue and, 126–35
    in Common Credo, 18–19, 150,
        151, 153, 155, 197
    debts incurred by, 153
    freedom as, 30–31
    as goal in itself, 222
    large, 120, 121, 145, 153, 211,
        214
    in liberalism and conservatism,
        121–25
    self-interest and, 127–31
    small vs., 11, 12, 82, 107, 120,
        124–25, 153, 212, 214
    sufficient, Founders' desire for,
        119, 120–21, 125
    uncontrolled expansion vs., 215–
        17
    welfare state and, 155
government programs, 12, 37, 48–49,
        122–24, 214, 215, 216

cost/benefit analyses of, 123, 249$n$
economic dependency on, 180–84
housing assistance, 43, 160, 181,
    189, 215
job creation, 64, 73, 152, 175–77,
    180–81, 189
job training, 152, 155, 174
poverty, 49, 181
technical training, 174, 193
unemployment assistance, 12, 73,
    152, 169, 181, 189, 214, 215,
    216
wasteful spending in, 120, 122–
    23, 124
government regulation, 30, 39, 81,
    89–90, 91, 92, 121, 124, 128,
    151
    as cause of income inequality,
        67–70
    in Common Credo, 152–53, 155–
        56
    compulsion vs., 99–100, 101–2,
        112, 247$n$
    enforcement of, 90
    of environmental pollution, 105–6,
        107, 214
    of financial industry, 159
    of free-market economy, 73,
        74–75, 81, 82, 89–90, 91, 126
    of health care, 22, 96–97, 99–101,
        153
government spending, 7, 10, 21, 83,
    111, 122, 129, 130, 215–18
    relative to GDP, 125, 215–16
    wasteful, 120, 122–23, 124, 197,
        215, 217–18
    *see also* budget deficits

grants of stock, 58, 61, 172
Great Britain, 94, 119, 189
Great Depression, 5, 42–43, 156, 171
Great Recession (2008), xi, 5, 7, 13,
    45, 63, 80, 86, 124, 140, 167,
    216, 227–28, 229
  cause of, 51, 70–72
  emergence from, 57
  personal experiences of, 182–83
  warning signs of, 8
  workers' compensation and, 56,
    59, 65, 70–72, 74, 75, 156–57,
    171
green energy, 111
gross domestic product (GDP), 8, 13,
    48, 55–56, 57, 58–59, 73, 86,
    170, 195, 222
  corporate tax payments in, 68
  debt ratio to, 185
  as economic measure, 205, 207,
    208
  federal spending relative to, 125,
    215–16
  potential, 257n–58n
  public-sector research and devel-
    opment spending relative to, 111
guaranteed minimum income pro-
    grams, 49
Gutfeld, Greg, 215

Hamilton, Alexander, 246n
Hanauer, Nick, 69, 245n
Hand, Learned, 126
Handbook for Congress (Cato Insti-
    tute), 68
Hatch, Orrin, 124, 127–28
Hayek, Friedrich, 44, 48, 241n

health care, xii, 17, 56, 92, 94–104,
    124, 168, 176, 189, 213, 241n–
    42n
  collective provision of, 114, 115
  coordination systems of, 95, 96,
    187
  data- (evidence-)based medicine
    in, 96, 187–88
  free market in, 94, 97, 99–100,
    102, 103
  free-riding in, 92, 97–102
  government intervention in, 22,
    96–97, 99–101, 153
  malpractice suits in, 188
  market failures and, 92, 93,
    96–104, 153
  medical errors in, 95
  outcomes of, 94–95, 96–97, 187
  oversupply in, 96
  overtreatment in, 96, 186
  pollution's effect on, 104–5
  quality of, 94
  2010 health-care reform act and,
    22, 99, 169, 187, 247n
health-care costs, 90, 94–98, 114,
    228
  in budget deficit, 185–89
  for businesses, 95, 103
  and compulsory medical services,
    98
  controlling, 102–4, 185–89
  deductibles in, 187
  doctors' fee-for-service payment
    in, 93, 96
  European, 94, 103
  pharmaceutical drugs in, 103, 188
  in policy solutions, 165, 185–89

health-care insurance, 92, 94, 103,
    152, 169, 181, 184, 186–88
    mandated, 96–102, 249*n*
    perverse economic incentives of,
    93, 95–97
    Supreme Court ruling and, 97,
    100–102
    unhealthy personal habits and,
    100, 249*n*
Heritage Foundation, 12, 99
Hewlett-Packard, 63, 65
homelessness, 160
Homestead Act (1862), 37–38
House of Representatives, U.S.,
    22–23, 124–25, 136, 218–19
    *see also* Congress, U.S.; represen-
    tatives, elected
housing assistance, 43, 160, 181,
    189, 215
housing prices, 71
Human Genome Project, 248*n*–49*n*

Illinois, 140
immigration control, 213
income distribution, 12, 39–40, 113,
    205, 207
    in Senate's policy responsiveness,
    199–200
income inequalities, 10, 16, 53–86,
    149, 168, 170–75, 177–78, 253*n*
    appropriate, 41, 76, 80
    consumer demand pulled from
    economy by, 79, 156, 244*n*, 246*n*
    economic problems caused by,
    60–64, 157
    educational attainment in, 58, 59,
    60, 63, 66–67, 70

global competition in, 60, 64–66,
    70
    heavy burden of government in,
    60, 67–70
    increasing, 84
    and low- vs. high-income spending
    habits, 71, 78, 81, 244*n*–45*n*
    social effects of, 83–85, 157
    *see also* wages and salaries
independence, 32–42, 167, 176–77,
    180–84, 241*n*–42*n*
    of elected representatives, 137,
    138, 146, 200
    in natural law, 32–33, 34
Indiana, 65
individual autonomy, 28–29, 30,
    36–37, 44, 150–51, 161
individualism, 20, 29–31, 39, 44,
    48–49, 100, 144, 158, 228, 231,
    237*n*–38*n*, 241*n*
industrialization, 42
industrial market economy, 42–45
industrial pollution, 92
information technology, 65
infrastructure, 13, 91, 113, 115, 124,
    153, 208, 213
    aging, xii, 21, 228
    as natural monopoly, 91
    in policy solutions, 176, 177, 191
initiatives and referenda, 142, 143,
    144
innovation, product, 17, 108–11, 191,
    208
Institute of Liberty, 29
insurance, 107, 194, 215, 216
    annuity coverage in, 184
    social, 48

insurance (*continued*)
  unemployment, 43, 184
  *see also* health-care insurance
integrated circuits, 110
intellectual dishonesty, 128–35,
    145–46, 198, 208, 229
  news media exposure of, 132–33,
    134
  private trust for tracking of, 133–
    34, 198
  restrictive mechanisms for, 131–34
International Monetary Fund (IMF),
    77
interstate commerce, 101–2
inventions, 90
  free-giving and, 92
  patented, 108–9
investments, 7, 71, 156, 218, 245*n*
  capital gains of, 68, 73, 74, 170,
    179
  market fluctuations and, 182–83
  in policy solutions, 179–80
  of retirement savings, 182
  returns on, 58, 170, 171, 179
  self-interest of, 77–78, 80
  taxation of, 64
"It Takes a Village to Raise a Child"
    (Clinton), 10

Jamestown, 35
Japan, 64
Jefferson, Thomas, 15, 18, 35–38,
    119, 121, 185, 249*n*
  abolition of slavery favored by, 35,
    239*n*
  available economic opportunity
    favored by, 36–38, 240*n*

Declaration of Independence
    drafted by, 27–28, 30, 32, 34,
    239*n*, 241*n*
  on disinterestedness, 137, 251*n*
  Louisiana Purchase initiated by,
    37–38
  on unemployment, 36–37, 177–
    78, 180
job creation, 7, 11, 21, 67–68, 70, 73,
    74, 78, 170
  by consumer demand, 75, 156,
    175, 245*n*
  global competition and, 65–66
  top-down growth and, 69
job-creation programs, 64, 73, 152
  in policy solutions, 175–77, 180–
    81, 189
jobs, 22, 36, 41, 62, 122, 180, 206,
    252*n*, 253*n*
  layoffs from, 13, 69, 93
  long-term vacancies of, 174
  low-paying, 16, 81, 83, 84, 86,
    181
  outsourcing of, 7, 65
  paying less than living wage, 5–6,
    57–58, 59, 156, 168–69, 205–6
  paying living wage, 166, 167–70,
    175–77
  public, 43
  ready choice among, 42, 56
  requisite features of, 56–57
  sufficient number of, 166, 175–
    77
Jobs Corps, 174
job security, 85
job-training programs, 152, 155, 174
jury duty, 184

Katz, Lawrence, 66
Kennedy, John F., 171
Kennedy, Ted, 10
Kevlar, 110
Keynes, John Maynard, 19, 233
    Smith and, 80
King, Colbert I., 245*n*
Kinsley, Michael, 129–30
Kipp program, 193–94
Koch, Charles, 179
Koch, David H., 139–40
Kyl, Jon, 130

labor costs, 13, 64–65
labor force, 5–6, 57, 81
    *see also* workers
labor unions, 64, 141, 173, 218
landed property, 33–34, 36–38, 42
    ownership of, 36–37, 137, 251*n*
    public, 37–38, 42, 240*n*
law enforcement, 90, 126, 128, 151,
    215
    *see also* police forces
lawyers, 140, 219
left, *see* liberalism
legal aid, 124
liberalism, xi, xii, 1–23, 80, 82–83,
    129, 157–58, 169, 197, 214,
    228, 233
    collective action's benefits for,
    115–16
    economic goals of, 38–40
    economic model lacked by, 13
    equality as focus of, 10, 43–44, 83
    as failed ideology, 9–13, 228, 230
    fundamental dilemmas faced by,
    47–51

    goal of, 149
    limited government in, 121–25,
    217
    well-defined principles lacked
    by, 9–10, 14, 50, 83, 122–23,
    157–58, 217, 231–32
libertarianism, 99
Liberty Central, 29
Lincoln, Abraham, 37–38, 89, 90, 93,
    103, 112
living wage, 5–6, 42, 44, 156, 159,
    191, 235*n*–36*n*, 252*n*, 257*n*
    jobs paying less than, 5–6, 57–58,
    59, 156, 168–69, 205–6
    minimum wage as, 43, 113, 152,
    240*n*
Locke, John, 29, 33
Los Angeles, Calif., 104
Louisiana Purchase, 37–38, 249*n*

Madison, James, 15, 121, 145, 178,
    179, 180, 185, 200–201, 240*n*,
    251*n*
    on freedom, 29, 30
    on independence, 33–34
    on virtue, 126–27
Madoff, Bernie, 183
malpractice suits, medical, 188
Mankiw, N. Gregory, 39–40, 44, 47
Marcus, Stanley, 97–98
marginal product, 63
market efficiency, 44
market failures, 90–104, 112, 114,
    115–16, 150, 155, 194–96, 241*n*
    Common Credo and, 150, 152–53
    free-giving, 91–92
    free-riding, 92, 97–102

market failures (*continued*)
  natural monopolies, 91
  perverse economic incentives,
    92–93, 95–97, 103–4
marriage, 29, 213
Mason, George, 15, 34, 178
  Virginia's Declaration of Rights
    composed by, 32–33
Massachusetts, 99
  Declaration of Rights of, 33
Mathews, Thomas, 183
McCain, John, 244*n*
McCain-Feingold campaign finance
  reform, 140–41
McClatchy surveys, 69
*McConnell v. Federal Election Com-*
  *mission*, 140–41, 201–2
McDonald's, 36, 239*n*
Medicaid, 12, 95, 103, 114, 214,
  215
  controlling costs of, 188
Medicare, 12, 95, 96, 103, 114, 214,
  215, 216
  controlling costs of, 186–88
Mexico, 64–65
Michigan, 218
military defense, national, 22, 91,
  113, 114, 115, 129, 152, 184,
  213, 215
minimum wage, 4, 73, 76, 159, 254*n*
  lifting of, 169–70, 191–92, 252*n*–
    53*n*
  as living wage, 43, 113, 152, 240*n*
  real, 64
monopolies:
  natural, 91
  of patents and trademarks, 108–9

morality, 35–37, 154, 158, 167,
  230–31
  absolute vs. relative, 45–47
Muller, Richard, 248*n*
Museum of Failed Products, 218

nanotechnology, 111
National Federation of Independent
  Business, 69, 74–75
*National Federation of Independent*
  *Business vs. Sebelius*, 100–101
national parks, 214
national public radio, 214
national security, 91, 215
Native Americans, 35
natural law, 31–33, 34, 35–37
  Earth as common stock in, 33,
    36–37, 177–78
  freedom in, 28, 32, 33, 34, 35–36
natural monopolies, 91
Nelsen, Ron, 75
Nelson, Richard R., 110
New Deal, 42–43
*New York Times*, 63, 65, 128, 133,
  139–40, 220
Nixon, Richard M., 169
noncognitive deportment skills, 194
Norquist, Grover, 124–25
*Notes on the State of Virginia* (Jeffer-
  son), 137, 239*n*
Novella, Steven, 127–28
Nozick, Robert, 39, 44, 48
nursing, 67

Obama, Barack, 10, 122, 129, 251*n*
  in 2008 campaign, 38–39
  in 2012 campaign, 20

2013 State of the Union Address of, 169

obligatory sharing, 47–50, 76–80

occupational therapy, 67

O'Donnell, Lawrence, 245*n*

oil, 114, 196

national dependency on, 165–66, 194, 228

oligopoly, 91

opportunity, *see* economic opportunity

outsourcing, 7, 65

of government services, 152, 188–89, 220–22

patents, 108–9, 126

Pennsylvania, constitution and Declaration of Rights of, 34

Pepsi, 218

perverse economic incentives, 92–93, 95–97, 103–4

pharmaceutical industry, 103, 188

publicly funded research exploited by, 109

philanthropy, 49, 50

Pickett, Kate, 84

Pioneer Overhead Door, 75

Planned Parenthood, 130

police forces, 11, 91, 114, 115, 152, 176, 213, 215

policy solutions, 152, 163–208

carbon emissions in, 165–66, 194–96

charges effected by, 191–92

children of welfare state in, 158–60

controlling budget deficits in, 165, 185–90

decentralization of, 166

dignified standard of living in, 166, 167–70, 176

economic measures in, 205–8

economy in, 165, 166–77

education in, 174–75, 177, 181, 191, 192–94

as fostering dependency on government, 180–84

free-market economy and, 177–79

getting ahead in, 166, 167, 176–77

health-care costs in, 165, 185–89

improving schools in, 165, 174–75, 176, 193

infrastructure in, 176, 177, 191

investment in, 179–80

job-creation program in, 175–77, 180–81, 189

jobs paying living wage in, 166, 167–70, 175–77

labor unions in, 173

lifting EITC in, 169, 175, 181

lifting minimum wage in, 169–70, 191–92, 252*n*–53*n*

political process in, 197–205

public fee in, 195–96

questions regarding, 177–184

rising compensation with increasing productivity in, 166, 170–75

student assistance in, 174

sufficient number of jobs in, 166, 175–77

taxation in, 105, 106, 171–74, 179–80, 189–90, 196

postal service, 109, 215, 218

poverty, 178, 191, 193, 208, 257*n*
    *see also* welfare state
poverty line, 206–7, 235*n*–36*n*
poverty programs, 49, 181
product innovations, 108–11, 191
products, failed, 218
Project on Government Oversight,
    220–21
property, 104, 137, 151
    condemning, 113
    distribution of, 35, 36–37, 177–
        78
    means of acquiring, 32–33
    *see also* landed property
property rights, 29, 36–37, 89, 113,
    126, 178
prosperity, xi, xii, xiii, 6, 15, 45, 51,
    55, 56, 59, 60, 90, 114, 149,
    150, 190, 205
    obligatory sharing of, 47–50,
        76–80
    postwar period of, 43, 165
public assistance programs, 37, 43,
    48–49
public choice theory, 217
public-employee retirement, 215,
    216
public fees, 195–96
public good, 126–31, 137, 153–54,
    217
public lands, 37–38, 42, 240*n*
public ownership, 91, 92, 152

Reagan, Ronald, 39, 55, 59, 125, 181,
    216
recessions of 2008, *see* Great Reces-
    sion

relativism, moral, 45–47
religion, 29, 46, 121
religious institutions, 113
representatives, elected, 120, 126–
    46, 200–205
    as beholden to select few, 137,
        138–45, 146, 154, 200, 203–5
    disinterestedness as quality of,
        137, 251*n*
    of gerrymandered districts, 134,
        135, 142, 154, 198, 256*n*
    independence of, 137, 138, 146,
        200
    intellectual dishonesty of, 128–35,
        145–46, 198, 208, 229
    national needs vs. constituency of,
        128
    as property holders, 137, 251*n*
    reelection of, 217
    self-interest vs. public good sup-
        ported by, 126–31, 137, 217
    special access to, 139–40, 141,
        143, 202
    undue influence on, 140–41,
        143–44, 202–5, 222
    *see also* Congress, U.S.; election
        campaign finance; House of
        Representatives, U.S.; Senate,
        U.S.
republicanism, 136, 200, 201
Republican Party, xi, 12, 19–20,
    38–40, 125, 129, 130, 140, 179,
    190, 191–92, 218
research, *see* basic research
retirement, 56, 182–83, 241*n*
    public-employee, 215, 216
    *see also* Social Security

Revolutionary War, 35, 178
*Reynolds v. Sims,* 136–37, 138, 145, 202
Rich, Frank, 132
right, *see* conservatism
Rolls-Royce, 65
Romney, Mitt, 12, 99, 192, 218, 251*n*
Roosevelt, Franklin, 42–43
Ross, Dennis, 218–19
Ryan, Paul, 19–20, 186

Say's law, 244*n*–45*n*
Scalia, Antonin, 97
schools, 159–60
    improving of, 174–75
self-interest, 119, 132, 198, 233
    in free-market economy, 75, 77–78, 80, 92–93, 156–58
    public good vs., 126–31, 137, 153–54, 217
self-reliance, 31, 37, 40, 41, 42, 44, 45, 75, 76, 82, 90, 151, 167, 180–84, 208
semiconductors, 108, 110
Senate, U.S., 10–11, 124–25, 127–28, 130, 138, 140
    constituents' income distribution in policy responsiveness of, 199–200, 257*n*
    filibusters in, 130–31, 134–35, 154, 199, 252*n*
    *see also* Congress, U.S.; representatives, elected
Shank, Kenneth, 239*n*
Simpson, Alan, 140
Singapore, 64–65

single-parent families, 169–70
slavery, 35, 38
    voluntarily selling oneself into, 48
Smith, Adam, 19, 36, 57–58, 233, 244*n*–45*n*
    "invisible hand" metaphor of, 77–78, 110, 156–57
    Keynes and, 80
Smith, John, 35
socialism, 113
social problems, 83–85, 157, 191
Social Security, 12, 43, 152, 169, 181, 190, 214, 215, 216, 254*n*
    as earned pension, 184
    privatization scenarios of, 182–83
South Carolina, 65
space program, 214
special interests, 7, 93, 138
spending habits, 168, 175
    of low- vs. high-income families, 71, 78, 81, 244*n*–45*n*
standard of living, 6, 40, 70, 157, 208, 229
standard of living, decent, 33, 36, 37, 38, 40, 41, 56, 57–58, 76, 79, 81, 151, 155, 167, 206, 240*n*, 241*n*–42*n*
    in policy solutions, 166, 167–70, 176
state governments, 136–37, 153, 176, 198
stock market, 182–83
stock options, 58, 61, 172
super majorities, 154
super PACs, 141, 201, 251*n*
Supplemental Nutrition Assistance Program (SNAP), 12, 189, 215

Supreme Court, U.S., 100–102, 129,
    200–202
  civic equality ruling of, 136–37,
    138, 143, 200, 204
  election campaign finance rulings
    of, 140–42, 143–45, 201–2, 204

Tamraz, Ray, 138
Taphandles, 56
taxation, 10, 11, 12, 21, 48, 83, 121,
    124–25, 152, 184, 215
  capital gains, 68, 73, 74, 189
  as cause of income inequality,
    67–70
  congressional power of, 101–2
  corporate, 68, 190
  cuts in, 21–22, 64, 68, 69, 74, 79,
    80, 125, 171, 173
  deductions in, 173–74, 181, 190
  Eisenhower, 172–73, 179, 180,
    190, 254n
  enforcement of, 126
  on environmental pollution, 105,
    108
  health-insurance mandate as, 129
  of investments, 64
  lower, 30, 31, 68, 73–74
  medical free-riders and, 98–99
  offshore havens from, 190
  in policy solutions, 105, 106,
    171–74, 179–80, 189–90, 196
  as proportion of GDP, 73
  top rates of, 171–73, 179–80, 190
  of workers' compensation, 64
tax cheaters, 189
technical training programs, 174, 193
technological advances, 65, 108–11

technology, educational, 175, 194
teenage pregnancy, rates of, 84–85
Teflon, 110
Tennessee, 65
$10,000 college degrees, 174, 193,
    256n
termination benefits, 63
Texas, 138
tobacco industry, 140, 141
tort reform, 140, 141
Toyota, 65
trade dislocation, 196
trademarks, 108–9
trade secrets, 108
Treasury Department, U.S., 196
trial, fair, 154, 155
Truman, Harry S., 171
Tucson, Ariz., Giffords's 2011
    attempted assassination in,
    22–23

Uncommon Schools program, 193–94
unemployment, 62, 169, 170, 176,
    182–83
  of college graduates, 67
  and earning less than living wage,
    57–58, 59, 66, 156, 205–8, 227,
    242n–43n
  global competition and, 66
  in Great Depression, 42–43
  Jefferson on, 36–37, 177–78, 180
  measures of, 205–7
  see also employment; welfare state
unemployment assistance, 12, 73,
    152, 169, 181, 189, 214, 215,
    216
unemployment insurance, 43, 184

unemployment rate, 5–6, 43, 175–76, 191, 253n

unions, labor, 64, 141, 173, 218

Ventana Medical Systems, 110

Veterans Health Administration, 103, 188, 213

Virginia, 65

Virginia Constitution, 239n
    Declaration of Rights of, 32–33, 238n

virtue, civic, 126–35, 153–54, 158

Volkswagen, 65

votes, voting rights, 135–37, 142, 203–4, 229
    equal civic weight of, 136–37, 138–39, 143, 199, 202–3
    majority of, 154
    self-interest in, 119

wages and salaries, 31, 37, 55–86, 103, 214
    benefits in, 170, 219
    of CEOs, 61–64
    commensurate with productivity improvement, 3–6, 16, 42, 43, 48, 56, 58–64, 66, 67, 69, 70, 72, 74, 78, 79, 81, 83–84, 86, 155, 156, 166, 180, 191, 242n–43n, 244n–45n
    debt ratio to, 70, 71
    distribution of, 61, 63, 81
    economic efficiency and, 75
    of employees vs. management, 58, 60–64, 65
    flatlined, 16, 61, 66, 72, 74, 83–84, 85, 86, 156, 183, 227

forced labor vs., 100–101
    and fundamentals of freedom, 56–59
    government influence on, 64, 70
    Great Recession of 2008 and, 56, 59, 65, 70–72, 74, 75, 156–57, 171
    median, 59, 60–61, 63, 65, 67, 68, 79, 156, 169, 171, 175, 190, 205
    in 1920s, 171–72
    in policy solutions, 166, 170–75
    in private sector, 63–64, 67–70, 218–21
    in public sector, 218–21
    raises in, 61–62, 67, 156, 244n
    real (inflation-adjusted), 6, 43, 58–59, 60, 61–62, 64, 67, 157, 171, 205, 207, 229
    subsidized, 152, 159
    total, 61, 63, 65, 66, 67, 68, 70, 171, 245n
    of upper-level management, 60–61, 65, 68, 69–70, 71, 74, 81, 156, 171–73, 219–20, 229, 244n
    of U.S. president, 63
    see also income inequalities

Walker, Scott, 68, 139–40, 218, 219

Wall Street Journal, 99, 133

Warren, Elizabeth, 10–11

Washington, George, 15, 35, 178

Washington Post, 129–30, 132

water pollution, 104–6

Wealth of Nations (Smith), 36

Webster, Noah, 35

welfare state, 50–51, 152, 155, 206, 241n

welfare state (*continued*)

    abuses of, 112–13

    assisting children in, 158–60

    limits and boundaries of, 82–83

    1996 reform of, 159

Wilcox, W. Bradford, 85

Wilkinson, Richard, 84

Will, George, 29, 237n

wind-turbine technicians, 174

Wisconsin, 68, 139–40, 218

Wood, Gordon, 136, 251n

workers, 51, 83, 165

    anger and resentment in, 72, 83–84

    blue-collar, 3–5, 228–29

    compensation of, *see* wages and
      salaries

    debt levels of, 8, 72

    diligent, 4, 7, 41, 56, 151, 167

    distressed, 205–7

    as human capital, 176, 242n

    increased work hours of, 70–71

    in manufacturing, 37

    shortages of, 67, 174

    unions of, 64, 141, 173, 218

    wages of, *see* wages and salaries

worker safety, 30, 47, 214

World War II, 4, 43, 63, 72, 79, 165

wrongful harms, 29, 30, 184, 237n

    prevention of, 89–90, 104–7, 112,
      127–28, 151, 154–55

Wyden, Ron, 186

Wyoming, 140

Zandi, Mark, 244n